Milton and the
Science of the Saints

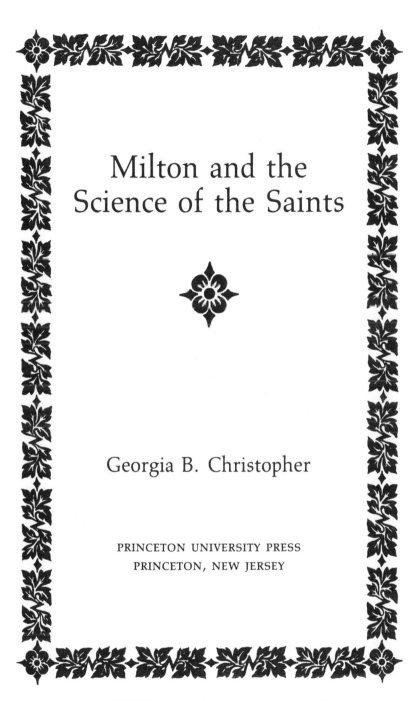

Milton and the
Science of the Saints

Georgia B. Christopher

PRINCETON UNIVERSITY PRESS
PRINCETON, NEW JERSEY

Copyright © 1982 by Princeton University Press
Published by Princeton University Press, 41 William Street,
Princeton, New Jersey
In the United Kingdom: Princeton University Press,
Guildford, Surrey

All Rights Reserved

Library of Congress Cataloging in Publication Data will be
found on the last printed page of this book

Publication of this book has been aided by a grant from the
Paul Mellon Fund of Princeton University Press

This book has been composed in Linotron Aldus

Clothbound editions of Princeton University Press books
are printed on acid-free paper, and binding materials are
chosen for strength and durability

Printed in the United States of America by Princeton
University Press, Princeton, New Jersey

for
Laura Cooper Christopher

Contents

Preface

Dante's theology and the hermeneutic he outlines in his "Letter to Can Grande Della Scalla" figure prominently in discussions of the *Commedia*, but the esthetic consequences of Milton's "theology of the word," if considered at all, are assumed to be purely negative. Milton had a metaphysical investment in the assumption that language conveys personal presence. Books, he claimed, treasure up "the lifeblood of a master spirit." Likewise, he assumed that when one read the Bible or any redaction of it, the Master Spirit might be present. This "sacramental" assumption that God is present to man through verbal speech lends a Reformation dynamic to Milton's texts and calls for a reassessment of the alleged flaws in his major poems. Because Milton chose biblical "fables" and classical forms, his major works inevitably evoke readings as pluralistic as the religious and intellectual traditions of his audience. I have no wish to impose an orthodoxy nor to curtail the polyphonic potential of Milton's texts. Rather, I wish to suggest that among these possibilities be included—perhaps as a base line—a reading that takes seriously the Reformation hermeneutic that Milton himself affirms.

Preliminary versions of this study have been given as lectures or seminar papers at the Modern Language Association, the New York Milton Seminar, the Folger Institute Colloquium, Bryn Mawr College, the Hollins College Classical Symposium, Mary Washington College, and the University of Essex, England. Other versions have been published, and here reprinted with permission, in *ELH* (37, 1970; 43, 1976), *MLQ* (41, 1980), and *PMLA* (91, 1975), and I owe much to Stanley Fish, William

ix

S. Matchett, and Arnold Stein for early encouragement. In addition, I wish to thank the American Council of Learned Societies and the Folger Shakespeare Library for fellowships that enabled me to do most of the reading and to write a major draft, and to the University of Richmond for a sabbatical leave during which I completed the manuscript. The kindness and patience of Mrs. Erwin Davis of the University of Richmond Library, Dr. John B. Trotti of the Union Seminary Library, and Nati Krivatsy of the Folger Library meant much to me during this time. Sister Ann Case, Bettie Forte, Charles Frey, Diane Hatch, John H. Leith, Jeanne Addison Roberts, Jason Rosenblatt, Sally Yeates Sedelow, and Dewey Wallace read various chapters and, with their helpful comments, taught me what is meant by "the community of scholars." Wayne H. Phelps cast a critical eye over the entire manuscript and offered advice just before it went to Mrs. Gordon English and Wendy P. Thompson for expert typing, and to Katherine Sweeney for proofreading.

My largest debts are to the generosity of Joseph H. Summers and Mary Ann Radzinowicz, who read the manuscript for Princeton University Press, and to George P. Hayes, F. T. Prince, B. A. Wright, Maynard Mack, and Louis Martz—for precept and example.

G.B.C.

List of Abbreviations

All quotations from Milton's poetry are taken from *John Milton: The Complete Poems and Major Prose*, ed. Merritt Y. Hughes. New York: Odyssey Press, 1957.

Aen.   *The Aeneid of Virgil*, ed. R. D. Williams. 2 vols. New York, St. Martin's Press, 1973.

CD   John Milton, *Christian Doctrine*, ed. John Carey. Vol. VI of *The Complete Prose Works of John Milton*, gen. ed. Don M. Wolfe. New Haven, Yale University Press, 1973.

CE   *The Works of John Milton*, gen. ed. Frank Allen Patterson. 18 vols. New York, Columbia University Press, 1931-1938.

Inst.   John Calvin, *Institutes of the Christian Religion*, ed. John T. McNeill, trans. Ford Lewis Battles. 2 vols. Philadelphia, Westminster Press, 1960.

LW   *Luther's Works*, gen. eds. Jaroslav Pelikan and Helmut T. Lehmann. 55 vols. St. Louis, Concordia, and Philadelphia, Fortress Press, 1955-1976.

PL   *Paradise Lost*

PR   *Paradise Regained*

SA   *Samson Agonistes*

TT   Martin Luther, *Table Talk*, trans. Henry Bell. London, 1650.

YP   *The Complete Prose Works of John Milton*, gen. ed.
     Don M. Wolfe. 8 vols. New Haven, Yale University
     Press, 1953————.

Unless otherwise indicated, italics in the quotations are those
of the original text.

Milton and the
Science of the Saints

❖ 1 ❖
Milton's "Literary" Theology

I

The studie of scripture is . . . the only true theologie.

(CE 6.80)

The gospel loseth his whole authority, unless we know and be also fully persuaded that Christ being alive, speaketh to us from the heavens.

(Calvin, *Commentary upon Acts*, p. 36)

When Erasmus translated *Logos* (λόγος) as *sermo* (speech) rather than as *verbum* (reason) in his 1516 edition of the New Testament, he prepared the way for Luther to cast aside the entire philosophical tradition in which the eternal Son was understood as the mind and instrument of God.[1] Luther, who was working on his commentary on Romans at the time, immediately availed himself of Erasmus' scholarship and proceeded

[1] *Novum Testamentum*, in *Opera Omnia*, Amsterdam, 1701, VI, 335. Though Ficino had earlier translated *Logos* as *sermo*, it was Erasmus who influenced the usage of Luther and Calvin and ultimately the piety of the English puritans.

to work out an antiphilosophical theology that dealt in literary categories. He conceived of God, not as *Actus Purus*, but as a person who "speaks." Seizing upon the naïve analogy that Father and Son are related as "speaker" and "speech" (*TT*, p. 181), Luther found Christ mystically present and speaking in each divine utterance in the Old Testament, especially in any promise for the future. When properly "opened," these promises spoke of redemption in Christ, and when *heard*, they connected man with God. Luther had not set out to abolish the Mass, but he nonetheless introduced an alternative means of grace that shifted the locus of religious experience from visual symbol and ritual action to verbal action.

The Bible, as the setting of "sacramental" action, took on supreme importance and a somewhat new shape. Luther, who knew the exegetical tradition mainly from Lyra and Carrensis, complained of the lack of commentary on the Old Testament (*LW* 3.26), for he was coming to see the Old Testament less as a thesaurus of types than as a history deserving close attention in itself. The issue of faith, he held, was the same for the patriarchs as for his contemporaries: man was confronted by God's oracle. Luther's relative deemphasis of typological symbolism in favor of a "realistic" reading seems to be part of a cultural trend also evident in the interpretation of epic, but its ultimate causes are beyond the scope of this book. Suffice it to say that Luther's "realistic" interpretation redefined the unity of the Scripture in a way that was to have far-reaching consequences for English poetry. Traditionally, Scripture was assumed to adhere to the analogy of faith; that is, it was assumed to be in accord with the classic creeds of the Church. With Luther, the analogy of faith became more specifically an analogy of the word—an analogy of the verbal promise of redemption, or what Milton was to call the "*analogy* of Evangelick doctrine" (*YP* 2.338).

Recent studies of Milton's poetry have tended to blur the hermeneutic break between the Reformation and Catholic tradition, just as earlier ones had tended to make the differences absolute. MacCallum and Madsen have demonstrated that the

Reformers, for all their insistence upon the literal level, never completely abandoned typology.[2] Lewalski has reminded us that Aquinas never disavowed the literal or historical level and considered the figures in the text to be part of the literal level.[3] Despite these important qualifications, the Reformers' hermeneutic differed considerably from the classic system of typology outlined by Aquinas. We will have a better picture of the hermeneutic that Milton inherited if we ask not whether typology is present at all—MacCallum has shown that Milton was more conservative on this score than most Protestants[4]—but how Old Testament history is valued, what the literal level is discovered to be, and how an interpretation is validated.

The most profound hermeneutic changes of the Reformation occurred on the literal level. Where one discovered the figures in Scripture made all the difference. Foxe's *Book of Martyrs* contains numerous stories of dissenting mechanicals who argued with Marian bishops about whether "is" should be a metaphor or a true designation in Jesus' words "This is my body" (Matthew 26:26). Typically, Luther discovered figures in a text in order to include a promissory allusion to the Son or in order to preserve narrative consistency. When Moses seemed to nod, Luther found simile, allegory, irony, hypallage, metonymy, or synecdoche to be present, so that Deuteronomic history appeared trustworthy, as in the following passage:

> Note, however, that in this passage *the people are described by Moses as godless*, when he says that they do what seems right to them, not to God. . . . Does this agree with the statement in Num. 24:6-9, where *this nation is called*

[2] Hugh MacCallum, "Milton and Figurative Interpretation of the Bible," *University of Toronto Quarterly*, 31 (1962), 397-415; William G. Madsen, *From Shadowy Types to Truth*, New Haven, Yale University Press, 1968. See also Barbara K. Lewalski, *Milton's Brief Epic*, Providence, Brown University Press, 1968.

[3] Barbara K. Lewalski, *Protestant Poetics and the Seventeenth-Century Religious Lyric*, Princeton, Princeton University Press, 1979, p. 115, cited hereafter as *Protestant Poetics*.

[4] MacCallum, "Milton and Figurative Interpretation of the Bible," p. 407.

blessed and is so magnificently praised by Balaam? It will agree in this way, that in both cases *the matter is understood to be stated by synecdoche*; that the larger part was godless and the lesser part pious. However, the whole nation is praised on account of the Word of God, which was in the Godly ones among them just as in Rom. 3. 1-2 Paul praises circumcision, that is, the whole people, because the oracles of God were entrusted to them, although many did not believe.

(LW 9.125-126, author's italics)

Discovering tropes was a method that could be employed for special pleading, and indeed often was. Milton himself was to argue that "fornication" was a mere synecdoche of the many wifely lapses that Scripture allowed as grounds for divorce (*CD*, p. 378). That Scripture so often was used to justify a course of action like divorce or regicide is less remarkable than the way in which "the analogy of the word" remained in force regarding the central question of salvation throughout the century of Puritan Revolution. Luther himself admitted that Scripture could be an infinitely malleable "wax nose," but held, especially in his writings prior to the Peasants' Revolt, that the analogy of the word and the prompting of the Holy Spirit would prevent grievous error.

For Luther, and even more so for Protestants after him, the Holy Spirit provided the experiential authentication for a reading of Scripture. This was the most radical aspect of his hermeneutic, for Aquinas had discussed the whole topic of revelation without mentioning the Holy Spirit. According to Luther, the discovery of clarity in Scripture waited upon an epiphany of the Holy Spirit.[5] Discovering clarity usually involved a shift

[5] "There are two kinds of clarity in Scripture, just as there are also two kinds of obscurity: one external and pertaining to the ministry of the Word, the other located in the understanding of the heart. If you speak of the internal clarity, no man perceives one iota of what is in the Scriptures unless he has the Spirit of God. All men have a darkened heart, so that even if they can recite everything in Scripture, and know how to quote it, yet they apprehend and truly understand nothing of it. They neither believe in God, nor that they themselves are crea-

6

of referent—regarding the speaker, the object of address, or a word that made an entire passage metaphorical. The Holy Spirit's work, formally considered, was that of rhetorical expertise. In a very important sense, faith became a "poetic" activity—a passionate reading of a divine text (in which the figures were identified and read aright) followed by a reading of experience through this text. With the Reformation, religious experience, to an overwhelming degree, became "literary" experience. In sum, Luther's revisionist reading of the Scripture proceeded on two principles: one essentially mystical (the Holy Spirit's epiphany) and the other rational (the analogy of the word). The latter he observed very strictly, even to the point of rejecting the Book of James because it does not mention the promise of Christ. Haller virtually ignored this "objective" principle and assumed that the Reformation made what in Catholic practice had been visual and corporate into something impalpable and inward.[6] To be sure, the Reformation does emphasize the action of grace upon individual consciousness, but the innovation of the Reformation cannot adequately be described as a referential shift inward. It would be more accurate to describe it as a shift of the sacramental medium from things to words, which demonstrably can be both intimate and communal. Because physical symbols do not transliterate into verbal ones in any easy point-by-point fashion, and because the laws of their deployment are stubbornly incommensurate, any attempt to describe Reformation piety in terms of Catholic images and the philosophical assumptions attached to them will be misleading. Luther's exegesis makes a radical shift from physical to *verbal*, not simply from physical to mental, reference. In nearly every

---

tures of God, nor anything else. . . . The Spirit is required for the understanding of Scripture, both as a whole and in any part of it. If, on the other hand, you speak of the external clarity, nothing at all is left obscure or ambiguous, but everything there is in the Scriptures [and] has been brought out by the Word into the most definite light" (*LW* 33.28).

[6] For a discussion of puritan inwardness, see William Haller, *The Rise of Puritanism*, New York, Columbia University Press, 1938, pp. 195-217, especially p. 211.

case, the referral of images to verbal matters calls in question the power of visual images to describe the motions of faith.

For example, in Reformation commentary, "sacrifice" becomes a verbal action, though not entirely an inward one: sacrifice becomes "praise." There is no simple and obvious point of comparison between Protestant praise and Old Testament sacrifice (or that of the Mass), except in the very broad sense that they are acts of worship. When Luther rings changes on Hosea 14:2 ("We will render the calves of our lips") and exhorts us to offer up to God "the fruit of lips" (*LW* 29.176), the metaphor sheds no particular light upon the nature of verbal sacrifice; he has to explain that uttering words alone becomes a sacrifice only if the words are offered "in the midst of sufferings," or "when a man in the midst of bitterness of heart and in the agony of death even sings to God, saying (Ps. 119:137): 'Righteous art Thou, Oh Lord . . .' " (*LW* 29.176). Praise, in Luther's view, is giving God credit for being God and finding evidence for his goodness even in the face of counter-evidence. Accordingly, the dominant protocol for praise is simply that of "telling His wonderful works" (*LW* 16.167)—in creation, history, or personal experience; hence, praise takes a variety of literary forms—a catalog of the natural world, an historical narrative, a doctrinal summary, or an autobiography. All such "sacrifices" Milton will offer in the course of *Paradise Lost*, the most moving of which will be the narrator's sacrificial song in his "shady covert hid."

In a similar way, other time-honored images of the Christian tradition are referred to verbal activity. The Kingdom of God "consisteth in the 'preaching' of the Gospel." The "secrets" of the Kingdom, grasped only by its members, turn out to be a very public arcana—Christian doctrine.[7] The "gate to paradise" is God's promise when it is believed.[8] Even when Luther's ex-

---

[7] John Calvin, *Commentary upon the Acts of the Apostles*, trans. Christopher Fetherstone, ed. Henry Beveridge, Edinburgh, Calvin Translation Society, 1859, I, 15. Cf. *LW* 26.27; John Calvin, *The Mystery of Godliness and Other Selected Sermons*, Grand Rapids, Mich., Eerdmans Press, 1959, p. 50.

[8] *LW* 34.337; John Calvin, *The Mystery of Godliness*, p. 122.

egesis seems most medieval, he finds that the purport of the allegory he is expounding concerns verbal matters: "You see, there is no doubt that the two cherubim before Moses and Isaiah indicate the ministry of the Word . . . . [They] are winged because the Word flies; it runs swiftly. That is what poets, too, wanted to picture with their Mercury, the winged messenger of the gods, and that is how his name was chosen, why he should be called 'Hermes.' So also Vergil described rumor as winged . . ." (*LW* 20.59-60).

The Reformation imagery that causes the most difficulty to latterday readers has to do with "vision" and "opened eyes." These terms do not treat direct perception of the Empyrean, nor that of a fresh visible world in the sands we tread underfoot. Routinely, the Reformers make the caveat that heavenly things like God's throne cannot be seen except by the "eyes of faith" (*LW* 13.7). To them, "seeing" is verbal understanding, a grasping and taking to heart of a divine locution. Indeed, "seeing" is believing some very definite divine words, for Luther maintained that in doctrine we see the face of God (*LW* 1.309, 22.157). On a number of occasions, he carefully distinguishes this "verbal vision" from an ineffable, mystical one. "It is the true contemplative life," he declared, "to hear and believe the spoken Word" (*LW* 3.276)—a contemplative life exemplified by the narrator in Book III of *Paradise Lost.* Nothing more clearly demonstrates how the Reformation forged new patterns, rather than merely psychologizing old ones, than this dissolving of the distinction between the contemplative and the active life. The *viseo dei* was understood to be readily available in this life and was to be sought in a "literary" account, as Calvin explained:

> He appeareth to us daily by His gospel. Although He dwelleth in His heavenly glory, if we open the eyes of faith, we shall behold Him. We must learn not to separate what the Holy Ghost hath joined together.[9]

[9] John Calvin, *The Mystery of Godliness*, p. 50. Cf. *Inst.* 1.9.3, and *LW* 26.287: "And this grasping of Christ through faith [by 'an intellect that has been illumined'] is truly the 'speculative life.' . . . The speculation by which

One result was to give extraordinary authority to verbal experience and to inject into daily life a "minimal mysticism." Contemplation thus verbally defined became the hallmark of the active life. Though the absence of required "works" was a favorite theme for Luther and Calvin, their commentaries make a *de facto* requirement: "Christ desireth nothing more of us, then that wee speak of him . . . [which is] the true service of God: hee loadeth no heavie burthens upon us, neither to cleav wood, nor to carrie stones; but will onely have that wee believ in him, and preach of him" (*TT*, p. 132). The works urged are "literary" ones—reading, studying, meditating upon God's word and then professing, confessing, or testifying about one's grasp thereof. "To read the word, to heare the word, and to teach the word," claimed Luther, are "heavenly works" assisted by the Holy Ghost.[10]

Not surprisingly, in the commentary of Luther and Calvin, the ethical strictures of Holy Writ, via a referential shift, often turn into "literary" strictures. Pride, at its root, said Luther, "is Lying" (*TT*, p. 162). "The mind of the flesh" is not lasciviousness, but a certain hermeneutic stance, a wanton disregard of God's word. Accordingly, a staggering drunkard becomes an image for an ungodly teacher who "waver[s] hither and yon" (*LW* 16.242). The injunction to sobriety in I Peter 1:13 urges "not temperance only in eating and drinking, but rather spiritual sobriety, when all our thoughts and affections are so kept as not to be inebriated with the allurements of this world," but focused steadily upon God's word. "Sobriety" in these commentaries, as often as not, means walking in the word and not "swarving" from it. In a similar way, "Chastity" is regularly defined as fidelity to divine words.[11] Luther comes close to mak-

Christ is grasped is not the foolish imagination . . . ; it is a theological, faithful, and divine consideration of the serpent hanging from the pole, that is, of Christ hanging on the cross for my sins."

[10] Martin Luther, *A Commentarie Upon the XV. Psalmes, called Psalmi Graduum*, trans. Henry Bull, London, 1587, p. 7 (cited hereafter as *Gradual Psalms*).

[11] John Calvin, *Commentaries on the Catholic Epistles*, trans. John Owen, Edinburgh, Calvin Translation Society, 1855, p. 44.

ing sodomy a literary offense when, in commenting upon the story of Lot, he claims that the main offense of the Sodomites was not "ordinary" debauchery (which he itemizes), but their unforgivable hermeneutic stance—their "contempt of the Word" (LW 3.233). Virtue similarly is defined in a "literary" way so that writing of or preaching the word becomes an activity of great merit. As Milton himself said, "it is a deed of highest charitie to help undeceive the people" (CE 6.45).

One can scarcely overemphasize the way in which the images and rhetoric of Scripture, in the hands of Reformation exegetes, make reference to God's (verbal) word. As William Whitaker put it, "The sense of scripture is the scripture itself."[12] Even when one finds "faith," rather than "words," to be the explicit referent in a passage, one need not read far to be reminded that faith is bound up with "words"—as its external occasion, its external manifestation, and its psychological texture. The tacit equation of virtues and vices with literary stance and action is but one difficulty in reading with precision today what the puritans wrote. The appropriation of biblical language and imagery that makes puritan writing colorful also makes interpreting it problematic, because a given biblical phrase may be used for devotional, ethical, political, and autobiographical purposes and may indicate something different in each case. Hence, any reading of puritan texts—the locating of its metaphors and their referents—will be only as accurate as one's grasp of puritan experience. Luther liked to point out that such experience was as important as a knowlege of rhetoric and grammar:

> When a philologian unfamiliar with the subject matter hears the proverb "There is a wolf in the story" [Lupus est in fabula], he thinks that the story is being discussed.

[12] William Whitaker, A Disputation on Holy Scripture, trans. and ed. for the Parker Society, Cambridge, Cambridge University Press, 1849, p. 459: "For whatever hath the supreme authority of assigning the sense of the scripture, upon that our faith, in the last resolution, must bottom itself and rest. For our faith reposes upon that which gives the most certain sense of scripture, and judges of all doctrine . . . .

"God alone made the scriptures. Therefore God alone hath supreme authority to interpret the scriptures. . . . The scripture itself, therefore, is its own faithful

But if there is a wolf in the story, it follows that the wolf is being discussed. Who would not laugh at such a scholar? Yet great men [those who "know only the meaning of the words"] permit the same thing in the most serious discussions.

(*LW* 3.67)

The commentaries of Luther and Calvin demonstrate how they believe Christ to be "in" the biblical narrative. When considered in large swaths rather than in isolated, annotative detail, their commentary reveals the core of puritan experience for the next several centuries: the conviction that Scripture will become plain enough to anyone making a devoted study and the conviction that one encountered the Real Presence in biblical promise. The welter of conflicting positions on ethics, politics, and church polity that claimed scriptural sanction during the seventeenth century makes it difficult to see how the central emphasis upon grace by "hearing" divine words remained remarkably constant. The work of Luther and Calvin provides an appropriate starting point for a study of Milton, not because his views agree with the fine doctrinal shadings of the Reformers—although Milton's position on liberty was very close to that of Luther, and his understanding of the Holy Spirit is very close to that of Calvin—but because their commentary presents the phenomenology of this word-based piety with particular clarity. They often make explicit—and vivid—experience that Protestant scholastics like William Ames or William Perkins take for granted or reduce to arid formula. In particular, Luther and Calvin convey the sense of excitement, even numinosity, in reading sacred texts, and they set forth the major ways by which a text was rendered "changeable" under the operation of the Spirit.

Milton's indebtedness to Luther and Calvin for exegetical detail is not the concern here, though borrowing is probable in

---

and clear interpreter, and the Spirit of God in the scriptures illustrates and explains himself."

many instances. Rather, it is important to show that Milton shared their attitude toward sacred texts and their belief in a "verbal" sacrament. Since the focus is upon what is central to the Reformation tradition, I shall, for the sake of concision, often refer to Luther and Calvin as "the Reformers." The most difficult point to grasp about their exegesis is the variety of interpretive routes available. Traditional typology was still in use, but it no longer enjoyed the status of norm or the underpinning of natural theology. The assumption that the meaning of scriptural locutions had been fixed by God at Creation, that verbal meanings emerged from the structure of the universe and the providential order of history,[13] gave way to the assumption that the work of the Spirit governed scriptural meaning in accord with the analogy of the word.[14] Alternate readings were common in the work of the Reformers. Luther, on various occasions, interpreted "the head of the serpent" in the prot-evangelium (Genesis 3:15) as presumption (*LW* 26.307), as the Devil (*LW* 1.191), as the works of the Law (*LW* 26.332-333), and as doubt and uncertainty (*TT*, p. 15). On the same verse, Calvin differed with Luther about the meaning of "the Seed" (thinking it designated Christians rather than Christ himself [*Inst.* 1.14.18]) without fundamentally altering the shape of Luther's biblical theology. So long as the analogy of the word was honored, a passage might be grasped afresh when a type was perceived as a trope, when metaphor gave way to metonymy, and when (an occasional) allegory gave way to a simple, plain designation. The alternate routes did not always comprise a choice among the traditional fourfold meanings, but often a

[13] See Barbara K. Lewalski, *Donne's "Anniversaries" and the Poetry of Praise: The Creation of a Symbolic Mode*, Princeton, Princeton University Press, 1973, pp. 144-145 (cited hereafter as *Donne's "Anniversaries"*); and *Protestant Poetics*, p. 111.

[14] For example, William Whitaker, writing in 1588, abandons neither classic typology nor a respect for the Church Fathers, but he places the Holy Ghost above the Church in the rule of faith and shares the Reformation emphasis upon the verbal sacrament: "But we affirm the whole essence of the sacrament to be delivered in the sacred writings" (*A Disputation on Holy Scripture*, pp. 484, 500). See n. 12 above.

choice between contradictory meanings. Moses might be seen as a type of Christ, as synecdoche of the Old Dispensation (and hence a personification of the Law), or as a complicated Christian saint—and each would be correct so long as the analogy of faith obtained.

II

The Holy Spirit is the best rhetorician and
logician, and therefore He speaks most clearly.
(LW 16.117)

For if I rightly understood and did believ but
onely these few words . . . that God (who
made heaven and earth, and created all crea-
tures, and hath all things in his hand and power)
were my Father, then I should certainly con-
clude by my self, that I also am a Lord of
heaven and earth, that Christ is my brother,
that *Gabriel* is my servant, that *Raphael* is my
coachman, that all the Angels in my necessities
are my attendants. . . . To conclude, it must
needs follow, that everie thing is mine.

(TT, p. 6)

Whatever the claims of nineteenth-century fundamentalists,
God's word in the first two centuries after the Reformation was
not equated with the lexical surface of the Bible, nor with the
exact wording of any particular passage. The promise of re-
demption through Christ could be communicated by a variety
of verbal arrangements—and in any language from Hebrew or
Greek to the English vernacular. Luther had at first identified
God's "word" with its oral proclamation in preaching, but he
himself found the *viva vox Christi* also in the lonely reading
of Scripture. Formally considered, the Reformers' Bible was a
referential Möbius strip; it was a word about the word about
the Word. What kept religious experience from being a verbal
shell game[15] was the belief that when comprehension of the

---

[15] Malcolm Mackenzie Ross describes the Protestant Communion thus: "The
'bread' stands for the written word only; it cannot *be* the living Word. It is

Promise occurs, "God really speaks to me" (cf. *LW* 26.375), and that one's status was thereby subjectively and metaphysically changed. God's verbal communication was not "sacramental" in the sense that it joined one to God's "substance"; rather it was an overlapping of souls of the sort described by Milton as an agreement in mind and heart and intent. Milton jettisoned the philosophical categories that "substance" implies in favor of the rhetorical category of "persuasion," which he used to gloss "substance" in the famous Pauline definition of faith (Hebrews 11:1): "Faith is the [persuasion] of things hoped for, the demonstration of things which are not seen" (*CD*, p. 472). This persuasion, however, was not without a supernatural component and was thought to be a real and mysterious joining of man and God.

If one attempts to read *Paradise Lost* while keeping in mind Milton's stated intention to be a "doctrinal" power beside the pulpit, then any "literary" epiphany that may arise during the course of a reading—discovery of a metaphor in an innocent word like "wandering," of a new referential aptness in a long-familiar line, of a contextual definition for a doctrinal phrase like "grace implanted," or of a fresh correspondence to the reader's own experience—all would be understood as the work of the Holy Spirit, as the *viva vox Christi* breaking through the text. With such discoveries, the text would take on enormous authority and affective power. Ultimately, the success of Milton's poetry lies less in the local effects of style than in the "poetic" power of his set of beliefs, in the combinatorial possibilities of his doctrinal system, and in the broad strategies that convey the power of this doctrine. If we grant that ideas could affect the sensibility of John Donne and move him passionately, must we not also allow that doctrinal ideas could have a strong emotional valence for Milton and the puritans of his day? One has only to read Golding's paraphrase of Calvin to catch some-

---

not the Word, but the word that *tells* of the Word," *Poetry and Dogma*, 1954, reprint New York, Octagon, 1969, p. 76.

thing of the passionate investment made in this theology of the word:

> And David speaking by the same spirite, exhorteth you by his owne example to set your whole delight in [the scriptural word], too occupy yourselfe in it day and night, too lay it up in your hart, too set more store by it than by riches, to be mindeful of it, to make it your counsayler, to stick too it, too talk of it afore Kings and great men, to love it too make your songs of it, to remember it night and day, too count it sweeter than Honey, too take it as an heritage, and to make it the ioy of your hart.[16]

A cardinal point of evangelical doctrine was that the Holy Spirit breathes where he lists and that his movements could never be predicted in advance, just as one can never predict the exact moment or point in a text when a literary classic like *King Lear* will yield a profound insight. In Milton's poems, as in poetry generally, the curve of an individual's response in the course of a reading is unique and essentially mysterious. Nonetheless, we can locate the formal features of Milton's text that allow for an almost infinite number of doctrinal epiphanies, we can describe the expectations that a reader must have for an epiphany, and we can discuss Milton's persuasive strategies that are of larger compass than the diction of doctrinal formula.

Unlike Shakespeare, Milton's grounding in Reformation doctrine is beyond dispute. His own father left home in his youth, rather than abandon biblical theology, and Milton's tutor, Thomas Young, was an earnest Calvinist who risked the high seas for his particular brand of faith. The religious views learned at home probably got Milton in trouble with his Laudian tutor at Cambridge. If so, suffering rustication the way his father had suffered disinheritance must have only reinforced his beliefs and etched them deeply in his psyche. Though Milton moderated the strict Calvinism of his early tracts, the distinguishing fea-

---

[16] *The Psalmes of David and others With M. John Calvins Commentaries*, trans. Arthur Golding, London, 1571, p. ii.

17

tures of his belief-system remained those of a Reformation theology of the word. This theology is more important to the esthetic success of *Paradise Lost* and Milton's major poems than generally is supposed. It provides the "filter" through which Milton read the Church Fathers and the literary classics alike. He finds Athanasias, for example, voicing the Protestant caveat against adding to the word (*YP* 1.564) and concludes "that the Fathers referre all decision of controversie to the Scriptures, as all-sufficient to direct, to resolve, and to determine" (563). Similarly, Milton quotes "three [of] the famousest men for wit and learning"—Dante, Ariosto, and Chaucer—to support Luther's distinction between the civil and spiritual realms (*YP* 1.558-560). In short, the Reformation hermeneutic provided Milton with a lifelong structure of apprehension, as well as a dynamic structure for his poetry.

It may now be as difficult to participate imaginatively in Milton's world view as it is to participate in Vergil's civil religion and applaud the sacrifices of bullocks that he describes in the *Aeneid* in bloody detail. The sociology of religion works against our taking the sacramental aspect of Milton's poetry very seriously because those who hold his precise doctrinal views today may be on the fringes of society and display an antagonism toward education and high culture that would have made Milton gasp. It is difficult therefore to discuss Milton's theology of the word and the way in which it informs his poetry without making the poet appear culturally declassé. In Milton's youth it was far otherwise. If Calvinism was not still the latest intellectual word from the Continent that it had been in the 1580s, it was, as Auden remarked, as "modish as shepherds and goddesses."[17] It was "the creed of progressives" espoused by a few nobility, some gentry, and many enterprising lawyers and scriveners who had gone to the university, who kept the booksellers in business, and who engaged tutors for their sons. The fierce political fervor that attached itself to this theology kept it in the forefront of

[17] W. H. Auden, *A Certain World: A Commonplace Book*, London, Faber and Faber, 1971, p. 45.

political as well as intellectual consciousness during the years when Milton was coming of age. One of the purposes of this study is to suggest something of the emotional weight and timbre of Milton's theology and to show that, properly considered, this theology helps to make his poetry simple, passionate, and even sensuous.

Demonstrating the simplicity or underlying unity is easy enough. Milton's poetry draws upon three large, interconnected formal patterns: the Bible understood with the function and shape given it by the Reformers, the doctrinal system extracted from this Bible, and the classical epic read through the lens of Reformation doctrine and biblical exegesis. The various forms that "the word" takes and the various powers it was understood to possess are spelled out in the commentary of Luther and Calvin in an informal and repetitive fashion. The English puritans, who were not theological innovators, soon honed the thought of these Reformers into systems of fine Ramian reticulation, as, for example, in the compendia of Ames, Wollebius, and Milton himself. One pattern that these compendia assume, but do not spell out, is what one might call the transformational grammar of "the word." Though the "word" was always *one*, it took at least seven major forms—the complete biblical narrative from Creation to Judgment Day, the verbal promise given in a single sentence from Scripture, a doctrinal abstract of the Bible, a retelling of a biblical story with elaboration and commentary, an inventory of Creation, a review of the history of the world, and finally, the mere name of Christ, which covered and implied the rest. These basic forms of "the word" constituted a sevenfold system of puns (or "notation" in Renaissance rhetoric). A coincidence of any two or more forms of "the word" would yield an epiphany in reading. To take an example that has become almost a critical cliché, the "fruit" of that forbidden tree (*PL* 1.1) refers, in turn to what Adam and Eve ate on the fateful day of the Fall, to their lascivious lovemaking, to their sense of sin and guilt, and to their darkened vision; but it also refers to the fruit of their loins, who was to appear in history as the Messiah, and to their rehabilitation by God's promise of

19

the Seed. The way in which "fruit" consecutively takes on new and *corrected* meanings—as one "fact" in a narrative, as a doctrinal generalization, as a momentous turning point in history, and as a sacramental apprehension—illustrates the way in which *Paradise Lost*, like the Reformers' Bible, "interprets itself"[18] via a large circle of cross-reference.

The chief esthetic problem of Milton's poetry is that "the word" in his theology, if not wholly discursive, contains an irreducible discursive element, for the "Promise" of the Incarnation and the Crucifixion could not satisfactorily be conveyed by pure narrative. Explicit statement about its promissory meaning was needed before the events narrated could prove "sacramental." Doctrine was related to biblical narrative, much as literary criticism, or at least thematic criticism, is related to fictional narrative, except that doctrine held an exalted rather than a derivative status in puritan thought. The quasi-abstractions issuing from the mouth of God in *Paradise Lost*, reflect Milton's view that to connect doctrinal statement and biblical narrative (and life) is to hear God speaking. Contrary to the perennial judgment that Milton falters when he includes bare doctrine, I shall argue that explicit doctrine is not only the center of coherence in Milton's poetry, but a source of poetic energy as well. To be sure, many have shared Pope's view that Milton's God is a school divine and that his heaven is no more mysterious than the average schoolroom. Cassirer's analysis of abstract language seems to confirm Pope's judgment, for he argues that transparent, conceptual language invokes the categories of theory versus practice, while concrete language invokes the categories of the sacred versus the profane.[19] The language of the spirit, Cassirer maintains, clings to bodies, to the opacity of

[18] William Whitaker, "Scripture is its own interpreter" (*A Disputation on Holy Scripture*, p. 488); "Scripture [is] the sole interpreter of itself to the conscience" (*CE* 6.7).

[19] Ernst Cassirer, *Mythical Thought*, in *The Philosophy of Symbolic Forms*, trans. Ralph Manheim, New Haven, Yale University Press, 1953-1957, III, 29-59.

20

concrete objects. If so, the speech of Milton's God is inherently antipoetic and constitutes a grandiose defect in his poetry.

This view fails to take into account the extraliterary properties that God's "word" was presumed to have in Milton's religious tradition—properties that ultimately derive from Hebrew idiom. As Luther was quick to note, *dabar* (דָּבָר), unlike *sermo*, has an almost palpable weight and can be translated as "thing," "cause," "order," "something," as well as "word" and "speech" (*LW* 16.27). Behind the propositional language of doctrine, the puritan scholastics still felt the enactive force of *dabar*, which was understood to unite speaker and speech to hearer in one mighty deed ("Swift are the acts of God . . ."). This unity of divine deed governs the web of metonymies that make Reformation rhetoric almost impossible to label and fix in a doctrinal taxonomy, because often the same biblical phrase is used to describe the God who speaks, the language that conveys the divine word, the Spirit who underlines it, and the heart (or faith) that hears the word. This unity of deed makes the puritan esthetic, as it were, a "syntactical" esthetic. Spiritual mystery resided, not in *being*, but in grasping, via words, the *relation* between beings: Luther held that God was to be encountered, not in his substance, which was unknowable and terrifying, but "in the category of relation" (*LW* 3.122). In Milton's tradition, the Spirit clings, not to bodies, but to language itself and skips like Ariel along the tucks and gaps in the syntactical chain forming metaphor, metonymy, and other tropes. Spiritual adventure in Milton's poetry lies in the very changeability of his text, which can appear startlingly altered whenever a new metaphor is discovered, when an old one is flattened, or when a fresh referential connection is made that reorders the reader's grasp of the entire text—and possibly himself. Moreover, Milton's explicit doctrine is not so naked after all, because he gives it various coverings (or at least coordinates) chosen from the stock of literary conventions and rhetorical tactics available to a Renaissance poet.

─────── III ───────

If my opponents could show that the doctrine
they defend was revealed to them by a voice
from heaven, he would be an impious wretch
who dared to raise so much as a murmur against
it.

(CD, p. 204)

"On the Morning of Christ's Nativity" is a veritable Milton
sampler displaying the major ingredients of his esthetic of "the
word." Though the poem is generally conceded to be a product
of puritan spirituality, it is still taxed for not being a sensuous
icon on the grounds that "the doctrine of the incarnation cannot
be expressed unless the artist can manage a flesh-and-blood
baby."[20] Puritan spirituality, on the contrary, took God's word
on the matter and proceeded on the assumption that God's
actions could not be properly understood without the reportorial
powers of language. They believed that the mysterious reach
of language could connect, in a single moment, a grand historical
deed, the God who performed it, and the motions of a human
heart (see Chapter 4). In the Nativity Ode, as one might expect,
Milton treats the Incarnation as a "speech act," and his poetic
strategies belong in the category of *event* rather than *icon.*
Milton is not giving instructions to a painter, but offering an
elliptical narrative, a scenario for history, with the nodal points
starred, as it were.

The Advent is announced immediately and linked to the Cru-
cifixion and to its *interpretation* as a definitive legal transaction:

> The Babe lies yet in smiling Infancy,
> That on the bitter cross
> Must redeem our loss.
>
> (16.151-153)

---

[20] See, for example, John Carey, *Milton*, New York, Arco Press, 1970, p. 30;
Ross, *Poetry and Dogma*, p. 190.

22

To excerpt a doctrinal pronouncement, however, is to distort a major excellence of the Ode, that is, the way in which doctrine serves as the armature of the poem without being homiletically importunate. Martz observes that the poem is really about the *effect* of the Incarnation, or Redemption.[21] The presence of the poet in Milton's epic, which has received the best critical attention of late, needs to be considered here.[22] The presence of the poet makes the Ode a dramatization of the Protestant "sacrament"—the verbal transaction in which "objective" Promise is implanted in consciousness, a transaction signaled here by a celebratory repetition of doctrine. The poet-swain establishes in the proem that the Ode itself is his verbal offering, and with it he proceeds to perform one of Luther's "heavenly works" and "join [his] voice unto the Angel Choir" (Proem 4.27). Despite Milton's headnote on how the poem came to him one Christmas morning, and despite the intimation that he speaks at the behest of the Holy Spirit ("From out his secret Altar toucht with hallow'd fire" [4.28]), the poet's inner motions are handled with extreme reticence. The Ode brilliantly bonds the poet-swain's subjective awareness to objective events; both his heart's motions and points of doctrine are presented as *events*. The revolution that grace makes in the consciousness of the poet is expressed in the familiar pastoral paradigm, according to which a swain's response to his beloved is described as a radical change in nature. This familiar paradigm from the Renaissance miscellanies has considerable numinous potential, though it often becomes a routine strategy for compliment. A fresh use of the paradigm, when Nature is made to embody the power of the beloved and the adoration of the lover in equal measure, usually evokes a sense of mystery. The paradigm had already been applied to Christ in a rudimentary way in English Christmas carols,[23] but Milton's use of it is extended and more so-

[21] Louis L. Martz, *The Poetry of Meditation*, New Haven, Yale University Press, 1954, p. 165.
[22] See Arnold Stein, *The Art of Presence: The Poet and Paradise Lost*, Berkeley, University of California Press, 1977.
[23] See, for example, Edmond Bolton's "The Sheepheards Song," in *England's*

Milton and the Science of the Saints

phisticated. Nature's response is first generalized by a personification:

> Nature in awe to him
> Had doff't her gaudy trim,
> With her great Master so to sympathize.
> (1.32-34)

Then individual aspects of nature display the kind of animate response that had been offered to many a Phyllis and Astrea during the preceding thirty years, the kind that Marvell was to lay at the feet of Maria in "Upon Appleton House":[24]

Helicon, 1600, 1614, ed. Hyder Edward Rollins, Cambridge, Mass., Harvard University Press, 1935, I, 132, ll. 24-31:
> After long night, vp-risen is the morne,
> Renowning *Bethlem* in the Sauiour.
>   Sprung is the perfect day,
>   By Prophets seene a farre:
>   Sprung is the mirthfull May,
>   Which Winter cannot marre.
> In *Dauids* Cittie dooth this Sunne appeare:
> Clouded in flesh, yet Sheepheards sit we heere.

[24] Rosamund Tuve thought that the Nativity Ode would not have been considered a pastoral in the seventeenth century, despite the inclusion of shepherds, because "the basic metaphors of pastoral are absent" (*Images and Themes in Five Poems by Milton*, Cambridge, Harvard University Press, 1967, p. 42). The Nativity Ode, however, uses a pastoral paradigm common both to the Christmas carols of the miscellanies and to Marvell's sophisticated praise of Lord Fairfax's daughter in "Upon Appleton House":
> See how loose Nature, in respect
> To her, it self doth recollect;
> And every thing so whisht and fine,
> Starts forth with to its *Bonne Mine*.
> The *Sun* himself, of *Her* aware,
> Seems to descend with greater Care;
> And lest *She* see him go to Bed;
> In blushing Clouds conceales his Head.
>
> So when the Shadows laid asleep
> From underneath these Banks do creep,
> And on the River as it flows
> With *Eben Shuts* begin to close;
> The modest *Halcyon* comes in sight,

24

> The Winds, with wonder whist,
> Smoothly the waters kiss't,
>   Whispering new joys to the mild Ocean,
> Who now hath quite forgot to rave,
> While Birds of Calm sit brooding on the charmed wave.
>   (5.64-68)

If we read the pastoral paradigm aright, Nature presents a simultaneous description of the swain's heart and of the power of his God—exactly the reverse of Adam's situation in *Paradise Lost*, where *real* nature needs a priest to offer up its praise. Once we see that pastoral Nature "speaks" intimately for the poet, the Ode does not appear nearly so remote and cold as sometimes claimed. The "foul deformities" and "guilty front" belong to the poet whose sins are now "covered" by snow. It is his heart to which "meek-ey'd Peace" and the (Turtle) dove descend from the clouds. Just as the grounds of Appleton House are transformed into a paradise when Maria comes, so the poet-swain's redeemed consciousness becomes a pastoral idyll. Milton's conspicuously original touch is to combine the halcyon days of Nature with the halcyon days of the Augustan Age— "No War, or Battle's sound/Was heard the World around" (4.53-54). This widening of the pastoral response to include history shows again how relentlessly the poem is organized by *event*, rather than by *pictura*.

Milton's second major strategy is likewise a dynamic one; from the very first, his stanza form, with its trimeter lines suggesting the folk meter of naïve English carols,[25] has linked musical and doctrinal apprehension. This association becomes explicit when he presents doctrine *heard* as the sudden change

---

> Flying betwixt the Day and Night;
> And such an horror calm and dumb,
> *Admiring Nature* does benum.

(*The Poems and Letters of Andrew Marvell*, ed. H. M. Margoliouth, Oxford, Clarendon Press, 1967, I, 79, stanzas 83-84).

[25] See Martz, "The Rising Poet, 1645," in *The Lyric and Dramatic Milton*, ed. Joseph H. Summers, New York, Columbia University Press, 1965, p. 27.

from silence to song. That the swain hears the unheard music of the spheres in the nativity *Gloria* is Milton's musical version of the Reformation *topos* that to have faith is to be let in on God's "secrets" of well-published doctrine. It is a brilliant stroke to present a system of doctrine with unoffensive succinctness by giving each tenet an auditory correlate. The morning stars in chorus, *Gloria in excelsis*, Satan's clanging chains, and the trump of doom invoke, respectively, the doctrine of Creation, the Incarnation, Redemption, and the Second Coming. This equation of musical with doctrinal apprehension helps to artic-ulate the paradox of the Kingdom, which is difficult enough for verbal syntax and clumsy, if not impossible, in the visual arts. Angelic choruses easily knit together the once and future king-dom that

> now begins; for from this happy day
> Th'old Dragon under ground,
> In straiter limits bound,
> > Not half so far casts his usurped sway.
> > (18.167-170)

The anticipation of a remembered tune brilliantly conveys the conundrum of the Kingdom that is, has been, and is yet to be. Lest we miss the point, Milton invokes the circular structure of Vergil's Messianic Eclogue ("For if such holy Song/Enwrap our fancy long,/Time will run back, and fetch the age of gold" [14.133-135]), in order to amend Vergil's scheme ("no,/This must not yet be so"). Defining eschatology as musical repetition has the further advantage of giving doctrine the passionate es-thetic coloring that it is said to lack in *Paradise Lost*. The place of eros in Reformation piety becomes clear when Milton de-scribes an access of faith (*hearing* the word) as apprehending such music

> As never was by mortal finger struck,
> Divinely-warbled voice
> Answering the stringed noise,
> > As all thir souls in *blissful rapture took*:

26

The Air such *pleasure* loath to lose,
With thousand echoes still prolongs each heav'nly close.
                    (9.95-100, *author's italics*)

Milton's contrasting styles of reference are yet another way by which he gives the poem decisive movement. The divine Birth is treated in three brief notations (1.29-31, 8.85-92, and 27.237-244). In each case, the reference is simple and direct and itself takes on "semantic" value. After the conceited indirection of the first seven stanzas on nature's toilet, we turn once more to direct statement about the shepherds and the babe "kindly come to live with them below" (8.90), as if we were returning, after elaboration in a minor mode, to the key signature. In this way, the referential organization of the poem pits flirtatious obliquity against unambiguous directness—charm against truth—in a way that makes direct reference climactic, as it should be in a piety that defines grace as clarity discovered. In the latter half of the poem, Milton announces his view of the pagan gods as straw men,[26] rather than as unwitting Christian oracles, and he conveys their insubstantiality as much by style of reference as by auditory association—all those hysterical "shrieks" and neurasthenic "sighs." The catalogue goes on with ever more oblique and windy ways of proclaiming absence ("In vain [the] Cymbals' ring" in Moloch's palace, nor is Osiris seen on "*Memphian* Grove or Green,/Trampling the unshow'r'd Grass with lowings loud" [24.214-215]), until the roll call of abdicating pagans seems to be all encrustation, a piling up of epithets and entire lines having eccentric reference to a vacuum. Milton's strongest contrast in referential style comes when he describes the sun at two figurative removes, first through the civilized screen of bed curtains, and then *per confusio* through the faeries' Moon-loved maze:

        So when the Sun in bed,
        Curtain'd with cloudy red,

[26] Philip Rollinson, "Milton's Nativity Poem and the Decorum of Genre," *Milton Studies*, VII, 180.

27

Pillows his chin upon an Orient wave,
The flocking shadows pale
Troop to th'infernal jail;
    Each fetter'd Ghost slips to his several grave,
And the yellow-skirted *Fays*
Fly after the Night-steeds, leaving their
                    Moon-lov'd maze.
                            (26.229-236)

Milton may not have intended to contrast "poetic" obfuscation
with the clarity of divine revelation, but we cannot miss how
he tries "to clothe the sun" with conceits, then follows it with
a naked statement about the infant Son. The contrast in ref-
erential style makes the child being put to bed seem very real:

But see! the Virgin blest,
Hath laid her Babe to rest.
Time is our tedious Song should here have ending.
                            (27.237-239)

At last we are invited to look at the Advent as Nativity *scene*,
and we have a sense of journey completed as the goal of the
Wise Men, announced in stanza 5 of the proem, is finally *shown*.
The last stanza has the strongest visual appeal of any in the
poem, and Louis Martz observes that it is the kind that typically
might begin a Catholic meditation.[27] Milton withholds any vis-
ual statement until its doctrinal import has been presented *and*
apprehended, apparently valuing *pictura* as the Reformers did,
that is, merely as a means of rhetorical emphasis. Milton, like
Rembrandt, knew that the elimination of color and light gives
unusual intensity to what remains. So it is here when *pictura*,
though only the outline of a crèche, comes as a bold rhetorical
stroke summing up, or "sealing," the promise of history and
doctrine.

As if heeding Luther's caveats about substituting a tabloid
response to the *scene* of Christ's birth and death, instead of
"reading" its promise (*LW* 31.357), Milton avoids the risk of

[27] Martz, *The Poetry of Meditation*, p. 165.

sentimentality by suppressing domestic detail. The tenderness in the final scene is all the more powerful because of its indirect, masculine expression: love is defined by how power is used. What the last stanza "reveals" is that all of God's power is concentrated upon loving, tender care. All the "hevenly so-diers," as Tyndale calls them in his version of Luke 2:15, are put to minding the baby:

> Heav'n's youngest-teemed Star
> Hath fixt her polisht Car,
>   Her sleeping Lord with Handmaid Lamp attending:
> And all about the Courtly Stable
> Bright-harness'd Angels sit in order serviceable.
> (27.240-245)

In the Nativity Ode, Milton reveals his lifelong preoccupations—his understanding of God's love in terms of power and clarity, his description of faith as doctrine "heard," his view of doctrine as incipient history (and vice versa), and his belief in the momentous effects of God's speech. Milton later would abandon a pastoral view of history, would give the pagans their dark due, and would allow God's word to speak more on its own; but here his theology of the word proves no esthetic liability because he brilliantly uses musical association and pastoral paradigm as poetic "cover" for the naked word.

⚜ 2 ⚜
Masque à Clef

———————— I ————————

Yet some there be that
by due steps aspire
To lay their just hands
on that Golden Key
That opes the Palace of
Eternity.
(*Comus*, 12-14)

In *Comus*, Milton covers "the word" all too well, making it
a puzzle rather than a mystery hidden in plain sight. The young
poet, toying with Spenser's dark conceit, makes it even darker
than Book I of *The Faerie Queene*, which it resembles in many
ways. Spenser at least provided sententia now and then, but
Milton—perhaps partly for political reasons—leaves us to guess
how much more is meant by "chastity" and "virginity" than
meets the ear, and we must guess from hints that are so con-
tradictory as to suggest either a failure of artistic control or
sheer playfulness. Fletcher rightly emphasizes the young poet's
delight in his poetic ingredients, and on the whole *Comus* seems
more fashionably playful than deeply felt.[1] The masque is no

[1] Don Cameron Allen, *The Harmonious Vision*, Baltimore, Johns Hopkins
University Press, 1954, p. 24. Angus Fletcher, *The Transcendental Masque:
An Essay on Milton's Comus*, Ithaca, Cornell University Press, 1971, p. 243.

less fashionable, however, in its ideology than in its "Elizabethan" poetic ingredients, for puritan doctrine was then the creed of progressives.

Milton seems to be playing with puritan doctrines and corresponding ideas from the ancients, much as he plays with diction from Shakespeare's pastoral comedies. He had just been reading the *Phaedo* and was well aware that such words as "form," "virtue," "chastity," and "nature" could invoke several different worlds of thought—the Platonic, Stoic, Patristic, Thomistic, Neo-Platonic, and Reformation. Much depends upon one's starting point when approaching the masque. If read with Christian assumptions, it seems to present Christian motifs *in terms of* classical ethics and Platonic *topoi*. Little adjustment is needed to equate Platonic eternity with the Christian one or to read an attendant Daemon as the Holy Spirit, but today it is less obvious that the Platonic categories of "spirit" and "flesh" in *Comus* convert to Reformation ones. For example, the Elder Brother's claim that owing to the power of chastity the body "by degrees [is turned] to the soul's essence,/Till all be made immortal" (462-463) becomes a transparent statement of the doctrine of sanctification.[2] Though classical and biblical warn-

---

[2] William Kerrigan, in "The Heretical Milton: From Assumption to Mortalism," *ELR*, V (Winter 1975), 125-166, sees the Elder Brother as proclaiming the "Assumption" of the body when he claims that the chaste "by degrees [are turned] to the soul's essence,/Till all be made immortal" (462-463). Kerrigan suggests that the Elder Brother's philosophy is a "fictive" one that may be translated into a "real" philosophy or theology. He finds the "breach between the real and fictive philosophy" to indicate Milton's "psychological discomfort" with orthodox belief in the mortality of the body. He concludes that there is a "pronounced, puzzling, and arguably damaging emphasis on the immortality of the flesh" (p. 136).

If, however, one reads *Comus* in the light of Reformation thought, the "fictive" philosophy concerning the soul's transformation of the flesh stands as a transparent equivalent to the doctrine of sanctification. Both Luther and Calvin held that the "flesh" was not simply body, but rather sin and selfish desire of all sorts. To some degree an extirpation of "the flesh" or sinful inclination took place in this life though there was never a complete sanctification until heaven. Here, as throughout the masque, Milton seems to be presenting Reformation motifs *in terms of* Platonic ones.

ings against self-indulgence may be lexically similar, they appear worlds apart if one takes the biblical counsel to "sobriety," "chastity," and "temperance" as ultimately having verbal reference, that is, as having to do with how one takes, holds, or keeps God's words. Usually, Christian interpretations of Comus have assumed a point of origin in either the Anglican liturgy or in the Thomistic tradition. Woodhouse's reading, which has dominated criticism of Comus for the last twenty-five years, is based upon the notion that there is a continuity between nature and grace and that virtue is the fulfillment of nature.[3] If, however, we approach Comus with the Reformation assumption that nature is inimical to grace and that virtue is extrinsic to man, the masque will appear remarkably coherent.

Milton turns the plot of The Faerie Queene, Book I, on its head and, instead of an unfaithful knight who is seduced by a witch, presents a faithful lady who is not seduced by a sorcerer, though she will also need to be rescued. When Spenser recounts how the Red Cross Knight takes off his armor, drinks from a drugged stream, and succumbs to the blandishments of a scarlet woman, the primary concern is not sexual morality, even though lust appears in the parade of deadly sins to be avoided. Likewise, Comus, who was given Christian valence by Erasmus[4] and con-

---

[3] A.S.P. Woodhouse, The Heavenly Muse: A Preface to Milton, ed. Hugh MacCallum, Toronto, University of Toronto Press, 1972, pp. 64, 75. For liturgical resonances in Comus, see James G. Taafe, who argues that "the collect in the Anglican service for Michaelmas celebrates that hierarchy which exists among earthly and heavenly guardians." See "Michaelmas, the 'Lawless Hour,' and the Occasion of Milton's Comus," ELN, 6 (June 1969), 259; and William G. Hunter, who argues in "The Liturgical Context of Comus," ELN, 10 (September 1972), 14-15, that Milton used the evening prayer for September 28, the morning prayer for September 29, and the communion service for St. Michael's Day "as his point of departure" in the composition of Comus.

[4] A number of literary sources for Milton's Comus have been suggested in which he is either a belly god or a latter-day Dionysus, notably Ben Jonson's masque, Pleasure reconcild to Vertue, and Puteanus' neo-Latin play, Comus sive Phagesiposi Cimmeria. See Ralph H. Singleton, "Milton's Comus and the Comus of Erycius Puteanus," PMLA, 58 (1943), 949-957. No instances, however, have been cited in which Comus appears in a Christian context. Having first appeared in Imagines by Philostratus the Elder, Comus is such a relative

latecomer to the classical pantheon that he does not have a clearly established equivalence to a figure in the Christian myth as do, say, Jove or Pan or Hercules. Apparently it was Erasmus who baptized Comus in his annotations to the Greek New Testament of 1516, giving him a Christian (albeit negative) valence. Consider the way in which Erasmus brings his purely literary knowledge to bear upon Rom. 13:13:

'Η νὺξ προέκοψεν, ἡ δὲ
ἡμέρα ἤγγικεν· ἀποθώμεθα
οὖν τὰ ἔργα τοῦ σκότους, καὶ
ἐνδυσώμεθα τὰ ὅπλα τοῦ
φωτός· Ὡς ἐν ἡμέρα
εὐσχημόνως περιπατήσωμεν,
μὴ κώμοις καὶ μέθαις, μὴ
κοίταις καὶ ἀσελγείαις, μὴ
ἔριδι καὶ ζήλῳ. Ἀλλ'
ἐνδύσασθε τὸν Κύριον
Ἰησοῦν Χριστὸν, καὶ τῆς
σαρκὸς πρόνοιαν μὴ ποιεῖσθε
εἰς ἐπιθυμίας.

Tamquam in die composite
ambulemus, non comessationibus
& ebrietatibus, non cubilibus
ac lasciviis, non contentione &
aemulatione.

Let us walk honestly, as in the
day: not in reveling and
drunkenness, not in chambering
and wantonness, not in strife
and envyings.

To this verse Erasmus appends the following note: "*Non in comessationibus* the preposition *in* is missing in the Greek, μὴ κώμοις, that is, *non comessationibus*: However, the addition is not wholly displeasing. For Κῶμος is the God of drunkenness for the Greeks and a rather shameless and lively party is described by the same name. But both lively songs and dances are called κωμάζειν by the Greeks: whence also the name *commoedia*. And they are said 'to revel' who garlanded and well-drunk break into another's party, not without their own music: as in Plato, Alcibiades crashed the party of Agathon. Athenaeus states in several places that this is the custom among the Greeks."

After a lengthy discussion of word order and alternative word choice, Erasmus adds: "Moreover, it is possible for this whole passage to be seen as an allegory. *Nox praecessit, dies appropinquavit, adjiciamus opera tenebrarum, sicut in die honesta ambulemus.*" (Desiderius Erasmus, *Novum Testamentum, Opera Omnia*, 1705, reprint London, Gregg, 1621, 5, 637. I am indebted for this point to John William Aldridge, *The Hermeneutic of Erasmus*, Basel Studies of Theology, No. 2, Richmond, John Knox, 1966, p. 121n).

Milton obviously had read the New Testament of Erasmus with some care because he cites it on some half-dozen occasions in his *Christian Doctrine*, including a comment on Romans 9:5; and Maurice Kelley concludes that Milton had Erasmus' New Testament at hand while composing his doctrinal tract (*CD*, pp. 242, 107n). Plucking a classical god from a scrap of Pauline diction is the kind of philological coup that Milton himself may have seized upon without any suggestion from Erasmus' note.

34

sidered by Luther to epitomize the lust of the flesh,[5] is extremely charming. Like Duessa, he represents a more profound and all-encompassing vision of evil than a mere illicit passion. In both cases, lust is the figure for a larger evil. A distinctly Reformation understanding of *concupiscentia* and its opposite, *virginitas fidei*, underlies the form of Milton's masque, giving it a striking unity, but making it enigmatic to modern critics. It is necessary to keep in mind two theological distinctions that now are all but forgotten, but that exercised Protestants to an extraordinary degree after the Council of Trent.

[5] Luther was lecturing on Romans when Erasmus' New Testament appeared and immediately availed himself of Erasmus' note in the following gloss: "[Romans 13:]13) *Not in reveling.* Just as the term *graecari* ('to live in the Greek manner') is derived from *Graecus* (Greek), so the word *comessari* ('reveling') comes, it seems, from *comos* ('a revel'). For the Greek κῶμος means a banquet, or rather a luxurious, wasteful, and immoderate preparation and celebration of a banquet. Indeed, the god of drunkenness is called Comus, and his feast bears the same name. In this the Greeks outdo the Germans and indeed the whole world, because they gave attention to banquets so enthusiastically that they even devised a god who was in charge of this as a useful activity. But the apostle teaches contrary to this in this passage and the positive side in 2 Cor. 2:6. For he wants us to devote ourselves to fasting and temperance and sobriety." (*LW* 25.481)

These lectures hardly could have influenced Milton, for until the nineteenth century they were extant only as student notes. Milton, however, could have found Comus in Luther's commentary on Galatians, which appeared in nine English translations prior to the publication of *Comus*. In the following, Luther is expatiating upon the works of the flesh: "Finally there is 'carousing,' which in Luke 21:34 is called dissipation. Just as drunkenness weighs down the hearts too much with drinking, so dissipation weighs them down too much with eating. And this widespread evil is having an astonishing growth even among the leaders of the people and the great ones of Israel, and with such extravagance, such pomp, and such an abundance and variety of dishes that with the effort they put forth they seemingly want to make a mockery of the notorious feasts of the ancients. The word 'carousing' (*comessatio*), however, comes from the name Comus, who was called the god of festivity and of dissipation by the Greeks. Thus just as sexual lust is named for Venus, so dissipation is named for Comus. Both, of course, are very powerful and closely related deities. The latter is served by the belly; the former, by what is under the belly. Comus sustains Venus and invigorates her. Otherwise, without Ceres and Bacchus, Venus is cold" (*LW* 27.370-371).

Concupiscentia is the term that Luther and Calvin used for original sin. They went further than the scholastic doctrine that viewed it as the absence of original righteousness. Sin had too much energy, they thought, to be merely a lack of something subjective in the will, a loss of illumination in the intellect, and a diminution of the strength of memory. Man's nature held a dark, aggressive bent, a seething ferment, a positive "delight in error and darkness." According to Luther, sin had warped all the faculties of body and soul; and Calvin echoed with, "the whole man is of himself nothing but concupiscence."[6] Luther noted that over and over in Scripture the depths of man's nature, indeed "our very nature itself," is condemned under the name of concupiscence (*LW* 25.350-351). Man's spiritual fornication, he explained, is "a terrible curving in on itself" (*incurvatus in se*)—a hermetic egoism that sees and understands "by its own reason and sense." It thinks all created things it sees "serve to its advantage, exist for it and are done for it."[7] *Concupiscentia* thus understood is embodied imaginatively in Milton's magician and the seething nature that he describes. The strangling fertility of nature is an apt parallel to the deadly fecundity of his argument, which doubles back upon itself time and again. Indeed *incurvatus in se* is the essence of the Elder Brother's definition of evil as a closed circuit: "eternal restless change/Self-fed and self-consum'd" (596-597). It is important to remember that for Luther and the Reformation generally, man's reason is included under the rubrics of "flesh" and "concupiscence." However much Comus may degrade his victims, it is he who traffics in "reasons not unplausible" (162) and who elaborately argues the "moral" demands of nature, ending his appeal with "Be *wise*, and taste."

---

[6] *LW* 25.299 and *Inst.* 2.1.8. See also *Lectures on Galatians* [1535], *LW* 26.174. Since Milton's *Indexus Theologicus* has been lost, it is difficult to determine what Milton read of Luther and when he may have read it. In any case, Milton, in "An Apology against a Pamphlet . . . ," says that Luther is the model for polemical bitterness just as he is of "any other vertue" (*YP* 1.901).

[7] *LW* 25.346. See also *LW* 26.174 and 27.67.

36

So much for Sin-as-Concupiscence. Who then is to play his opposite number, who but Righteousness-as-Chastity? So often in Reformation piety, especially in the context of Luther's commentaries, "righteousness" is a metaphysical synonym for faith. If the Lady in Milton's masque materializes from Pauline strictures just as Comus does, then she may be intended as *virginitas fidei*.[8] In any case, it is hard to dispute that the Lady is a virgin, since Milton mentions the fact three times (350, 437, 787); and that the Lady has faith. No sooner is she alone in a dark wood than she looks above and declares her belief: "the Supreme good . . . /Would send a glist'ring Guardian, if need were,/To keep my life and honor unassail'd" (217-220). When the Lady touts the "serious doctrine of Virginity" (787), she indeed does mean "doctrine"—doctrinal virginity— which in a Reformation context would mean faith unadulterated, or *sola fides*.

With some justification, Luther has been accused of reducing theology to this single doctrine, and his commentary on Galatians, the single book most responsible for the dissemination of his ideas in England,[9] shows how important the conceptual clarity of faith was to his position. To mark off the distinct and inviolable borders of faith was his lifelong preoccupation, and with overwhelming repetition he distinguishes faith from love, on the one hand, and from reason on the other. Once faith became confused with either, he held, it was no longer faith.

Two of the celebrated cruces of *Comus* stem from Milton's concept of faith and easily resolve themselves if one understands what the Reformation considered to be faith's essence or "form." First of all, faith was not to be confused with love. The famous

---

[8] *LW* 26.113. For the Latin version see *Kritische Gesamtausgabe der Werke D. Martin Luthers*, Weimar, Nachfolger, 1911, XL, 204, cited hereafter as *WA*. My reading does not rule out the possibility that the Lady is also *ecclesia*, as Alice-Lyle Scoufos suggests in "The Mysteries in Milton's *Masque*," *Milton Studies*, 6 (1975), 113-142.

[9] Editions of this commentary appeared frequently—in 1575, 1577, 1580, 1588, 1603, 1615, 1616, 1635. For the origins of Luther's thought in England, see William A. Clebsch, "The Elizabethans on Luther," *Interpreters of Luther: Essays in Honor of Wilhelm Pauck*, ed. Jaroslav Pelikan, Philadelphia, Fortress Press, 1968, p. 100.

triad in lines 213-215 in *Comus*—"Faith," "Hope," and "Chastity"—makes a glaring alteration in Scripture in order to maintain a key doctrinal distinction. The difficulty was that I Corinthians 13:13, with its proclamation of "faith, hope, and charity," was a favorite proof-text for the Catholic position. Milton must have wanted to avoid all suspicion of a *fides charitate formata*.[10] The idea of charity as the "form" of faith would have seemed to him a papist legalism, for then love could be said to produce faith—an arrangement thought to be tantamount to salvation by human love and works. The Protestant position, of course, put things the other way around: faith produced love and good works. In *Comus*, Milton charmingly presents this doctrine as a fairy tale principle to remember when meeting strange men in the woods: none but such as are good men can do good works.[11] Though less adamant than Luther, Milton nevertheless is in general agreement with him. In *Christian Doctrine*, we find him arguing against classic Catholic proofs, one of which, for example, is the story of how Mary Magdalene washed the feet of Jesus with a rich perfume. The difficulty was that the Gospel had said: *her many sins are forgiven, for she has loved much.* Milton has to construct an elaborate chain of inferences from the context in order to conclude:

> It should be noticed that love was here not the cause but the sign or even the effect of forgiveness. . . . Obviously the quality which saved her was the quality which justified her, *and that was not love, but faith.*
>
> (*CD*, pp. 493-494, *author's italics*)

It would seem, then, that the famous triad in *Comus*—Faith, Hope, and Chastity—represents a determined attempt to keep faith distinct from love. Milton is attempting to preserve the virginity of the concept of faith against any contamination from

---

[10] *LW* 26.88-89. For a detailed discussion of this distinction, see B. A. Gerrish, *Grace and Reason: A Study in the Theology of Luther*, Oxford, Clarendon, 1962, pp. 26-37; and Gerhard Ebeling, *Luther: An Introduction to His Thought*, trans. R. A. Wilson, Philadelphia, Fortress Press, 1970, pp. 141-173.

[11] "Before doing any good work the person must be good" (*LW* 3.85).

works, even loving ones. If one keeps in mind that chastity is a pervasive metaphor for faith among the Reformers and that they have a tendency to meld faith with hope,[12] then the famous substitution of "chastity" in line 215 becomes tantamount to a triple iteration of "faith" for rhetorical effect.

What then was the "form" of faith? Milton, like the Reformers, held that in a realist sense Christ himself was the form of faith. Luther explains the matter in his commentary upon Galatians:

> *Nevertheless, I live: yet not I, but Christ lives in me.*
> . . . This "I" Paul rejects; for "I," as a person distinct from Christ, belongs to death and hell. This is why he says: "Not I, but Christ lives in me." Christ is my "form," which adorns my faith as color or light adorns a wall. (This fact has to be expounded in this crude way, for there is no spiritual way for us to grasp the idea that Christ clings and dwells in us as closely and intimately as light or whiteness clings to a wall.) "Christ," he says, "is fixed and cemented to me and abides in me. The life that now I live, He lives in me. Indeed, Christ Himself is the life that I now live."
> (*LW* 26.167, cf. *CD*, p. 498)

Such indwelling was not considered to compromise Christ's transcendence in any way, and Milton could claim without fear of sacrilege or self-deification that he was "incorporate" with Truth (*YP* 1.871). The same should be understood of the Lady because Comus recognizes that her breast is the "hidd'n residence" of the holy (246-248). The Attendant Spirit corroborates the point. Her song, he says, has the power "that might create a soul/Under the ribs of Death" (561-562), as if within she possessed the great Word who made creation. One more example will suffice to illustrate how pervasive doctrinal intimation is in the masque: At the climax of the seduction scene, the

---

[12] Luther tended to minimize distinctions between faith and hope, claiming that they were inseparable like rhetoric and dialectic in a single oration. Thus he was wont to make such comments as, "In fact, therefore, faith and hope are scarcely distinguishable" (*LW* 27 [1535].23).

Lady breaks off in righteous indignation that Comus dares "Arm his profane tongue . . . /Against the Sun-clad power of Chastity" (781-782). If Milton intends the pun "Son-clad," then it is one more verbal hint that chastity in the poem is to be equated with the righteousness of Christ. It is a pun recalling the *armor lucis* of the Red Cross Knight, which gleamed even in the Cave of Error; it likewise recalls the verses before and after Romans 13:13, the verse that may have been seminal for the masque:

> Let us therefore cast off the works of darkness and let us put on the *armour of light*. . . . But put ye on the Lord Jesus Christ.
>
> > (v. 12, 14, *author's italics*)

The garment metaphor is but one of the images in Scripture for the mysterious union of the believer and Christ. Milton was to use it to dramatize prevenient grace in Book X of *Paradise Lost* when the Son puts his cloak around Adam and Eve. In *Comus* the mystic powers that folklore had associated with virginity[13] suggest the mystery of such a union with Christ.

The mystery of *Comus* is not sheer mystery, as Angus Fletcher would have it, but the mystery of faith. Fletcher contends that Milton is always mediating from image to rhetoric to song to symbol in such a way that the system of references finally

---

[13] And not only folklore. Melanchthon makes chastity a key attribute of God. "Chastity," he said, "provides a very clear distinction between God and the impure spirits and men." He explains, "God is a pure, chaste, orderly being, and wants us to acknowledge him as such; and while we cannot see him physically and may not embrace him physically, he nevertheless wants us to keep him in our hearts as a pure, chaste, orderly being and to distinguish him from all irrational, unprincipled, impure natures. . . . This virtue, chastity, constitutes a very clear, evident distinction between God and the devils" (*Melanchthon on Christian Doctrine: Loci Communis*, 1655, trans. Clyde Manschreck, New York, Oxford University Press, 1965, pp. 112 and 138). The *Commonplaces* of Melanchthon is the book that Ascham gave to Queen Elizabeth "as best suited, after the Holy Scriptures, to teach her the foundations of religion" (T. W. Baldwin, *William Shakespere's Small Latine & Less Greeke*, Urbana, University of Illinois Press, 1944, I, 259).

points, not beyond itself, but "into its own vitals"[14]—a conclusion that makes *Comus* merely a frivolous tease. It is more likely that Milton's concept of faith holds together all the variegated poetic ingredients and makes them cohere in a significant pattern. The final reference point, then, is not just another internal reference, but the unnamed object of faith—Christ being the "something holy" lodging in the Lady's breast and also an inhabitant of eternity above those "silver linings" where she looks for help. Faith and, in turn, its "form" operate as the formal principle of the work.

The "form" of faith (considered in its transcendent sense) provides the key to the most "classical" moment in the poem. If one remembers who the "form" of faith is, the Lady's vision of the forms, for which a Platonic source usually is cited, takes on a strong Reformation coloring:

> O welcome pure-ey'd Faith, white-handed Hope,
> Thou hov'ring Angel girt with golden wings,
> And thou unblemish't form of Chastity,
> I see ye visibly . . .
>
> (213-216)

Milton may be punning upon the Platonic notion that the chaste of body can apprehend the forms of the intelligible world, thereby suggesting that only the virginity of faith can apprehend Christ, who is the "glorious Form," to borrow an epithet from the Nativity Ode (Proem 1.8). One scarcely needs to go back as far as Gregory of Nyssa in order to find a parallel to this moment in the masque.[15] The Reformers themselves are touched with

---

[14] Fletcher, pp. 250, 175-176; Cleanth Brooks, *Poems of Mr. John Milton: The 1645 Edition with Essays in Analysis*, New York, Harcourt Brace, 1951, p. 232, sees the "mystery" in *Comus* rather as a final apocalyptic consummation—"the Marriage of Christ and His Bride."

[15] William G. Madsen, "The Idea of Nature in Milton's Poetry," *Three Studies in the Renaissance: Sidney, Jonson, Milton*, 1958, reprint Hamden, Conn., Archon, 1969, pp. 207-208, quotes Gregory of Nyssa's *On Virginity* as a source in the Western tradition for the notion that "the Beauty which is essential" will become visible to true innocence or virginity. It is interesting to note that Milton himself appears not to have read *De Virginitate* until after

a Platonism deriving from St. Augustine, and it is possible to give them a heavily Platonic reading simply by emphasizing references "upward" and any mention of the invisible. Calvin, for example in his commentary on Romans 13:13, particularly stresses that in faith the "brightness of the celestial life . . . . is set before our eyes."[16] In a similar vein, Luther says, speaking of faith, "The vision that enters or leaves my eyes does not come from the flesh" because "chastity of the vision comes from heaven" (LW 26.171). To talk of supernatural vision—the contemplation of things not seen—is the Reformers' routine way of referring to faith, even when they are taking a conspicuously nonmystical position.

Similarly, the word "virtue" can be read in any of several traditions. Again Comus appears coherent if "virtue" takes its content from Milton's concept of faith. Even if one assumes that "virtue" in Comus is Christian, there are alternate possibilities. The Lady's "virtue" generally has been viewed in the tradition of St. Thomas Aquinas as the fulfillment of nature and reason. Thus Woodhouse, and Madsen after him, have assumed that the Lady's virginity represents the perfection of nature in grace.[17] John Demaray, however, has shown that Mil-

---

1639, that is, after the publication of Comus. James Holly Hanford, "The Chronology of Milton's Private Studies," PMLA, 36 (1921), 279, found that the edition of De Virginitate quoted by Milton in his Commonplace Book is the Paris edition of 1639. Rosamund Tuve, Images and Themes in Five Poems by Milton, Cambridge, Harvard University Press, 1957, pp. 144-149, suggests that the "unblemish't form of Chastity" which the Lady sees is visible as the moon.

[16] John Calvin, Commentary upon the Epistle of Saint Paul to the Romans, trans. Christopher Rosdell, ed. Henry Beveridge, Edinburgh, Calvin Translation Society, 1844, p. 374.

[17] A.S.P. Woodhouse, The Heavenly Muse, p. 64. See also p. 75: "there is an ascending scale of values, . . . grace builds upon foundations laid in nature." Madsen, "The Idea of Nature in Milton's Poetry," p. 212, says: "From the traditional Christian point of view virginity is in a sense not a denial of nature at all, but its fulfillment." Angus Fletcher, The Transcendental Masque, p. 159, claims that his reading "does not overthrow the main proposition according to which Woodhouse structured his original essay."

ton uses "virginity" and "chastity" interchangeably,[18] so that there is no longer a need to question the logic by which one *arrives* at an apex of virginity. Precisely because virginity cannot be achieved, it is a fitting symbol for Reformation faith. Luther explained, "if [a virgin] were seeking to become a virgin by some law, would she not be out of her mind?" (*LW* 27.378).

In Reformation thought, "virtue" is a *donné* rather than an achievement or a natural endowment. Nature in this tradition is considered hopelessly concupiscent, and "virtue" is read as a preemptive term—as the power through which God is mighty in faith. In his early exegesis of the Psalms, Luther adopted the Vulgate's use of *virtus-virtutis*, and ever after in his works "virtue" was never to mean human rectitude but always the power and righteousness of God.[19] For Calvin, too, as any reading of the *Institutes* will show, merit and virtue totally belong to God. Thus, if one reads *Comus* against a background of Reformation thought, "virtue" becomes almost a synonym for faith and for God's righteousness conferred thereby: "What, then, are human powers, where faith and the Word reign," asks Luther, "except masks of God?" (*LW* 9.41).

[18] John G. Demaray, *Milton and the Masque Tradition*, Cambridge, Harvard University Press, 1968, p. 93.

[19] Ebeling, p. 71n. In *Christian Doctrine*, Milton subsumes temperance, chastity, and sobriety (724-737)—like all virtues—under "good works" (647), whose efficient cause is God.

—————————— II ——————————

> The conscience must be as unaware, in fact,
> as dead toward the Law as a virgin is toward
> a man.
>
> (*LW* 26.349)

If the Reformers felt that keeping faith distinct from love was a matter of life and death, they saw an even more urgent need to keep faith distinct from reason. Luther denigrated reason because he associated it with the concept of Law. The sweet reasonableness of the assumption that one could earn one's place before God was for him the chief enemy to faith, for he had a keen sense of how strong the human impulse to self-justification was and how difficult it was to accept a conferred righteousness. Law and reason, then, Luther considered to be "hostile" to faith: "As soon as reason and the Law are joined [to it], *faith immediately loses its virginity*" (*LW* 26.113, *author's italics*).

One must add quickly that Luther, like Calvin, saw reason as an enemy only as regards grace and faith. Reason had its own proper sphere: the natural world, the political world, the home (where "smiles from reason flow"), and the care and functioning of the body. Here reason was no danger at all, but a divine gift (*LW* 26.174). Using language he borrowed from mysticism, Luther urged the separation of the order of reason from the order of grace: "Ascend into the darkness, where neither the Law nor reason shines, but only the dimness of faith. . . . Thus the Gospel leads us above . . . where the Law and reason have no business" (*LW* 26.113-114). At another point Luther put it this way: "There is a double life: my own, which is natural or animate; and an alien life, that of Christ in me" (*LW* 26.170).

Comus appears to be a celebration of this *aliena vita*, which is distinct from and counter to our natural existence, including reason. Madsen, continuing the line of interpretation set forth by Woodhouse, has argued that Comus and the Lady start from the same assumption—that nature is ethically normative, but that Comus reasons in a libertine fashion so that he concludes with the formulation of a pixilated natural law.[20] It is important, however, to see that the nature from which Comus argues, as is always the case in a pastoral, is merely a fictive reflection of the shepherd's heart. Colin Clout's dead forest in the January eclogue of *The Shepheardes Calender*, like the wintry scene in the Nativity Ode, mirrors the poet's condition and nothing more. Neither the January woods of which Colin sings nor the ferocious fertility of which Comus raves has any claim, in the context of pastoral, to be God's green world. The difficulty is not that Comus reasons badly from the right starting point in nature, but that his premise is really himself. The Reformers understood that human reason was part of "the flesh" and that its ultimate premise was always the self. In spiritual matters, reason and (human) nature bid the same—to dismiss faith as absurd. This Reformation disjunction between reason and faith is seen in Comus' elaborately reasoned invitation and in the Lady's reply that is simply doctrinal assertion (780-787). The Doctrine of Virginity, in any case, is something neither Comus nor reason has the ear to apprehend. Given a Reformation context, what else is an argumentative attempt to seduce *virginitas fidei* but an attempt to penetrate faith with reason?

The reasons of the self indeed constitute the verbal sorcery that has delighted readers of *Comus* for generations, with little recognition that Milton's sorcerer is tailored to the specifications of Reformation commentary. Luther held that Satan could touch the senses with illusion but that "bewitchment of the spirit" by false persuasions was the principal danger (*LW* 26.192). The devil's deceptions were overwhelmingly doctrinal, or to be more precise, they were aimed squarely at the doctrine of faith. "Those who are persuaded that they are justified by the works of the Law or by the works of human tradition," says Luther, "are bewitched" (*LW* 25.197). Hence Luther took voluminous pains to define faith, so that his readers could "learn to recognize the

[20] "The Idea of Nature in Milton's Poetry," p. 198.

illusions and crafts of this sorcerer"; there was constant danger, for

> day and night he prowls around, seeking to devour every-
> one individually. And unless he finds us *sober and equipped
> with spiritual weapons,* that is, with the Word of God and
> faith, he devours us.
>
> <div align="right">(<i>LW</i> 26.193, <i>author's italics</i>)</div>

Calvin, for his part, warns Christians to be on guard when God's dictates are "made the subject of merriment and ridicule."[21] The kind of argument to expect, he says, is one in which indulging one's lust is hailed as "a trivial fault." The argument will run thus:

> Fornication is viewed by God as a light matter. Under the
> law of grace God is not so cruel. He has not formed us so
> as to be our own executioners.[22]

In all ages, Calvin warns, "*Satan raises up sorcerers of this description,* who endeavour . . . [to] exercise a kind of fascination over consciences."[23]

Comus, like Calvin's sorcerer, makes satiric jibes at divine strictures, notably at the sixth commandment (739-742), and, like Luther's sorcerer, he makes his ultimate appeal to moral sensitivity. With his rural weeds, he momentarily fools the Lady about his identity, but illusion of the senses gets him nowhere; nor do his proposed sensual pleasures. He very soon leaves off mention of the "Primrose-season" (671) and turns instead to the "moral" demands of nature, notably the Lady's *duty* to be seduced.

Comus first of all wittily twists Calvin's doctrine of steward-ship into a doctrine of "curious taste." Calvin had claimed that "all those [earthly] things were so given to us by the kindness of God, and so destined for our benefit, that they are, as it were, entrusted to us, and we must one day render account of them"

---

[21] *The Epistles of Paul to the Galatians and Ephesians,* p. 307.
[22] Ibid., p. 308.
[23] Ibid., p. 307 (*author's italics*).

(*Inst.* 3.10.5). Milton took this doctrine seriously, as "Ad Patrem" and the sonnet on his blindness indicate. Here he gives the doctrine of stewardship and its investment imagery to Comus, who accuses the Lady of welching on a loan:

> But you invert the cov'nants of her trust,
> And harshly deal like an ill borrower
> With that which you receiv'd on other terms.
> (682-684)

The bulk of Comus' argument is that the Lady is transgressing the doctrine of stewardship, and he has an impressive array of rhetorical strategies by which he imputes guilt to her. She is guilty of hubris, because in refusing his sleeping potion, she is "Scorning the unexempt condition/By which all mortal frailty must subsist" (685-686). She will be a murderer of Nature, "Who would be quite surcharg'd with her own weight,/And strangl'd with her waste fertility" (728-729). Above all, she will be selfishly depraved, *incurvata in se*, if she keeps her beauty to herself when she should be sharing it with her admirers (745-747). And just as Calvin had warned that the argument would run, she would be the executioner of her own posterity (739-744).

Comus' ingenious arguments may bemuse us, but their danger is neither a confusion of logic, a starting point in nature, nor a warped notion of nature. The difficulty is that each point is a moral imperative—the whole harangue being a decalogue for foolish virgins. This "one must" is precisely the temptation which Luther saw as endangering *virginitas fidei*—the impulse to *do something* to get oneself out of the woods of guilt, as it were, rather than to rely completely upon grace. The metaphoric equation of faith with sexual purity and of "works righteousness" with loose lasciviousness occurs in many variants throughout Luther's works. The equation is stated baldly in his exegesis of Deuteronomy, which Luther wrote in the early days when he carefully appended an allegory to each chapter. "An Adulteress," he said, "always denotes a soul fornicating against Christ by deserting the Word and trusting in works" (*LW* 9.225).

A Lady, therefore, who is (and has) faith will not be seduced by any moral babble. Faith is impervious to moral smears and to imputed guilt. In Luther, especially, "good conscience" becomes almost an alternative definition of faith: Conscience "must be kept pure for Christ. . . . Therefore let conscience have its bridal chamber, not deep in the valley but high on the Mountain."[24] It is no wonder that with Conscience as her "strong siding champion" (212), Milton's Lady does not quaver before all the guilt that the magician imputes to her. She will not justify herself, will not apologize, will not explain.

The experience of temptation, Luther held, demonstrated the importance of his distinction between faith and love: Love always yields, but faith gives way to nothing (*LW* 26.119). *Virginitas fidei* is quite properly rigid and frigid. Where faith is concerned, one should be "invincible, inflexible, stubborn, and harder than adamant" (*LW* 26.103). And the Lady in Milton's masque is exactly so. She spurns love as a natural imperative and scorns reason for urging it as a moral imperative. The Lady, however, does not conquer her opponent by a better love or by a superior reason. She silences her opponent by the "word"— by a proclamation of the "serious doctrine of Virginity" (787). She baffles Comus with the Reformers' ultimate weapon against temptation: "By the proclamation of this doctrine [of faith], moreover, the devil is overthrown, and his kingdom is cast down."[25]

---

[24] *LW* 26.120. See also *LW* 26.137-138 on the priority of faith over loving works: "This Bridegroom, Christ, must be alone with His bride in His private chamber, and all the family and household must be shunted away. But later on, when the Bridegroom opens the door and comes out, then let the servants return to take care of them and serve them food and drink. Then let works and love begin."

[25] *LW* 26.14. This interpretation accords with John M. Steadman's view that Moly and Haemony represent Christian knowledge and belief. See " 'Haemony' and Christian Moly," *History of Ideas News Letter*, 4 (1958), 59-60, and "Milton's *Haemony*: Etymology and Allegory," *PMLA*, 77 (1962), 200-207.

But he that will mould a modern Bishop into
a primitive, must yeeld him to be elected by
the popular voyce, undiocest, unrevenu'd, un-
lorded, and leave him nothing but brotherly
equality, matchles temperance, frequent fast-
ing, incessant prayer, and preaching, continual
watchings, and labours in his Ministry, which
what a rich bootie it would be, what a plump
endowment to the many-benefice-gaping mouth
of a Prelate, what a relish it would give to his
canary-sucking, and swan-eating palat, let old
Bishop *Mountain* judge for me.

(*YP* 1.548-549)

But why does the Lady who is Faith speak for Temperance?
Madsen argues that lines 764-780 show her to be an exponent
of the reason and moral principles of order to be found in
nature,[26] but one just as easily can argue from this passage that
the Lady is Reformation Faith speaking to our natural exist-
ence—that realm of the body and society in which reason prop-
erly operates, that realm in which the good works flowing from
faith are to be performed. The passage is much too brief, really,
for us to determine theological niceties from it with any cer-
tainty; but in the light of what we know of Milton's puritan
rearing and youthful religious commitment, the appropriate
gloss seems to be the Reformer's commentary on the necessity
of temperance and soberness to the life of faith.

The Lady indeed seems to have read her Calvin, for she very
well could have drawn her temperance lecture from this passage
in the *Institutes*:

[Let this] continually resound in our ears: "Render account
of your stewardship" [Luke 16:2]. At the same time let us

---

26 "The Idea of Nature in Milton's Poetry," pp. 202-203.

remember by whom such reckoning is required: namely, him who has greatly commended abstinence, sobriety, frugality, and moderation, and has also abominated excess, pride, ostentation, and vanity; who approves no other distribution of good things than one joined with love; who has already condemned with his own lips all delights that draw man's spirit away from chastity and purity, *or befog his mind.*

(3.10.5, author's italics)

Here, concisely linked, are the functions of a disciplined life before and after grace. Discipline is necessary to perform the good works that flow from grace. One must live according to "sober laws" (766) if nature's blessings are to be "well dispens't/In unsuperfluous even proportion" (772-773). In addition, such discipline of life is vital if one is to keep the faith. The Lady knows that he who lives profligately befogs his mind and "Ne'er looks to Heav'n" (777). Even Luther, who never for a moment would suggest that a virtuous life could win heaven, counseled against chambering and drunkenness on the grounds that "it renders the mind unprepared over against divine matters" (*LW* 25.482).

The case of St. Augustine nicely illustrates the relationship between personal purity and an access of grace. St. Augustine gave up his life of epic fornication and ceased philandering some time before his famous conversion. Even when physically chaste, he was still complaining of spiritual fornication (*ita fornicatur anima*).[27] He endured a period of stasis in which he seemed to hang between two worlds. Then came the celebrated moment in the rose garden when he suddenly heard mysterious singing that told him to take up the Scripture and read. He did so and his eyes lit upon Romans 13:13, which he took as a command: "Let us walk honestly, as in the day: not in reveling and drunkenness, not in chambering and wantonness, not in strife and envyings." Only after this moment of grace did chastity of

[27] *St. Augustine's Confessions,* trans. William Watts, 1631, London, Heinemann, 1912, I, 86.

body coincide with chastity of soul. Chastity, in the Reformation tradition, is merely a probable precondition for grace—not a necessary symbol. Milton avoids the suggestion that there is a cause-and-effect relation between chastity and grace because he chooses a Lady who is already chaste. The masque is not concerned with an initial access of grace at all, the Lady's problem being to guard her chastity, to keep the faith. In this context, fornication and swinish drunken revelry do become necessary symbols for the absence of grace. Most of the pigs of Comus, says Milton, taste the drugged cup "through fond intemperate thirst" (67), rather than through a deliberate choice to forgo their [heavenly] home. Riotous living simply precludes spiritual awareness.

Notice that at this point Platonic and Reformation doctrine agree that physical self-indulgence precludes spiritual apprehension.[28] The final counsel of the masque, then, can be read in either a classical way or a puritan way. If for Plato in the *Phaedo* chastity and temperance are necessary to gain a glimpse of the intelligible world, in the Reformed tradition they are necessary to keep the "chaste vision" of faith till the end. Milton's parting admonition—that "virtue" (understood as chastity and bodily discipline) "can teach ye how to climb/Higher than the Sphery chime" (1020-1021)—is either the promise of reaching the top of Plato's ladder or the promise of reaching heaven at last. Milton's masque seems to be built upon such large conceptual puns. Its very structure is a giant metaphysical conceit, in which Christian doctrine and classical ethics meet in key words like "chastity," "form," "nature," and "virtue." This system of classical and Christian puns is compounded by the

---

[28] For Platonic interpretations, see B. A. Wright, "Above the Smoke and Stir," *TLS*, 27 October 1945, p. 511; Irene Samuel, *Plato and Milton*, Ithaca, Cornell University Press, 1947; John Arthos, *On "A Mask Presented at Ludlow Castle,"* Ann Arbor, University of Michigan Press, 1954; Sears Jayne, "The Subject of Milton's Ludlow *Mask*," 1959, reprinted in *A Maske at Ludlow*, ed. John S. Diekhoff, Cleveland, Press of Case Western Reserve, 1968, pp. 165-187; and J. B. Savage, "*Comus* and Its Traditions," *ELR*, 5 (Winter 1975), 58-80.

paradoxes of the doctrine of faith, especially that of the "identity" of the believer with Christ. This means that there is both a human and a divine reference in such phrases as "the power of Chastity" and "Follow Virtue." Cleanth Brooks observed that when the theme of Grace enters, "Grace and Virtue are essentially the same."[29]

The Lady's imprisonment in the enchanter's chair also rings a witty change upon a motif in classical mythology. It is reminiscent of the silver-studded throne in which Circe seats her victims, Hephaestus' golden chair whose invisible fetters trapped Hera, and the Chair of Forgetfulness, which, according to Apollodorus, was the fate of Theseus in Hades.[30] None of these, however, offers an exact parallel because the Lady does not forget her home nor is she surprised by an illicit passion. The wicked magician, with all his wiles, has not touched the freedom of her conscience and her mind. This highly verbal Lady caught in the magician's chair is a vivid image of the central tenet of Reformation faith—that the Christian is both sinner and justified saint (*simul iustus et peccator*)—at once bound and free. This paradoxical condition, said Luther with a play upon the verbs *abesse* and *obesse*, meant that "the desires and the conflicts of the flesh will not *vanish*; yet they will not *vanquish*" (*LW* 27.80, author's italics). The man of faith becomes "dead to sin, the devil, death and hell, all of which still remains." It seems that Milton has chosen what one might call Luther's archetype, as we see when Luther continues:

When Christ arises from the dead, He is free from the grave; and yet the grave remains. Peter is liberated from prison, the paralytic from his bed, the young man from his coffin, the girl from her couch; nevertheless, the prison, the bed, the coffin, and the couch remain. . . .

The righteousness of grace simply does not pertain to the flesh. For the flesh must not be free but must stay in the grave, in the prison, and on the couch.

(*LW* 26.157-158)

[29] Brooks, p. 212.   [30] Arthos, p. 46.

And, one might add, in the chair of Comus.

Comus' chair and Sabrina's releasing magic represent two halves of the Reformation paradox: the persistence of sin despite the most triumphant faith, and the final freedom from sin effected at death. Sabrina's magic, of course, is typologically complex, standing also for the daily gift of grace, no less than for its metaphysical mechanics as the Reformers understood them. The symmetry of the myth, however, stresses the opposition between a paradoxical freedom and a complete freedom. The problem posed is that of a chair imprisoning a Lady who has a free mind and faithful spirit. Sabrina's graceful magic effects a release of her flesh and a *final* homecoming. Thus, the teasing opalescence of *Comus* yields a suprisingly firm and coherent structure if one approaches it with the Reformation assumptions about faith. Much depends upon whether the reader can make a "literary" commitment to a puritan set of beliefs during the course of a reading. Milton himself seems to acknowledge that he has written a masque *a clef* when he has the Attendant Spirit hint in an aside: "List mortals, *if your ears be true*" (997, author's italics).

Comus may also be a masque *a clef* in a more conventional sense. It may make a covert political statement in which terms like "libertine," "sorcerer," and "revels"—as well as "chastity," "Lady," and "sober song"—are counters for well-known political attitudes.[31] With its contest of true and false shepherds, *Comus* is probably also an antiprelatical masque. By the time of Elizabeth I, the terms "conjurer," "sorcerer," "necromancer" and "enchanter" had become code words for "recusant priest," and the puritans soon turned these epithets against the Anglicans in antiepiscopal controversy,[32] as Milton, for example, does

[31] See John D. Cox, "Poetry and History in Milton's Country Masque," *ELH*, 44 (1977), 622-640, which argues that the opposition in *Comus* represents the generalized division between the aristocracy and the puritan bourgeoisie (that is, between corrupt court and virtuous country) that would later ripen into the Civil War.

[32] See Keith Thomas, *Religion and the Decline of Magic*, New York, Scribner's, 1971, pp. 51-77, especially p. 68.

in *Of Reformation* (YP 1.581). Only three years after *Comus*, Milton is making a vehement attack upon clerical shepherds who creep into the fold "for their bellies' sake" ("Lycidas," 1.114). The episcopacy (and false-shepherd imagery) had been a focus of political tension since the 1580s, and Milton himself notes that "our admired *Spencer* inveighs against" the episcopacy in *The Shepheardes Calender* "not without some presage of these reforming times"; he notes especially that "the Poet lively personates our Prelates" in the "false Shepheard *Palinode* in the Eclogue of *May*" (YP 1.722). It is probable, then, that Milton's antiprelatical tracts offer a gloss for political allusion in his pastoral masque. At least, the first of his antiprelatical tracts, *Of Reformation* (1641), uses rhetorically the same oppositions that occur visually and dramatically in *Comus*. The prelates, called "Wizzards" and "drunken *Preists* [*sic*]," are scored for their self-indulgence, for the "pride, and gluttony of their owne backs, and bellies" (YP 1.596, 594, 610). In a way recalling the masque's concern for "unsuperfluous even" distribution, Milton accuses the prelates of filling their "epicurean paunches" from the alms that ought to go to "the blind, the lame, the impotent, the aged, the orfan, the widow" (YP 1.611). Milton especially seems to be angry that educational opportunities are thus lost and decries

> these expences thus profusely throwne away in trash, [when] rather *Churches* and *Schools* might be built, where they cry out for want, and more added where too few are; a moderate maintenance distributed to every painfull Minister, that now scarse sustaines his Family with Bread, while the *Prelats* revell like *Belshazzar* with their full carouses in *Goblets*, and *vessels* of *gold* . . . . (YP 1.590)

Of Reformation further excoriates a lax episcopacy for being a threat to the monarchy because, he argues, it will surely bring in a "Popular Commotion" which "slides aptest into a Democraty [*sic*]" (YP 1.592). He thinks that holy days have been perverted and laments that "at such a time . . . men should bee pluck't from their soberest and saddest thoughts, and by *Bishops* the pretended *Fathers of the Church* instigated by publique Edict, and with earnest indeavour [be] push't forward to gaming, jigging, wassailing, and mixt dancing [which] is a horror to think" (*YP* 1.589). If Milton in 1641 is still decrying James I's Book of Sports (which prohibited interference with "May Games, Whitson Ales, and Morris-dances, and the setting up of Maypoles &c other sports therewith used" [*YP* 1.589 n]), then there probably is a political slur in the Morris dance of the sorcerer's rabble rout in *Comus*, which was written shortly after the Book of Sports was reissued on May 3, 1633. In the tract, Milton is not simply repelled by drunken dancing and dissolute behavior, but argues that indulging the people makes them politically inert. Then he clinches his argument by invoking a classical fable of bestial metamorphosis parallel to that of Circean Comus:

> To make men governable in this manner [the prelates'] precepts mainly tend to break a nationall spirit, and courage by count'nancing upon riot, luxury, and ignorance, till having thus disfigur'd and made men beneath men, as *Juno* in the Fable of *Iö*, they deliver up the poor transformed heifer of the Commonwealth to be stung and vext with the breese, and goad of oppression under the custody of some *Argus*.
>
> (*YP* 1.572)

Comus the magician seems to sum up what Milton considered to be wrong with England. The magician is a Lord of Misrule— of the village festival; of ungoverned appetite; perhaps of imminent "uproare and combustion, and . . . the brand of Civill Discord" (*YP* 1.613); certainly of "the mis-rule, and turbulency of the *Prelats*" (*YP* 1.588)— they were "Libertines" and great "hinderers of *Reformation*" (*YP* 1.541). In 1634 revolutionary zeal may not have fired Milton as it did in 1641, when he called for "the Axe of Gods reformation" (*YP* 1.582). He may not have been as angry as he was in 1637, when he made a more opaque call for the ax in "Lycidas" (he was to claim in his first volume of poems that in this elegy he had foretold "the ruin of our corrupted clergy then in their height"). In 1634 Milton may have been concerned mainly about the kind of shepherd that he wanted to be. In "Ad Patrem" he obviously was feeling some pressure to set poetry aside and take up Holy Orders without delay, and in his masque he may have been working out the solution to his vocational dilemma, dissociating himself from false shepherds (high-living high churchmen who blessed Whitsun Ales) and identifying himself instead with the shepherd as singing master (the poet who has garnered flowers—or rather herbs—from the garden of Meliboeus and then used them to help creatures lost in a dark wood). Milton, as it turned out, would choose the path of heaven-sent Thyrsis: he would undertake a work suitable "for a spirit of the greatest size, and divinest mettle." He would take it upon himself, by pamphlet and poem, to guide the nation "in true wisdom and vertue" (YP 1.571).

Milton begins the task in Comus, by presenting the Lady as a model of faith, personal discipline, true church discipline, and hence national well-being. As Milton sighs in Of Reformation:

> Alas Sir! a Commonwealth ought to be but as one huge Christian personage, . . . compact in vertue as in body; for looke what the grounds, and causes are of single happines to one man, the same yee shall find them to a whole state.
>
> (YP 1.572)

If the Lady is one such composite "Christian personage," her sobriety represents the "one right discipline" (YP 1.605), that is, the "compresbyterial" arrangement that Milton then advocated instead of episcopacy. Insofar as the Lady is England, she may reflect Milton's youthful confidence in the goodness and staunchness of his countrymen, his firm belief that the sober sort would prevail on the issue of church polity and so finish the Reformation. In words that could well sum up the Lady's character, Milton claims

the *wisdome*, the *moderation*, the *Christian Pietie*, the *Constancy* of our Nobility and Commons of *England* be ever forgotten, whose calme, and temperat connivence could sit still, and smile out the stormy bluster of men [most] audacious and precipitant.

(YP 1.596)

Perhaps the Lady is the embodiment of English liberty, the result of such "vertue." In *Comus*, as well as the later tract, Milton seems to boast of "the impregnable situation of our Liberty and safety, that laught such weake enginry [belonging to the proponents of episcopacy] to scorne" (*YP* 1.596-597). Does the Lady represent True Faith who resists the blandishments and "witcheries" of prelatical apologists, but is nevertheless caught in their institutional chair? If so, a politically inspired Thyrsis is expected to free her.

Such a reading is highly problematic, because it is impossible to disentangle the pious, the personal, and the political strains in *Comus* or to determine which is foremost. The Spenserian conceit, shorn of its guiding sententia, is so utterly ambiguous that it becomes a test of the adept, a cabala to be read aright only by men of like faith and politics. If in one pastoral fable Milton is attempting to assert the invincibility of his political cause and to display the mystery of his faith, then his attempt has gone somewhat awry. He has made faith an esoteric matter, rather than an open secret, and has made it more murky than mysterious. The difficulty is that Milton's new and darker version of the Spenserian conceit is fundamentally at odds with his religious faith, which rests upon a divine promise of utter clarity. "The very essence of Truth," Milton says in *Of Reformation*, "is plainnesse, and brightnes; the darknes and crookednesse is our own" (*YP* 1.566).

Never again was Milton to play with the pious sense of a poem at two or three removes from its lexical surface. In his mature poetry he would repeat God's promises in full, not merely

57

intimate them; but he would discover strategies of poetic in-direction that did not obscure doctrinal *claritas*. Milton's ex-pectations of victory for the Reformation of course would be disappointed, as would his dreams of personal happiness, but his sense that faith was a mystery would deepen painfully. Never again would the pagans serve him as easy analogues to Christian doctrine, but in *Paradise Lost* would yield a full-fledged antagonism.

3
The Crooked Scripture

I

Hell is hell not because punishment is there,
but because praise of God is not there.
(*LW* 29.176)

In *Paradise Lost* Milton returns to the esthetic announced in the Nativity Ode, in which God's word as explicit doctrine governs the world of the poem. Evil is no mere clank of chains or the swingeing of a Dragon's tail in Milton's epic, but has its own voice, articulate and strong enough to contest—some would say undermine—the supremacy of God's voice. The epic will be seriously misread unless we understand that Satan and God do not speak the same language. Vergil, following common epic practice, has both the Greeks and the Trojans speak Latin—a minor epic convention that raises no problem in the *Aeneid.* No question of verisimilitude arises when the foreign murmur of Greek soldiers is heard in the streets of burning Troy (*ora sono discordia signant* [*Aen.* 2.423]). In *Paradise Lost,* however, all manner of confusion has followed from the fact that both God and Satan speak English. Milton's piety assumes that the words of God and Satan are incommensurate and that God's speech has certain well-defined extraliterary properties, which are discussed in the next chapter. Suffice it to say here that Satan takes the Primal Decree of God (5.600-615) as if it were human or creaturely speech, whereas Milton's epic assumes that it constitutes all reality. If we grant this premise, as we would easily grant the premise of a fairy tale, the problem of epic coherence and balance becomes one of accepting this "literary" point of faith.

Such acceptance need not be part of the reader's *a priori* equipment; Fish has argued that our acquiescence to Satan's views in the early books is a deliberate part of the poet's grand strategy, so that by the time of Adam's fall the reader is forced to acknowledge an identification with Adam.[1] The reader, however, need not accede to the rules of Milton's epic universe precisely at the moment when Adam falls, and in any case Milton's intent seems to go beyond that of convicting the reader of sin. But if, early or late, the reader reaches a point of accepting these epic rules, his perception of the entire poem will undergo a rapid reorganization, the change in perceived shape being facilitated by a poetic structure of finely reticulated cross-reference.

That God's speech, in a very active sense, "constitutes" reality is a proposition that perforce must be demonstrated serially. Milton's procedure is to present us with various "Interpretants" of God's speech. Not only Satan, but the steadfast angels, the blind poet, Adam and Eve, Creation, and history—all by their responses help to "illustrate" God's *speech*. In *Paradise Lost* the meaning of God's words is their "operation" in the world of the poem. Milton does not treat God as an inaccessible unity imitated by the multiplicity of the world, but as a "character" whose speech is a unity interpreted by a multiplicity of creaturely responses: the adamantly negative response (Satan), the adamantly positive (Abdiel and the good angels), the tenuous (Adam and Eve in the garden), the automatic and blatant (Creation), the automatic but often hidden (history), and finally the response that is both hard won and given (the blind poet, Adam

[1] Stanley E. Fish, *Surprised by Sin: The Reader in "Paradise Lost,"* Berkeley, University of California Press, 1971, p. 271.

and Eve in the wilderness). The effect of God's word on each of the respondents provides a fractional but reliable gloss.

In Books I and II God's words are absent entirely—and that is Milton's definition of Hell. Satan's cry of *"injur'd* merit" is a grim joke from a poet reared in the Calvinist tradition, in which merit belongs to none but God. Satan epitomizes what the Reformers meant by "the flesh": enmity toward God (*CD*, p. 389). Except for one leer in Paradise, bodily awareness plays little part in Satan's characterization. He comes to us primarily as a style of consciousness and a style of rhetoric—*peccatum cum voce*. Satan is the "voice of experience," the voice of human failure and pain and self-defense, to which readers always in some degree respond. He epitomizes the cry of human failure throughout literature—from Oedipus at Colonus, who in old age accepts no blame at all for having killed his father Laius, to the greasy ship captain who assassinates Lord Jim in Conrad's novel, all the while carrying *right* "within the envelope of his common desires."[2] The opening books of *Paradise Lost* present the response of the quintessential loser. Or rather they present a spectrum of typical responses: Moloch's immediate impulse to physical aggression, Belial's inclination to withdrawal, Mammon's urge to sublimate failure into art, and Beelzebub's (really Satan's) penchant for aggression delayed but shrewdly channeled. He does not get mad, but would get even—he is the dangerous kind of loser.

Satan's contention that he has been treated unfairly by the powers that be is given tacit support by the way in which the opening books of *Paradise Lost* parallel the beginning of the *Aeneid*. The storm with which Vergil's epic begins *does* come from the malice of a god and has no relation to the hero's meritorious behavior on the voyage out from Troy. The similarities between the opening book of Vergil's epic and that of Milton's are so striking that it is little wonder nineteenth-century poets who had shed their Christian dogma, but retained a

---

[2] Joseph Conrad, *Lord Jim*, ed. Thomas Moser, New York, Norton, 1968, p. 246.

schoolboy love of Vergil, perceived Satan as the hero. The *Aeneid* begins with allusive comparison between its hero and Homer's Odysseus so as to announce a New Odysseus, who, instead of making a long, perilous journey home to Ithaca, is about to make a long, perilous journey to a new and as yet unknown home. In a similar way, Milton invites us to see Satan as a new and ironically "better" Aeneas, who will go to a new land, not to build but to destroy, and who paradoxically will not get anywhere, as his blank shield intimates.

At first glance, however, Satan and Aeneas may seem to be temperamentally far apart, but that is part of Milton's strategy. We are invited to watch a "perfected" Aeneas, who meets all the situations that Vergil's hero encounters, but with perfect poise and aplomb. Satan, like Aeneas, is an exile, storm-battered and awash on perilous seas. As Aeneas watches the welkin explode with lightning, he is paralyzed with fear (*Aeneae solvuntur frigore membra*) and wishes he had fallen on the plains of Troy with Hector and his countrymen (*Aen.* 1.92; 94-101). Satan is subject to an elemental violence even more spectacular, for he has been "Hurl'd headlong flaming from th'Ethereal Sky/With hideous ruin and combustion down" to a "fiery Gulf" (1.45-46); yet he is no reluctant hero. Apparently without fear, he displays a "fixt mind" and "high disdain," a near Stoic reaction to defeat: "What though the field be lost?/ . . . the unconquerable Will" remains (1.105-106).

For some time, both epics follow a similar course. After the storm, each hero puts ashore with his troops, surveys the strange new land, and rallies his troops with a heartening speech that recalls dangers past and urges renewed courage. Then each sets about to reconnoiter the new land and organize the common life. Satan performs firmly and successfully every task facing Aeneas, never giving an outward indication of uncertainty. He is ever "steadfast" and "obdúrate" in his mission as he conceives it. He displays a sense of corporate responsibility when he marshals his troops—"Awake, arise, or be for ever fall'n" (1.330)—and he organizes life in the burning land with a dispatch and grandeur that out-Romans the Romans. Unlike the lonely, vulnerable Aeneas, Satan is never in danger of being deflected from his mission by female entanglement. When Lady Sin approaches him at the gate of Hell, recalling their amour and begging him not to go, Satan handles the situation with a tact and finesse that Aeneas could well have used when he left Dido.

Even Aeneas' Stoic flaw—the compassion that has endeared him to so many readers over the centuries—is given to Satan, but in such a way that it is made into a martial virtue. The leader of the fallen angels shows "Signs of remorse and passion to behold" his troops so overwhelmed, just as Aeneas mourns the plight of his fallen comrades (*Aen.* 1.216-222). Otherwise he hides his despair under a perfect martial front, just as Aeneas *spem vultu simulat* (*Aen.* 1.209). Even in small details, Milton marks Satan's iron nerve, noting, for example, that he walks barefoot "Over the burning Marl" (1.296). Satan's finest hour, though, comes when he stands at the threshold of Hell, about to plunge into the vast Abyss. He faces a nature so turbulent as to make the storm that Neptune raises in Book I of the *Aeneid* seem like a tempest in a teapot. He faces nothing less than "Eternal Anarchy, amidst the noise/Of endless wars" where "hot, cold, moist, and dry, four Champions fierce/Strive . . . for Maistry" (2.896-897, 899). The scene gives Satan pause, but he spreads his "Sail-broad Vans" for flight and plunges in. And he perseveres in the face of total disorientation and nonbeing with a doggedness that one cannot but admire: "So he with difficulty and labor hard/Mov'd on, with difficulty and labor hee" (2.1021-1022). When Satan at last emerges from the Abyss and arrives at the verge of the created world, "like a weatherbeaten Vessel" (2.1043-1044), he appears to be the ultimate Stoic hero, whose *vita temperata* has triumphed over the most elemental *furor*.

In the long view, of course, Satan does not qualify as a Stoic hero, for when alone he drops this mask, and Uriel watches with alarm as a veritable masque of unreason passes over Satan's countenance (4.114-115). Satan then appears more like Turnus, whose passions are about to boil up from the cauldron of his heart: "a lower deep/Still threat'ning to devour [him] opens

63

wide" (4.76-77; cf. *Aen.* 7.462-466). He is like Mezentius too, in that he is fearless in battle and a reckless *contemptor divum* or, more precisely, a *contemptor sermonis dei,* for having once rejected the Prime Decree of God (5.600-615), he is utterly reprobate. The "success" of Satan's leadership in the opening books, then, is important to Milton's puritan argument about the futility of sheer performance. He provides a negative illustration of the Father's promise to give new life to those "who renounce/Thir own both righteous and unrighteous deeds" (3.291-292).

In epic terms, being a *contemptor divum* makes Satan a degenerate hero.[3] In the figure of Satan, moreover, Milton seems to have summarized the literary degeneration of Aeneas in Western literature. Milton had ample opportunity to observe what Calvin saw as the degenerative process of poetic invention in what had happened to Odysseus, for in Vergil's hands he had lapsed from Homeric wiliness into real malevolence. Aeneas similarly degenerates as he passes from narrative to narrative in succeeding centuries. He first appears in the *Iliad* cast in heroic mold, where he kills like "the war god" (13.500) and fearlessly attacks Achilles with all the proud posturing that we recognize in Satan in Books I and II. Notice how the Ur-Aeneas

> strode forth in menace, tossing
> his head beneath the heavy helm, and he held
> the stark shield
> in front of his chest, and shook the brazen spear.[4]

There is only one fleeting shadow on the portrait of Aeneas in Homer. We momentarily see him strike a pose of injured merit in Book XX: he is disaffected,

> at the uttermost edge of the battle
> standing, since he was forever angry with

[3] Francis C. Blessington, *Paradise Lost and the Classical Epic*, Boston, Routledge & Kegan Paul, 1979, p. 14.

[4] *The Iliad of Homer*, trans. Richmond Lattimore, Chicago, University of Chicago Press, 1951, XX, 161, 163, cited hereafter as *Iliad*.

brilliant Priam
because great as he was he did him no honour
among his people.

(Iliad 13.459-461)

Aeneas then passes into Vergil's hands and, as we have observed, becomes a more tentative, even reluctant hero. From a humanist point of view he may represent a civilized improvement over the single-minded Homeric warrior, but if Homeric valor is taken as the norm, then the hero of the *Aeneid* represents a decay, for he even thinks of abandoning his mission in Book V, line 700.

Legend was soon to make him a full-blown traitor. In both Dictys' *Ephemeris Belli Troiani* and Dares' *De Excidio Troiae Historiae*—accounts believed in the Middle Ages to be more reliable than Homer—Aeneas joins in a serious defection from Priam and even parleys with the Greeks.[5] Dares specifies that Aeneas helps Antenor to open the Scaean Gate by night to the invading Greeks and that he soon sailed away from Troy with the Grecian ships.[6] The latter version was known to Milton in a redaction by Joseph of Exeter, whom he commends in his *History of Britain* as "the only smooth Poet of those times" (*YP* 5.15). This twelfth-century work, *De Bello Trojano*, was bound in two editions of Homer used by Milton,[7] and it may be that very early he connected the disgruntled Aeneas of Homer with the treacherous Aeneas in Dares' sequel to the *Iliad*. Milton also was well read in medieval romance and may have known Benoit de Sainte-Maure's *Le Roman de Troie* (c. 1160), which presents the reputation of Aeneas at its nadir: Hecuba excoriates the once pious hero of Vergilian epic as "Satanas."[8]

[5] Arthur M. Young, *Troy and Her Legend*, Pittsburgh, University of Pittsburgh Press, 1948, pp. 52-55.

[6] Ibid., p. 56.

[7] French Fogle, *YP* 5.15, n. 42.

[8] Benoit de Sainte-Maure, *Le Roman de Troie*, ed. Léopold Constans, Paris, Firmin-Didot, 1908, IV, 26164. See also the section, "Trahison d'Anténor et Énéas," 24397-24824. I am indebted to Professor Bettie Forte of Hollins College for this point.

It is not so important to establish a new "source" for Satan as it is to show that a darker account of epic heroes than those assumed by Renaissance humanists was available to Milton.[9] The figure of Satan illustrates how many allusive vistas *Paradise Lost* opens up and how difficult it is to fix the boundaries of allusion to any set books. Satan, for example, may be seen simply as a "Homerized" Aeneas, since Book I of *Paradise Lost* offers a *contaminatio* of Vergilian plot and Homeric character. Alternatively, Satan may be seen as a Vergilian sampler, combining something of Aeneas, Turnus, Mezentius, and perhaps Juno's injured merit;[10] and it is tempting to argue that Milton is condensing all of Vergil's epic into the character of Satan, much in the way that Vergil compresses the fall of Troy into Book II of the *Aeneid*. Finally, one may view Satan as a summary of the literary decay of Aeneas' reputation from Homer onward, so that he stands as the embodiment of what Calvin saw as the downward course of vain imagination. Seen thus, he offers an instructive contrast between the mutability of fame that comes from "partial" songs and the enduring fame that comes from being enrolled in the Father's Book of Life.

[9] See, for example, Chapman's preface to his *Odysses* in *Chapman's Homer: The Iliad, the Odyssey and the Lesser Homerica*, ed. Allardyce Nicoll, New York, Pantheon, 1956, II, 5.

[10] See John M. Steadman, *Milton's Epic Characters*, Chapel Hill, University of North Carolina Press, 1968, p. 234: "Actually Milton invested this figure [Satan] with conventional attributes of at least three different types of heroes: the Achilles-type (represented by Ajax, Turnus, and Rinaldo) . . . ; the *dux* (exemplified by such generals as Agamemnon, Aeneas, and Godfrey) . . . ; and the Odysseus-type characterized by wiles, ruses, disguises and deception."

—————— II ——————

O what a fine time that was years ago, when
there was peace, joy, and God's help when the
people were godly. . . . Time was when. . . .
Troy had its day, and so did Ilium.

(*LW* 27.367)

If Milton's reading in medieval romance suggested to him
that Aeneas was a traitor, and even something of a Satan, his
reading of the Protestant Reformers complemented the view of
Trojan lore in these romances. Despite Milton's early enthu-
siasm for Spenser and Italian critics, the proximate models for
his assimilation of epic material to biblical poetry seem to be
Luther and Calvin, who read classical literature with all the
dogmatic intensity of thirteenth-century scholastics, yet with
the philological finesse of the humanists. In their view, Chris-
tianity corrected, rather than fulfilled, the classics—a relation
paralleling the disjunction between faith and reason in their
theology. Even if Milton himself had never read a single com-
mentary by Luther or Calvin—and his divorce tracts show that
he read several of them carefully—he most likely would have
read classical epic with much the same religious categories as
did the Reformers, because his tutor Thomas Young was a learned
Calvinist. He probably would have translated *superbia* in the
Aeneid as "sin" and drawn conclusions after the manner of
Luther: "Vergil says it was not the Greeks who destroyed Troy
but their own great sins" (*LW* 17.148). Like Calvin, Milton
must have found the poets sometimes proclaiming truth about
God under the name of Jupiter and sometimes letting Satan
speak "under the visor of Apollo."[11] Classical allusion in the
Reformers' commentary is sometimes that of medieval com-
monplace, but often suggests that a new theological "transfer-

[11] John Calvin, *Commentary upon the Acts of the Apostles*, trans. Chris-
topher Fetherstone, Edinburgh, Calvin Translation Society, 1859, II, 93, cited
hereafter as *Commentary upon Acts*.

ence" had taken place in their reading of ancient authors. They seem to have read the classical poets through a filter of their Reformation Bible and, in selected areas, to have reversed the process. In *Paradise Lost*, classical allusion reifies a similar "transference."

Luther invoked the classics in a wide variety of ways. Like Milton, he found Vergil to be a gold mine of information on subjects ranging from meteorology to rhetoric, all ultimately helpful to him in making biblical glosses.[12] But medieval exegetes had done as much. It is rather Luther's attention to the narrative texture that set the style for Protestant commentary. In a way that anticipates Auerbach, he noted that Old Testament stories were mere lattices, and urged the exegete to weave himself into the sense by filling in the interstices with details of situation and psyche from his own experience.[13] Much of Luther's experience, like Milton's, was literary experience, and he finds ancient authors a useful *amplificatio* of biblical narrative, especially for describing a character's consciousness. Cain and Orestes, for example, felt very much alike after murder: "they are so fiercely pursued by the Furies that they are indeed dumbfounded and think that heaven and earth have taken on another appearance; and they do not know where to flee. . . . Such an awful thing is this outcry of the blood and of an evil conscience" (*LW* 1.286-287). The builders of Babel defied prophecy, but had a divided consciousness like Ovid's Medea, who had expressed her inner state with a Pauline precision: "I see and applaud the better things, but I follow the worse" (*LW* 2.219-220). Typical of the way in which Luther weaves both his literary and his quotidian experience into the biblical story

[12] Vergil usefully records ancient customs like animal sacrifice (*LW* 1.247) and natural phenomena like the burning wind (*venti urentes*). The latter (apparently a *lapsus memoriae* because it is not actually to be found in Vergil) Luther considered helpful in explaining how the waters receded after the flood (*LW* 2.106).

[13] "The procedure of Moses is correct: he suggests by dots, as it were, situations that cannot be expressed in words. He does so in order by that brevity to stimulate the reader's feelings to pay closer attention to a situation" (*LW* 1.280). See also *LW* 3.303-304.

is his comment about Abraham watching the smoke of Sodom on the horizon:

> We must not suppose that Abraham was a block of wood and devoid of all human feelings. He was as godly and compassionate as anyone else. Consequently, he was concerned about the safety of the five cities and especially about the members of his family. Therefore he could not stay in bed. He gets up before daylight and has some hope that perhaps God will act more mildly. Full of hope, worries, and fears, he accordingly turns his eyes at once toward the well-known region to see whether it is still unharmed. Familiar are the sentiments we feel toward absent friends, *the way Terence's Mitio is anxious about his son, who is tarrying too long.* In like manner, I am anxious about my dear Philip while he is at Frankfort and now [early 1539] have a variety of thoughts about him. Hearts affected in this manner feel nothing but troubles and worries. They think: "Ah, what are my friend, my nephew, my children, my fellow citizens, and others now doing?" such was the state of Abraham's heart at that time; he was full of sighs and groans. Even though these facts are recorded by Moses in few words, they should not be looked at with carnal eyes; *you must make the mood, yes, even the effect of the events your own, put yourself, as it were, into the situation before us, and examine your heart as to what you would have thought or done had you been in such a position.*
>
> (*LW* 3.303-304, *author's italics*)

In sum, Luther does not search ancient authors for alternate types of Christ, such as Hercules, but for models of consciousness that he can use in explicating the experience of biblical characters.

The Reformers also found the ancients helpful in summarizing the ways of a world that proclaimed a *deus absconditas;* "But we know from experience," remarks Luther, and "from the examples of the poets, particularly the tragic poets," that there is no reward here and now (*LW* 3.49). Accordingly, his commentaries are sprinkled with the familiar proverbial lines from the *Aeneid* found in medieval *florilegia*. Calvin, however, is wont to quote Vergil more copiously on the ways of the world. To explain why Paul and Silas were put in jail one night for stirring up the citizenry only to be released the next morning, Calvin inserts the whole of Vergil's famous epic simile in which he likens Neptune's calming a storm to an orator's quieting a mob (*Aen.* 1.144-156), and then adds: "There is no other thing here set down but that which falleth out most commonly when sedition is once raised. For not only the minds of the common people begin to rage, but also the tempest carrieth away the governors also, no doubt perversely. For we know that of Virgil."[14] To the Reformers, ancient writers were the repository of all the "experience" of the Western world, their poetic inspiration coming "from no other fountain save only from nature and common reason."[15]

Ancient authors were deadly wrong, however, when they strayed beyond the realm of nature. On the question of the supernatural, a great gulf yawned between ancient poetry and Scripture, a distance parallel to that between faith and reason in their theology:

> In the historical accounts of the heathen there are certainly outstanding instances of self-control; of generosity; of love toward fatherland, parents, and children; of bravery; and of philanthropy. Yet we maintain that the loftiest thoughts about God, about the worship of God, and about the will of God are *a darkness* more than *Cimmerian*.
>
> (*LW* 2.42, *author's italics*)

Calvin put the matter more acidly: "the men of Athens, who, having buried and quite put out the remembrance of the true God, had put in place of Him Jupiter, Mercury, Pallas, and all that filthy rabble."[16] Milton makes a similarly sweeping and dismissive appraisal of what ancient authors have to say about

[14] John Calvin, *Commentary upon Acts*, II, 107.
[15] Ibid., p. 145.
[16] Ibid., p. 135.

70

God: they "accuse him under [false] names,/Fortune and Fate
. . ." (PR 4.316-317). Milton laments, "Alas! what can they
teach, and not mislead," except for things they know "By light
of Nature, not in all quite lost" (PR 4.309, 352). Nevertheless,
he and the Reformers never ceased adverting to the wretched
divinity of the ancients. Unlike Dante, who leaves Vergil behind
when he turns to explore the upper reaches of the Empyrean,
Milton finds Vergil's mistakes about God to have their uses
because they provide occasions to clarify Christian doctrine.

The enormity of the ancients' theological errors lay in the
point that they were degenerative mistakes, demonstrating that
men have a bent "naturally to deform God's Glory with their
inventions" until they come to present "ghosts instead of God."[17]
Flashes of resemblance to biblical matter in the work of ancient
poets underscored the doctrinal tragedy that they had once learned
something "from the ancient tradition of the patriarchs" (LW
4.90) or that they had once had some innate knowledge of God:

> For because men have naturally some perseverance of God
> [Aliquo Dei sensu imbuti sunt], they draw true principles
> from that fountain. And though so soon as they begin to
> think upon God, they vanish away in wicked innovations,
> and so the pure seed doth degenerate into corruptions; yet
> the first general knowledge of God doth nevertheless re-
> main still in them.[18]

And, Calvin goes on to say, "Paul's meaning is, that men do
never make an end of erring until God do help them" (pp. 148-
149). It is important to keep in mind both the disgust that this
tradition held for degenerate divinity and the respect that it had
for poetic traces of truth. Milton respected such traces enough
to include in his History of Britain the story of how Aeneas'
descendants had populated England, even though he thought
the story had little basis in fact: "Oft-times relations heertofore
accounted fabulous have bin after found to contain in them

17 Ibid., p. 137.
18 Ibid., p. 146.

many footsteps, and reliques of something true, as what we read in Poets of the Flood, and Giants little beleev'd till undoubted witnesses [that is, the biblical writers] taught us, that all was not fain'd" (*YP* 5.3, *author's italics*).

Looking at ancient writers through the lens of Scripture certified "reliques of truth" in them. Calvin insisted that God's help was needed in this process, and, presumably aided by the Spirit, he proceeds to demonstrate how to correct the ancients. St. Paul in his sermon on Mars Hill had quoted a half-line from *Phaenomena*, an astrological epic poem by the third-century Stoic poet Aratus—"For in him we live, and move, and have our being; as certain also of your own poets have said, *for we are also his offspring*" (Acts 17:28). Calvin comments:

> It is not to be doubted but that Aratus spake of Jupiter; *neither doth Paul,* in applying that unto the true God, which he spake unskilfully of Jupiter, *wrest it unto a contrary sense.*[19]

This "invention" of Aratus, Calvin goes on to say, "ought not to have hindered Paul from retaining a true maxim, though it were corrupt with men's fables" (p. 146). It may be that Milton deliberately borrows the same half-line from Aratus that St. Paul does, setting it in Raphael's speech to Adam: "If ye be found obedient, and retain/Unalterably firm his love entire/ *Whose progeny you are* . . ." (5.501-503, *author's italics*). Milton knew Aratus well, for he meticulously corrected the misprints in his copy of Aratus' *Phaenomena*, which he reviewed in preparation for teaching his nephews.[20] At least, Milton seems to have proceeded on Calvin's assumption that Aratus and St. Paul, Moses and Homer, Vergil and Calvin—all meant the same God:

> No man of a sound mind can doubt to apply that unto the true God which we read in Virgil touching the feigned and

[19] Ibid., p. 146, *author's italics.*
[20] Maurice Kelley and Samuel D. Atkins, "Milton's Annotations of Aratus," *PMLA* 70 (1955), 1090-1106.

false joy, that *All things are full of joy.* Yea, when Virgil meant to express the power of God, through error he put in a wrong name.

(p. 146)

When Milton invokes Urania in *Paradise Lost* and adds "the meaning, not the Name I call" (7.5), he is not abjuring nominalism, as is sometimes supposed, but correcting the eccentric reference of classical bards.

In contrast to humanist readings that emphasize the performance of the hero, the Reformers' reading of epic focuses intently upon the power of the gods and their verbal interaction with men. It is the speech of the gods, in council and in directed oracle, that makes epic and the Reformers' Bible analogous structures. Luther can compare Abraham and Aeneas, claiming for the patriarch a long-range destiny comparable to that of founding Rome: "The church of Abraham . . . is truly the church of God out of which the Savior of the human race is to be born. For Abraham was the father of the promise, and wherever he wandered, he carried with him the promise concerning Christ, who would be born from his seed; he did not carry gods with him, as Aeneas did" (*LW* 3.359). About the time that Luther was beginning to abandon allegory in biblical exegesis, the epic was also undergoing a hermeneutic sea-change. In contrast to Landino, who had read the *Aeneid* as an allegory about Man (Aeneas) from his nonage (the idyllic days of prewar Troy) to his death (the arrival in Italy in Book VII), Melanchthon read the *Aeneid* as being about a particular man whose religious rites he found shocking,[21] and a similar reading of epic is implied in the biblical commentary of Luther and Calvin. Allegory of course did not vanish as a way of reading either Scripture or epic, but *Paradise Lost* owes its allusive shape to a habit of reading both

[21] Don Cameron Allen, *Mysteriously Meant*, Baltimore, Johns Hopkins University Press, 1970, pp. 149-155; Domenico Comparetti, *Vergil in the Middle Ages*, trans. E.F.M. Benecke, New York, Macmillan, 1895, pp. 110-112; Clyde Leonard Manschrek, *Melanchthon: The Quiet Reformer*, New York, Abingdon, 1968, p. 395f.

the Old Testament and classical epics as "realistic" narratives about individual men and their encounters with God's oracles. Corrected for the gods and oracles, the epic became useful as a "Third Scripture."

Luther had jettisoned the Second Scripture (Nature), incidentally curbing an important poetic resource when he rejected natural theology in favor of a biblical one. Calvin follows him closely, except that he holds Nature to contain God's word in a confused and even terrifying manner. If read with the "Spectacles of Scripture," however, it would yield some Christian doctrine, but only the most general propositions about God's power (*Inst.* 1.6.1). Though a Reformed poet could not present an encounter with God as visual experience, a Catholic poet could appropriate, according to the Analogy of Being, any sensuous object from real or imagined Nature to symbolize God. So Dante presents both a Gryffon and a veiled Beatrice as Christ-figures in the last canto of the *Purgatorio*. Milton adheres to the rigors of his biblical theology and does not present God as a visual presence—not even before the Fall. He turns instead to the "voices" of classical epic, whose messengers and oracles offer him numerous "literary" images for divine encounter. These he appropriates according to the analogy of faith—an analogy of the (promissory) word in his tradition. Epic, considered as a system of poetic correspondences, has a different organization from the evenly graded hierarchy of symbolic value in the Great Chain of Being. Instead it offers two sharp differentiations of metaphorical distance—near (for the motions of natural man and his world) and far (for the character and speeches of God). In the latter case, the metaphorical and metaphysical distance is so great that one can scarcely speak of a synthesis of traditions.

Milton draws upon the "voice-images" of epic gods when he presents the Father in *Paradise Lost*, Book III, but the points of resemblance between pagan and biblical deities are so few as to emphasize the distance between a saving revelation and what any man might know through his *sensus divinitatis*. In other words, Milton uses his "Third Scripture" much as Calvin used

Nature—as a rhetorical device to emphasize certain of God's general attributes. Northrop Frye[22] has reminded us that the opening speech of Milton's defensive God—"whose fault?/Whose but his own? . . ." (3.96-123)—echoes the disclaimer by Zeus in Book I of the *Odyssey*:

> Well now, how indeed mortal men do blame the gods!
> They say it is from us evils come, yet they themselves
> By their own recklessness have pains beyond their lot.
> So this Aigisthos married beyond his lot the lawful
> Wife of the son of Atreus, and killed him on his re-
> turn;
> Knowing he would be destroyed, since we told him be-
> forehand.[23]

It is tempting to conclude that Milton's allusion to Homer here confirms a departure from Calvin on the matter of free will.[24] The allusion of itself, however, cannot certify Milton's position because Calvin also applauds Zeus' position on human responsibility, even chiding "Homeric Agamemnon" (*Iliad* 19.86) for blaming his "own wickedness" on the gods (*Inst.* 1.17.3). Calvin finds Homer confirming his own dark paradox that God does not cause evil, even if nothing happens in the world that is not according to his will. The allusive agreement between Odyssean Zeus and Milton's God encompasses no more than the point that God does not cause evil.

From this general revelation, the distance between God and Zeus opens up, inviting a variety of invidious doctrinal comparisons. For example, Zeus in the *Odyssey* considers the fall of the house of Atreus with detachment, while Milton's God observes the fall of the House of Adam and immediately devises a plan for its restoration. Or one might notice how the tender

[22] *The Return of Eden*, Toronto, University of Toronto Press, 1965, p. 99. Blessington also notes this in *Paradise Lost and the Classical Epic*, p. 47, but concludes that Milton "emphasizes the synthesis of Christianity with the epic tradition" (p. 49).
[23] *The Odyssey*, trans. Albert Cook, New York, Norton, 1974, I, 32-37.
[24] Cf. Blessington, p. 47.

concern of Athena parallels that of the Son, yet notice the great disparity between the geographical home that Athena seeks for Odysseus and the spiritual return projected for Adam. By the end of the divine colloquy in Book III, God has begun to "echo" Jupiter's first speech in the *Aeneid* in such a way as to invite eschatological comparison. As the Father outlines history and declares to the Son, "all Power/I give thee, reign for ever" (3.317-318), so Jupiter promises Venus that her son shall have a glorious destiny and says, *imperium sine fine dedi* (*Aen.* 1.271). This is a speech that Luther was fond of quoting to show how wrong the pagan prophets were: "Vergil said about Rome, 'The eternal city will continue without end,' but that prophecy is vain, unsure, and infirm. Thus all heathen oracles have evaporated," the Roman empire having fallen considerably short of eternity.[25] Milton also seems to be marking the distance between Vergilian prophecy and the Father's promise when he gives *imperium sine fine* a true referent as the "New Heav'n and Earth, wherein the just shall dwell" (3.335).

The way in which God's counsels play allusively, now against those of Zeus and Athena, now against those of Jupiter and Venus, makes God's speeches metaphysically conceited in the boldest and most radical way. What more violent yoking can there be than joining true and false prophecy? In Book III, one is invited to consider at the same time the decayed "reliques of truth" and the bright original. This allusive coincidence may be read in a variety of ways, depending upon the assumptions one brings to the poem. One may hear the voice of ancient reason subverting puritan rigor, if one does not take God's voice as the primary term of the conceit. On the other hand, if one takes God's voice as primary, one may hear Christianity building on classical reason, clarifying pagan prophecy into the revelation it had figured forth. Or, as more probable in Milton's tradition, one may take God's speeches as both prior and primary and hear a precise God discounting epic corruptions of truth. What had been accomplished in the Nativity Ode by the

---

[25] *LW* 17.51; cf. *LW* 14.250.

spectacle of a retreating procession of priests and oracles is accomplished here by speech. In *Paradise Lost*, the discovery of an allusion to classical epic provides an occasion to judge degenerate revelation by the true one and to hear the Bible correcting and silencing the crooked "Scripture." There is a good deal more being said and done by indirection in Milton's heaven than Christopher Ricks supposed.[26]

Paradise Lost alludes so variously, yet so constantly, to classical works that its structure is highly prismatic and offers the possibility of an almost unlimited number of epiphanies during the course of a reading. These discoveries depend upon the distance, or even antagonism, between two traditions, rather than their fusion. At the time Milton was writing, the antagonism between the two traditions was intensifying. In the 1650s there was discouragement from the literary left and the puritan right for anyone writing a biblical epic. Divines in the wake of William Perkins were condemning all reference to pagan gods in devotional writing, while Sir William Davenant was arguing that a Christian poet did not need "invention" and should not imitate the fables of epic poets who "meanly illustrate a probable heaven."[27] As early as *Areopagitica* and as late as the preface to *Samson Agonistes*, Milton felt the need to justify his use of the classical authors. He found his sanction for "intertextuality" in St. Paul, who had "insert[ed] into holy Scripture the sentences of three Greek Poets" (*YP* 2.508)—Epimenides in Titus 1:12, Euripides in I Corinthians 15:33, and Aratus in Acts 7:28. But even in Milton's apologia there remains the sense of risk underlying the liberty of using polluted texts while keeping a conscience that was "not defil'd" (*YP* 2.512). The poetic vigor of Milton's celestial dialogues depends upon our perceiving this fundamental enmity between classical and biblical texts *on matters of divinity*. To the extent that a *fusion* of these texts is perceived, the heavenly dialogues will be found flatly univocal,

[26] Christopher Ricks, *Milton's Grand Style*, Oxford, Clarendon, 1963, pp. 148-149.

[27] "Preface to *Gondibert*," in *The Works of Sir William Davenant*, London, 1673, reprint Benjamin Blom, 1968, p. 3.

and to the extent that the antagonism of traditions is felt, the poem will yield continual metaphorical gleams, as the pagans are sighted through the biblical word, across a vast gulf.

Other variables enter into a reading of *Paradise Lost* besides the theological and historical context. The extent of the reader's acquaintance with classical epic, the locus of the epic motif remembered—whether from Homer, Vergil, Ovid, Dante, or Spenser—and whether it leads to further allusion—are variables that will make a reading of this prismatic poem a unique one. Even if the reader tries to assume Milton's theology of the word, there may be several appropriate readings for any given allusion. Thus *Paradise Lost* is both firmly dogmatic and yet radically indeterminate. Today one might attribute the variance of reading patterns to the indeterminacy of allusion, but Milton no doubt would have credited such differences to the motions of the Spirit.

Aineias,
which one of the gods is it who
urges you to such madness
that you fight in the face of
[Achilles], against his
high courage
though he is both stronger than
you and dearer to the
immortals?

(*Iliad* 20.331 334)

Sin is not our nature but its
derangement.

(*Inst.* 2.1.10)

If classical epic is a skewed version of God's truth, the "classical hero" of *Paradise Lost* is deranged. Vergil's epic definition of sanity changes when Milton makes correction for the gods and oracles. In Vergil, Aeneas embodies, however imperfectly, the Stoic conception of reason and sound mind. Throughout the *Aeneid*, the *vita temperata*, characterized by competence, fidelity, and equanimity, is set in opposition to the madness of passions gone berserk—*furor, ira, mens insana*. In *Paradise Lost*, Satanic Aeneas makes "reason" his highest boast (1.248), but he embodies Reason in the sense labeled "madness" by Reformation commentary. Milton thus alters the central conflict of the *Aeneid*, changing it from *ratio* versus *furor* to *nova ratio* (faith) versus *mens insana* (the derangement of the reprobate mind). The governing definition of Reason in Milton's epic is not a philosophical one, but that of common parlance: reason equals sanity.

Given the facts of Milton's literary universe, Satan's voice as we first hear it in *Paradise Lost* is necessarily the voice of madness. Like a schizophrenic who has no trouble convincing a personnel manager of his competence, Satan is convincing because he can expound intelligently the version of reality he believes at the moment and because he includes no information in his discourse that may be used as counter-evidence. To perceive the distortion in what Satan (or a schizophrenic) claims, one must have other testimony of the reality alleged. In *Paradise Lost*, the conclusive testimony showing Satan to be mad does not come until midway in the epic; but from the outset there are warnings from the narrative voice, and from the dramatic situation itself, that we should not take Satan's claims at face value. Our attention is absorbed, however, by Satan's highly charged, subjective account of things. His opening speech—"All is not lost; the unconquerable Will/And study of revenge, immortal hate . . ." (1.106-107)—is so powerful that one scarcely can imagine its being delivered without an upright, martial bearing and a fist shaken at heaven. Yet this speech is declaimed from a horizontal position. Satan, like Dryden's Mac Flecknoe and Monarch Oaks, "supinely reign[s]"[28]—unsteadily so, "rolling in the fiery Gulf" (1.52). So great is the power of this rhetoric to make its own gesture that we generally miss the comic contradiction between defiant rhetoric and compliant posture, as well as the absurdity of heroic figures planning an attack while flat on their backs.

Also on first reading we generally miss two unsettling facts about the fallen consciousness: each devil in some respect has a better grasp of reality than Satan himself, and each devil, under the pressure of official rhetoric, abandons his best insight, just as Satan himself is to do in his soliloquy in Paradise (4.32-113). Beelzebub, the first angel after Satan to wake up on the dreadful lake, immediately understands that though their strength remains, they can only and inevitably

---

[28] John Dryden, "Mac Flecknoe," in *The Works of John Dryden*, ed. H. T. Swedenberg, Jr., Berkeley, University of California Press, 1968, II, 54, ll.27-28.

do him [God] mightier service as
his thralls
By right of War, whate'er his business be . . .
(1.149-150)

Beelzebub gives up this perception with alarming ease in the face of Satan's rhetoric, demonstrating the instability of devilish apprehension once its grounding in God's word has been severed.[29] Even Moloch, whose dullness makes him an easy target in debate, knows that, God's throne being "inaccessible" (2.104), they cannot win a heavenly war. Belial is a good deal sharper, but he has no sure grasp of the situation because he holds out the possibility that in time they will adjust (2.215-220). He is unaware that Hell contains regions of ice to provide a change of venue precluding adjustment. Nevertheless, he too shows a momentary grasp of things more comprehensive than that of his leader, when he argues that opposition to God is pointless:

for what can force or guile
With him, or who deceive his mind, whose eye
Views all things at one view?
(2.188-190)

Mammon, like Belial, is wide of the mark when he thinks that Hell has possibilities (2.270-273). He is clear-headed, however, about the sociology of heaven and knows that its sole propriety is bowing to the word—"subjection" he calls it. So each devil has a partial grasp of reality, no two of them sharing the same glimmer of truth, a fact that makes them an easy prey to the demogogic skill—and even more delusional worldview—of their leader.

It may be impossible to determine just what Satan knows at any given moment and thus to judge when he is lying and when he is deceiving himself. His errors are both systematic and random. When, like Iago, he gives three different motivations

[29] See Arnold Stein, *Answerable Style*, Minneapolis, University of Minnesota Press, 1953, p. 5.

81

for his trip to earth (2.354-370, 3.671-676, 4.938-940), he has obviously crafted lies to fit the victim. But no matter who is listening, Satan seems to assume that he in some way can hurt God through creation, and this systematic error in Satan's calculations suggests that from the first he is as mad as the old man who builds himself a set of paper wings and jumps off the garage thinking he can fly.

Perhaps it is going too far to see madness in the obsessive glints darting from the eyes of the oriental despot who in Book II sits

> High on a Throne of Royal State, which far
> Outshone the wealth of *Ormus* and of *Ind*,
> Or where the gorgeous East with richest hand
> Show'rs on her Kings *Barbaric* with Pearl and Gold.
> (2.1-4)

Nevertheless, this despot, whose subjects approve his policies out of fear and give obeisance by prostrating themselves, would have been labeled "mad" according to the rhetorical habits of Milton's prose, in which he accuses Emperor Theodosius of "tyrannicall madnes" (*YP* 1.607) and claims that "like all sinners, all tyrants too are quite mad" (*YP* 4.527). In Book X, this oriental despot meets a fate that is strongly reminiscent of Nebuchadnezzar, who disregarded the word of the Lord and therefore was stricken mad. He lost his tongue for speaking, fell to his hands, ate grass like an ox, and began to take on a bestial appearance, until finally "his hairs were grown like eagles' feathers, and his nails like birds' claws."[30] Satan's fate is analogous: his punishment for not heeding God's primal word (5.600-615) is that he falls to the ground as a serpent who, in an annual fit, gobbles up Sodom apples.

In a somewhat different key, the roll call of devils in Book II hints at madness defined in psychosexual terms. First comes

---

[30] Daniel 4:33. See Penelope B. R. Doob, *Nebuchadnezzar's Children: Conventions of Madness in Middle English Literature*, New Haven, Yale University Press, 1974, p. 69.

The Crooked Scripture

atrocity—Moloch, "horrid King besmear'd with blood/Of human sacrifice" (1.392-393), "lustful Orgies" (415), the transvestism of Baalim and Ashtoreth (422-424), and the matron in Gibeah who was exposed "to avoid worse rape" (505). This march of history as psychosexual disorder is summed up in the figure of Lady Sin, whose tortured nether parts and repellent genitality could only be the product of some imagination as mad as King Lear's[31]—and indeed she is, having sprung from the brow of Satan. As we shall see in the next chapter, she embodies the hermeneutic reason that constitutes madness in Milton's universe.

The hints thus far are only circumstantial, because the Arch Fiend is superbly controlled throughout the early books. It is only in Book IV that anyone perceives Satan's "mad demeanor" (129). When, thinking himself alone, he drops his Stoic front, Uriel becomes spectator to a veritable masque of unreason—"ire, envy, and despair"—playing across Satan's face in quick succession (4.115). He then appears a deeply troubled tempter whose "perturbation" Milton contrasts with the soundness of heavenly minds who "from such distempers foul/Are ever clear" (119-120). The moment is brief and fleeting, however, and it is not until the war in heaven that Satan's madness becomes unmistakable—and strongly comic.

The war in heaven presents a bold and extended image of the madness of the reprobate mind. The vocabulary of Bedlam threads its way through the somewhat impressionistic account of the battles. There is a great concatenation of "madding Wheels" (6.210) and "inextinguishable rage" (217), "Horrible discord"

31   Down from the waist they are Centaurs,
        Though women all above;
        But to the girdle do the gods inherit,
        Beneath is all the fiends': there's hell,
                there's darkness,
        There is the sulphurous pit, burning, scalding,
        Stench, consumption. Fie, fie, fie! pah! pah!
(*King Lear*, in *The Riverside Shakespeare*, ed. G. Blakemore Evans, Boston, Houghton Mifflin, 1974, 4.6.124-129)

(210), and such strife as "Tormented all the Air" (244). Everywhere about are a great many "Seraphim confus'd" (249), and even the landscape goes berserk with the "jaculation dire" of trees and hills. The speeches of the rebels quickly take on a lunatic cast. "This we style the strife of glory," Satan trumpets, and at once we are given demonstration of how his rhetoric overreaches reality. Moloch, playing Achilles, defies Gabriel and threatens "at his Chariot wheels to drag him bound" (6.358-359). Forthwith, the threatener, in a manner most un-Achillean, is "Down clov'n to the waist" (361), and so the poor forked angel leaves the scene of battle "bellowing" like a bull, more an Ajax than Achilles.

As Luther was wont to say, "blasphemy against Christ is immediately followed by a counterfeit reality" (*LW* 16.65), and so it is with Satan. The finer his calculations become, the more they approach the preciosity of farce. From the experience of one antic battle, he ironically rejoices that they have emerged from the first day of battle with their minds unscathed:

> perhaps more valid Arms,
> Weapons more violent, when next we meet,
> May serve to better us, and worse our foes,
> Or equal what between us made the odds,
> In Nature none: if other hidden cause
> Left them Superior, while *we can preserve*
> *Unhurt our minds, and understanding sound,*
> *Due search and consultation will disclose.*
> (6.438-445, author's italics)

What else is madness but supposing that with better munitions one can win a war lost from the outset? Satan and Belial, however, boast "in gamesome Mood" of their secret weapon, and the narrator notes that they are "highth'n'd" in their thoughts "beyond/All doubt of Victory" (6.629-630): they are out of their minds.

Satan's madness finally turns chilling on the last day of battle, when he is set upon by the Messiah's mysterious war machine. What does he do when confronted by visible evidence that he

84

The Crooked Scripture

has misinterpreted God's Prime Decree (5.600-615)? Just as
Abdiel had contended, the saints do seem to be "more illustrious
made" when they come marching in twin formation behind the
blazing chariot of the Messiah:

> about him fierce Effusion roll'd
> Of smoke and bickering flame, and sparkles dire;
> Attended with ten thousand thousand Saints,
> He onward came, far off his coming shone,
> And twenty thousand (I thir number heard)
> Chariots of God, half on each hand were seen:
> Hee on the wings of Cherub rode sublime. . . .
> (6.765-771)

Who would not want to be part of such a parade? For their part,
Satan and his rebel troop are not unwistful. At the sight of

> His Army, circumfus'd on either Wing,
> Under thir Head imbodied all in one,
> (778-779),

they "Took envy" (793). They should have been reasonable
and, like the uprooted hills, returned to their appointed places;
but the rebels, despite all, "stood obdur'd,/And to rebellious
fight rallied thir Powers/Insensate, hope conceiving from de-
spair" (785-787). So overwhelming is the force ranged against
them and so mad is any resistance at this point, that even the
narrator is moved to wonderment at their insane stubbornness
(788).

But so works God's *terribilitá*—hard hearts are hardened more
(6.791). Calvin's commentary on Ezekiel's chariot, which he
claims was a vision sent to warn a rebellious Israel, is relevant
here. The vision was both cautionary and punitive, "for as soon
as any one apprehends the anger of God, he is necessarily ag-
itated, and then, like a raging beast, he wages war with God
himself."[32] A revelation of God's anger could freeze men in

[32] John Calvin, *Commentaries on the First Twenty Chapters of the Book of
the Prophet Ezekiel*, trans. Thomas Myers, Edinburgh, Calvin Translation So-
ciety, 1849, I, 55.

85

their rebellion—or in their madness, for Calvin here makes the equation between derangement and hostility toward God that is typical of his commentaries:

> The vengeance of God, as soon as it is displayed, drives men to despair, and *despair casts them headlong into madness*.[33]

And so it is with the rebel angels, who flee before the Messiah's blazing chariot like maddened beasts of prey, "choosing" to jump off the crystal battlements. Just so, Achilles taunts Aeneas for fleeing:

> I tell you, you ran from my spear.
> Or do you not remember when, apart from
> your cattle, I caught you
> . . . and chased you in the
> speed of your feet down the hills of Ida
> Headlong, and that time as you ran you did not
> turn to look back.
>
> (*Iliad* 20.187-190)

At the moment when Satan jumps headlong from the crystal battlements, Milton marks the Fiend's deterioration as "epic" hero by inserting a simile that compares him and his fleeing minions to "a Herd/Of Goats or timorous flock" (6.856-857). Even when Satan is described by bestial imagery, he is far from the medieval devil of hairy limbs, multiple faces, and cloacal preoccupations.[34] Milton shows the mind opposing God suddenly reduced to the prerational terror of animals caught between fight and flight. It is the "*mind* of the flesh" that Milton's tradition found demonic. Just as the medieval demon often was represented by a melange of mismatched body parts (for example, Duessa stripped for her bath), so Milton's Satan is a

---

[33] Ibid. (*author's italics*).

[34] Roland Mushat Frye, *Milton's Imagery and the Visual Arts*, Princeton, Princeton University Press, 1978, pp. 65-91; plates 14, 46, 55, 56, 58, and especially 97.

mind whose parts do not function well together. Satan's intelligence works splendidly with respect to tactics, but he cannot relate his tactics even to his most accurate perception of things. By experience he has learned that God with his thunder is "stronger" (1.92), but this conclusion, which he can state so well, seems inaccessible to his strategic thinking. The affective part of Satan's psyche also works atomistically, his emotions being anything but "fixt" by conscious control. While he may talk an "obdúrate" game, he is subject to emotional whiplashes of the most arbitrary sort. One moment he is maintaining inner stability even against all of chaos, the next he is stunned into stupid goodness at the beauty of Eve, or maddened by the beams of the sun, or "abasht" at the "awful goodness" of young Zephon (4.846-847)—and always he expects a "lower deep" to devour him. Satan's punishment is to have his mental instability fixed in a yearly ritual.

In Satan's punishment, Milton seems to be challenging Dante's claim to have presented the ultimate serpentine metamorphosis.[35] Whereas a horrified Dante watches as a serpent steals the form of a wraith and leaves him prone and writhing as a viper,[36] Milton's narrator watches in amusement a potentially more horrible theft: Satan's "sanity" is snatched away. His mental equipment is sabotaged so that he compulsively eats ashen apples that he mistakes for real ones. Were the reader allowed to share Satan's perceptions at this point, as he is able to do in Book I, the terror of such mental malfunctioning would be

[35]
> Taccia Lucano omai là dov' e' tocca
> del misero Sabello e di Nasidio,
> e attenda a udir quel ch'or si scocca
> Taccia di Cadmo e d'Aretusa Ovidio,
> ché se quello in serpente e quella in fonte
> converte poetando, io non lo 'nvidio
> ché due nature mai a fronte a fronte
> non trasmutò sì ch'amendue le forme
> a cambiar lor matera fosser pronte.

(*Inferno*, 25, 94-97, in *The Divine Comedy*, trans. Charles S. Singleton, Princeton, Princeton University Press, 1970)

[36] Ibid., 103-141.

almost unbearable. Empathy, however, is impossible because *peccatum* is now *sine voce*. God's victory is climactically portrayed as a verbal act—as a silencing. Milton's hell finally depends upon a Reformation reading of Scripture, in which the ultimate punishment is "speechlessness," or being made to dwell "in the land of silence"—a biblical view of Hell that Luther found confirmed in Vergil.[37]

---

[37] "When Zacharias (Luke 1:18-22) does not believe the angel, he is punished with speechlessness for a definite time" (*LW* 3.208); "Thus the prophet [Isaiah] says that he was completely reduced to nothing, or reduced to silence, . . . For   means 'he was silent' and   means 'silence,' as in Ps. 94:17: 'Almost it would have lived in hell.' In Hebrew: 'My soul would soon have dwelt in the land of silence.' Poets say ghosts are silent, since there is no memory of them" (*LW* 16.72, cf. *Aen.* 6.264).

❈ 4 ❈
The *Verbum Reale*

───────── I ─────────

God either is, or is not, such as he represents
himself to be.

(*CE* 14.37)

To one who does not know what faith is,
the Word of God is a closed book.

(*LW* 16.92)

The act that sets Satan on his mad course occurs in the "Primal
Scene" of Book V. 600-615 and has no close precedent in hex-
ameral literature. Milton seems to have invented it to stand as
the Ur-drama of the Reformation: God speaking and the crea-
ture responding, for better or for worse. Just how far *Paradise
Lost* has come from the Platonic esthetic of *Comus* may be seen
if we look at Milton's version of the Fall in comparison with
that of Spenser and St. Augustine himself. *The City of God*
defines God's Word as an ideational template and cautions that
it is not to be thought of as a "vocall" word.[1] Spenser's account
of the Fall likewise presents God's Word as "Th' Idee of his

[1] St. Augustine, *The Citie of God*, trans. J. Healy, London, 1610, XI, viii,
415.

pure glorie"—as "celestiall beauties blaze."[2] The Fall in this tradition is a matter of inexplicable metaphysical taste: St. Augustine's angels simply turn from the vision of God's Word to something less beautiful.[3] Milton comes no nearer to explaining the Fall than his predecessors did, but he gives it a literary rather than a metaphysical cast: in *Paradise Lost* God's word *is* vocal. Unlike St. Augustine's angels, Milton's have to be told, because a dark cloud surrounds the Almighty's throne, and instead of a communal interpenetration of vision, "blessed vision" goes one way—from God's providential eye downward: the angels "from His sight *receiv'd*/Beatitude past utterance" (3.61-62, *author's italics*).

Milton's version of the Fall consists of two verbal gestures that approach the dramatic simplicity of a mystery play. The *Ludus Coventriae*, for example, depicts the Fall in two physical moves: God exits to survey the Garden (presumably on the floor of the pageant wagon below), and in his absence Satan gets up and sits in God's chair ("I wyl go syttyn in goddys se").[4] Milton cannot match the naïve power of such bold physical moves, but he does gain in intellectual subtlety when he treats the primal sin as a literary lapse, a misconstruction of a divine text. For the text of the proclamation that appears at roughly the midpoint of *Paradise Lost*, Milton chooses a text that appears at roughly the midpoint of the Bible, one that epitomized, for the Reformers, the Promise of all Scripture. Calvin took Psalm 2:6ff. to be God's solemn decree of the King-

---

[2] Edmund Spenser, "An Hymne of Heavenly Love," *Spenser's Minor Poems*, ed. Ernest de Sélincourt, Oxford, Clarendon, 1960, p. 463, ll. 284, 277.

[3] *The Citie of God*, XII, vi, 445.

[4] *Ludus Coventriae*, ed. K. S. Block, Early English Text Society, London, Oxford University Press, 1922, p. 18, l. 56. Spenser reduces the entire first episode of the *Ludus Coventriae* to three lines of rhetoric in "An Hymne of Heavenly Love," ll. 80-82, where the rebel angels

> gan cast their state how to increase
> Above the fortune of their first condition,
> And *sit in Gods owne seat without commission*. (*author's italics*)

dom,[5] and Luther called it "the highest article of our faith"
(*LW* 12.46):

> Then shall he speak unto them. . . .
> Yet have I *set my king* upon my holy hill of Zion.
> I will *declare* the decree: the Lord hath said unto me,
>   Thou art my Son; this day have I *begotten* thee.
>   (Psalm 2:5-7, *author's italics*)

Milton redacts this verse and removes it from its background
having to do with the "kings of the earth" and their heathen
rage. He eliminates the confusing change of speakers (from
Father to Son) and lessens the interval between metaphors, with
the result that in *Paradise Lost* the Divine Decree comes out of
the blue with the logical consistency of a conundrum:

> Hear my Decree, which unrevok't shall stand.
> This day have I *begot* whom I *declare*
> My only Son, and on this holy Hill
> Him have *anointed*, whom ye now behold
> At my right hand . . . .
>   (5.602-606, *author's italics*)

We immediately recognize the doctrinal nexus to which *beget-
ting*, *speaking*, and *anointing* belong: the *reference* to divine
persons is clear, but the *sense* of the metaphors is not. Because
this redacted verse is deliberately shorn of all context, its con-
flation of *fathering*, *speaking*, and *king-making* makes no sense
to ordinary experience or, initially, to puritan cognoscenti. This
doctrina doctrinarum is presented as pure oracle, open and ap-
plicable to all contexts. The proclamation is the rhetorical coun-
terpart of the geography of heaven, which, though filled with

[5] John Calvin, *Commentary on the Book of Psalms*, trans. James Anderson,
Edinburgh, Calvin Translation Society, 1845, I, 15-16. Milton also must have
drawn upon Hebrews 1:5-6 in constructing his "Primal Scene." Calvin, in
Commentaries on the Epistle of Paul the Apostle to the Hebrews, trans. John
Owen, Edinburgh, Calvin Translation Society, 1853, pp. 43-44, calls God's
announcement of "begetting," wherever it appears in Scripture, to be the "sol-
emn decree" of the Kingdom.

light, is "undetermin'd square or round" (2.1048). Milton has brilliantly solved the problem of how to make God's word an open secret, how to make it lexically clear, but dark and puzzling nonetheless. The oracle will be unriddled by gleams and fractions as the reader supplies specific reference for it during a reading of *Paradise Lost*, but only if *begot, declare,* and *anoint* are taken in some sense to be metaphoric. Milton is true to the hermeneutic set forth in his *Christian Doctrine*, where he declares that we must accept God's *mimesis* (representation) of himself. Scripture consistently uses human metaphors when representing God, and Milton underlines the point that God does not have hands and feet, wrath and repentance, in the way that human beings do (*CD*, pp. 133-134). God had revealed himself in literary categories, and men should adhere to them: "If, at any rate, [God] wants us to imagine him in this way, why does our imagination go off on some other tack? Why does our imagination shy away from a notion of God which he himself does not hesitate to promulgate in unambiguous terms?" (*CD*, p. 136). Because Milton holds God to be a metaphor-maker when he represents himself as a speaker, faith necessarily becomes a "poetic" reading of God's speech, one that acknowledges the important metaphor *of* God's speech, as well as the metaphors *in* God's speech.

In *Paradise Lost*, the reader has an advantage over Satan when approaching the Primal Text (5.600-615) because the network of associated commonplaces that the key metaphors invoke has been reviewed for him in Book III. This review is a prerequisite to, but not a guarantee of, solving God's oracle. Milton himself concedes that the *begetting* of Psalm 2:7 is a mystery that admits of no complete solution. He holds it to be *both* literal and metaphoric, concluding "Anyone who wants to be wiser than this is really not wise at all. Lured on by empty philosophy or sophistry, he becomes hopelessly entangled and loses himself in the dark" (*CD*, p. 212).

In Milton's Ur-drama, then, the "words of God" are deliberately made an offense to reason. With the accident of passing time, they have become an esthetic offense as well, bald authoritative or didactic statement now being perceived as anti-poetic. The offense, however, is ultimately serviceable, both to Milton's evangelical purposes and to an esthetic apprehension of *Paradise Lost*. Any epiphany that occurs during the course of a reading—as a felicitous referential connection is made between the Primal Word and some point in the earthly narrative—will be proportionate to the emptiness or illogic first perceived in the Primal Word.

Regardless of how the Prime Decree strikes the reader in Book V, this proclamation dramatizes the essential motion of faith. Because the decree cannot be certified by logic, experience, or desire, it calls for a "snap judgment" about God's character—in other words, a leap of faith. Taking a position on God's character comes before a reading of his words. Luther liked to point out that faith reverses the Ciceronian dictum to pay attention to *what* is being said rather than *who* is speaking. Milton concurs: divine testimony "gets all its force from the author."[6] If one recognizes God as *God*, the response to his words will be that of the good angels, who *bow* and sing hosannas. In every utterance of God there comes an implicit command that can be summed up as: Submit your reason to the word.[7] Satan, however, does not submit, and it becomes impossible to distinguish between his hostility toward God and his misinterpretation of the divine proclamation. Satan thus offers a textbook case of how *not* to interpret Scripture. His is the ultimate heresy: hearing God's truth and believing it to be bad. The Rebel Angel does not dispute that the Son has been made King—at least not at the beginning of Book V—but he does dispute that this arrangement is made for the benefit of God's creatures and that it will make them "For ever happy" (5.611). Instead, he thinks

---

[6] *CE* 11.283.

[7] Compare *CD*, p. 136 and *CE* 14.36-37. The Yale edition of *Christian Doctrine* translates *Qualis sit Deus, eos optime capere statuamus qui suum accommodant captum Dei verbo* as "they understand best what God is like who *adjust* their understanding to the word of God." The Columbia edition translates *accommodant* as "submit," which accords with Adam's response to Michael's exposition of the word: "I yield it just, said *Adam*, and submit" (*PL* 11.526).

93

God an aggressor who "hath to himself ingross't/All Power and [him] eclipst under the name/Of King anointed . . . (5.775-777). Satan's prime mistake is to take God's speech as ordinary language, all of which is another way of saying that his response indicates a profound misreading of who God is. As Milton emphasizes, "The whole of scripture proves the same point, and it is absolutely requisite that . . . he *who comes to God must believe that he is God*" (*CD*, p. 132, *author's italics*).

Satan's assumption that God speaks ordinary language means that he misses the metaphor in *declare*, and misses other metaphors as well. Satan reads *anointing* in ordinary political categories and calls into play the political passions applicable to the civil realm, thus confirming his sense of political injury. Those who marvel that Milton the Republican should depict God in *Paradise Lost* as an absolute monarch (and the Son as Regent) do not appreciate how implicitly he honored the metaphors God had used to present himself in Holy Writ. The metaphor of kingship was highly charged for those belonging to the Good Old Cause, "King" being a political title considerably besmirched, if not altogether discredited, by the time Milton was writing *Paradise Lost*. To insist upon the royal titles of Psalm 2 for the hero of a puritan epic was to yoke violently negative and positive associations. The literary work of faith was that of substracting for the dark passions attendant upon political monarchy and of reading the title "King" as a telling *a fortiori* statement of divine power.

Anyone reading *Paradise Lost* will fall into Satan's pattern of response, unless he deliberately takes a position that resists the workings of ordinary language with its mundane field of reference. The "natural" processes of language fuel Satan's rage and lend tacit support to his political reading of the Prime Decree. It is not just that "process" or linearity is involved, but that human speech always takes place *in medias res*. It has a paradigm of tenses implying preexistent time; an apparent capacity for reference, implying a preexistent world, and a semantic richness, implying a preexistent community of understanding. By its very nature, our language is not equipped to

94

treat of absolute beginnings. Satan ignores the disjunction between divine speech and ordinary language and so is able to pin the injustice of God's Decree on its timing, on the fact that it comes "now" (5.784) and, like Archbishop Laud, imposes a "new" (679) and unwonted discipline upon the angels. A good angel like Abdiel, however, does not trust to the workings of ordinary language. He reminds Adam that he is presenting the words of God as *Interpreted* in "the Dialect of men" (5.761, *author's italics*), thus nudging the reader as well to make the necessary allowances for the medium. Empson failed to perceive the metaphor in the medium and gives the definitive literalist exposition of the Primal Scene (5.600-615), in which Satan appears as the voice of reason seeking to amend a repressive society.[8]

Satan here is the embodiment of the Reason that Reformation commentary excoriated as the chief enemy of faith. This Reason is situation-specific and does not include the human faculty in its everyday uses where it is a divine gift. In a religious context, though, Reason was thought to be unfailingly presumptuous. Sometimes Luther and Calvin inveigh against the "demonstrative reason" of the late Scholastics, but usually it is an "adversary Reason" that they deplore, a Reason that aims the mind like a battering ram, now from this angle, now from that, *against* God's words. With characteristic hyperbole, Luther advises that when there appears to be a conflict between God's promises and human estimations, "we must honor the Holy Spirit by believing His words and accepting them as the divine truth . . . . the eyes of reason must be blinded, yes, gouged out, as it were" (*LW* 22.10-11). In matters of faith, the mind was no objective instrument, but always argued the dark reasons of the self.

Milton allegorizes this passional view of reprobate Reason in the parthenogenesis of Lady Sin, who is a re-presentation of the Lady of Wisdom in Greek mythology. Coming Athena-like from the brow of Satan, she is the pictorial counterpart of his

[8] William Empson, *Milton's God*, rev. ed., London, Chatto and Windus, 1965, p. 102.

cavils against the Prime Decree in Book V. She represents no simple Augustinian fornication or mere "turning" away from God, but the more tabloid depravity of the Reformers, the "turning in upon oneself" (*incurvatus in se*) of all human powers—a prostitution of human Reason and a never-ending intellectual incest. As a character, Lady Sin is all sweet reasonableness, for she tries to prevent a duel between father and son. What could be more civilized? She is the voice of Reason also in that she accurately reads the realities of Milton's universe and urges her paramour not to attempt a mission impossible. Her grasp of things, like her body, is committed to the service of the Father of Lies; she could well have materialized from Luther's favorite quip that Reason is "the Divel's Whore" (*TT*, p. 135)—a remark that Milton probably knew from Captain Henry Bell's translation of Luther's *Table Talk*, which caused quite a stir when it was published in London in 1652, purportedly for the first time anywhere.[9] If Satan's sin spawns an allegory of reason, his end may be imprisonment in an allegory in which the Sodom, or Sorbus, apples stand for a rival theological tradition that accords reason a high place. According to Luther's fanciful etymology, the Sorbonne, which he considered the "mother of many Errors," derived its name from its location, a street that had "strongly locked gates, called *Sorbona*; named, (as I take it) of the *Sorbus* Apples that grow on the dead sea, which on the outside are very

___

[9] Captain Henry Bell curiously claimed that he had been informed in a dream of the location of the manuscript in a Hamburg cellar and insisted that he was publishing Luther's *Table Talk* for the first time ever. Aurifaber, however, had included the *Table Talk* in an early German edition of Luther (cf. *LW* 54.xv). Milton's use of allegory in the presentation of Lady Sin accords with Luther's mature position on the subject: "Allegories or spiritual significations are fine ornaments of whores-hides, they are not of proof; wee ought not lightly to make use of them, except the principal caus bee first sufficiently proved with strong grounds and arguments. As wee see *St. Paul* did in the 4. Chap. to the *Galatians*, the bodie is the Logick, but Allegorie is the Rhetorick; now Rhetorick (which at length finely and amplie adorneth and enlargeth a thing with words) is of no value without Logick, which round and briefly comprehendeth a matter" (*TT*, p. 480).

fair to behold, but when they are opened within they are full
of ashes" (*TT*, p. 497).

Milton uses reason in such different senses throughout his
work that Tillyard and Grace concluded that there was a basic
ambiguity toward it that he never resolved.[10] But if Reason
takes its primary content from Reformation usage, Milton's
work takes on more coherence than is usually admitted. Milton's
resounding praise of Reason in his prose works usually concerns
its operation in worldly spheres (cf. *YP* 2.396). When he treats
the Kingdom of God, however, Reason appears somewhat less
exalted. For example, in *Paradise Lost* Milton poses the question
of God's goodness in terms of rationality or "justice," but he
answers the question in the "literary" terms of Reformation
commentary, where God's justice is not tied to rationality, but
to his speech. When in *Paradise Lost* God says that the Messiah
"by right of merit Reigns" (6.43), one of course can assume
this to be the rational God belonging to the tradition of Aquinas
and Hooker. The epic form with its celestial councils, however,
slants the possibilities in another direction, especially if one
remembers that it is God's speech that imputes merit to the
Son in the first place just as it is God's speech that imputes
righteousness to Reformation man. The question of whether
the Son in *Paradise Lost* is "rightfully" King by birth or worth
is an illusory question, because the Son is made filial, merito-
rious, and royal all by God's decree (5.600-615). In *Christian
Doctrine*, Milton flirts with heresy in order to stress the primacy
of God's verbal speech. Milton notes that "whatever measure
of Deity is attributed" to the Son in Scripture derives from "the
peculiar gift" of the Father (*CD*, p. 223). In the first 25 lines
of *Paradise Lost*, Milton locates his epic firmly in a Reformation
ethos when he announces that he will "justify" his God and
implies that to do so is merely to "assert" eternal providence.
That is to say, he will repeat God's promissory declarations.
The epic has been unfairly faulted for making an unconvincing

[10] E.M.W. Tillyard, *Milton*, London, 1930, reprint New York, Collier, 1966,
pp. 215-217; William J. Grace, *Ideas in Milton*, Notre Dame, University of
Notre Dame Press, 1968, p. 47.

"argument" when it is offered instead as proclamation—as a repetition of divine "testimony," which is amplified by the poet's own. As Milton explains elsewhere, "testimony" simply "affirms or denies that a thing is so . . . , it does not cause me to know or understand why things are so"; and yet it "brings about that I believe" (*CE* 11.283).

Abdiel's apology for God's justice, in any case, is based upon the sheer fact of God's utterance. He scolds Satan thus:

> Canst thou with impious obloquy condemn
> The *just Decree* of God, *pronounc't and sworn*,
> That to his only Son by right endu'd
> With Regal Sceptre, every Soul in Heav'n
> Shall bend the knee, and in that honor due
> Confess him rightful King? *unjust* thou say'st
> Flatly unjust, to bind with Laws the free, . . .
> *Shalt thou give Law to God*, shalt thou dispute
> With him the points of liberty, who made
> Thee what thou art, and *form'd the Pow'rs of Heav'n*
> *Such as he pleas'd*, and circumscrib'd thir being?
>   (5.813-825, *author's italics*)

This amounts to saying that God's decree is just because it is God who pronounced it and that the Son is rightful King because the Father is pleased to say so.

When God condemns the Rebels who "reason for their Law refuse," we can supply a Stoic or a Thomistic conception of Reason, or we can supply Luther's *recta ratio*, which, like the terms *nova ratio* and *nova iudicium*, becomes in his writings a synonym for faith.[11] In Reformation commentary, faith is treated as a quasi-faculty, as right thinking about God (*LW* 26.238) or as the hermeneutic stance that assumes God is faithful and "cannot lie" (*LW* 2.295). In Milton's heaven, then, the Law of Reason is none other than the "Law of Faith." The conditions of Milton's Empyrean, one should keep in mind, are the same

[11] B. A. Gerrish, *Grace and Reason: A Study in the Theology of Luther*, Oxford, Clarendon, 1962, p. 72. Cf. *LW* 26.262: "Another reason must come into being, which is the reason of faith."

as those on earth in one important respect: the angels are re-
quired to make the same stand that Reformation man does
(5.535-537). The angels are commanded irrationally, it seems,
to fight a battle that they cannot win; but such is the picture
of history that Michael gives in Books XI and XII. Adam will
finally leave the Garden to procreate new life that he knows
will end in family murder, intertribal marriage, and the general
decay of his people; but his faith, or *recta ratio*, submits to
God's speech, rather than to the logic of circumstance. Milton's
position will come into focus, if, in the following passage, one
substitutes for "reason" the name of the faculty that is part
literary discrimination, part reality-detection: the Almighty
commends Abdiel and predicts the defeat of the rebels,

> who reason [faith] for thir Law refuse,
> Right reason [*recta ratio* or faith] for thir Law,
> and for thir King
> Messiah, ...
>
> (6.41-43)

In *Paradise Lost*, faith is the principle of sound mind ("reason"),
for it is faith that accedes to the divine announcement of the
Son's Kingship, that truly perceives and respects reality. Mil-
ton's Ur-drama is cannily constructed so that Satan's misreading
of divine speech is also a rejection of Christ—and a gesture of
insanity. As the rebel host mobilizes for war, the narrator la-
ments,

> O Heav'n! that such resemblance of the Highest
> Should yet remain, where *faith* and *realty*[12]
> Remain not.
>
> (6.114-116, *author's italics*)

When God's speech is discounted, bedlam lies ahead. Satan's
aboriginal gesture has taken him across the great binary divide

---

[12] "Reality (*OED* Ia) or sincerity (*OED* 2) or both" (Carey and Fowler, p.
735).

of Reformation thought, beyond the pale of ethics into a dark region where all discriminations and distinctions become farcical—where intelligence, determination, stamina, rhetorical skill, and architectural achievement equally count for nothing—"Whatsoever is not of faith is sin."[13]

[13] Rom. 14:23, a verse that Milton and Luther like to cite as a great leveling principle. Cf. *CD*, p. 639. Luther made the point even more strongly: "Whatever is outside the promise and the faith of Abraham is under a curse and remains under a curse that is heavenly and eternal" (*LW* 26.250).

II

So shall my word be that goeth forth out of
my mouth: it shall not return unto me void,
but it shall accomplish that which I please.

(Isaiah 55:11)

The special properties that distinguish God's speech from
human speech are as contradictory as the particles and waves
that describe the physical properties of light. In Reformation
thought, God's speech was said to bear a "faint" analogy to
human speech and yet no analogy at all.[14] God's speech was
both performative and noetic, threatening and promising, eter-
nally inflexible and topically dramatic, transcendentally aloof
and urgently intimate. Usually only one of these characteristics
suggests itself at any given point in a narrative, but an epiphany
will occur whenever two of the paradoxical qualities or God's
speech are perceived at once.

The first distinction between God's speech and that of men
is one of enactment versus reference; God utters a *verbum
reale*—not just sound or empty air but "things very great and
wonderful, which we see with our eyes and feel with our hands"
(*LW* 12.32-33). Milton devotes all of Book VII to showing that,
with God there is no gap between word and deed, and that his
speech, rightly considered, is "concrete poetry." When God
said, "Let the Waters generate/Reptile with Spawn abundant,

[14] *LW* 22.9-10: "[T]here is no analogy between the word of mortal man and
the Word of the eternal and almighty God. There is a wide gulf between the
thoughts, discussions, and words of the human heart and those of God. . . .
No one has given Him His speech, His Word, or His conversation. What He
is, He is of Himself from eternity. . . . He alone has everything from Himself.

"Therefore this analogy of our word is very inadequate and vague. But
although our word cannot be compared to His Word, it affords us a faint idea.
Indeed, it impels us to ponder the matter and to obtain a better insight into its
meaning, comparing the thoughts and speculations of the human heart with
those of God. . . ."; and the word of God "is entirely different from my word
or yours" (*LW* 22.8).

living Soul" (7.387-388), we are to understand this utterance as bonded to the scene *subsequently* described:

> the Sounds and Seas, each Creek and Bay
> With Fry innumerable swarm, and Shoals
> Of Fish that with thir Fins and shining Scales
> Glide under the green Wave . . . .
>
> (7.399-402)

What obtains in Creation also obtains in the preservation of things: "when the sun rises, when the sun sets, God speaks" (*LW* 12.32). Reading God's word in nature, however, depends upon first hearing God's words "in grace" (*LW* 12.33), the "content" of nature being not redemptive but rhetorical. Creation was an "interpretant" of God's word only with respect to its power to act, order, and sustain. What Creation in Book VII demonstrates about God applies to the Primal Word (5.600-615), even though of itself the announcement is likely to convey a certain blankness and appear as the sheer assertion of authority:

> This day I have begot whom I declare
> My only Son . . . .
>
> (5.603-604)

This announcement has all constitutive powers of "Let there be light," but is more sweeping and inclusive. As Luther said of Psalm 2:7, upon which the Prime Decree is based, "This verse, rightly considered, fills heaven and earth so that nothing can be seen except it, no matter how great and splendid before the world" (*LW* 12.36). It is impossible to grasp all the implications of the Primal Decree, especially on first reading, because the announcement of the Son's Kingship constitutes the sum of reality, both visible and invisible—the creation, Incarnation, grace, and by implication all of history as well—including poem, poet, and reader. To use terms that Milton certainly would have rejected, this is the magical matrix of the poem.

Important narrative consequences follow from this understanding of God's speech as the *verbum reale*. Malcolm Mac-

kenzie Ross, who objects that *Paradise Lost* contains neither
eucharistic symbols nor a narrative of Christ's passion and death,[15]
fails to understand the special properties that the Reformation
attributed to God's speech. Consider the implications of the
Son's reply in which he volunteers:

> Behold mee then, *mee for him, life for life*
> I offer, on mee let thine anger fall;
> Account mee man; I for his sake will leave
> Thy bosom, and this glory next to thee
> Freely put off, and *for him lastly die*
> Well pleas'd, *on me let Death wreck all his rage* . . . .
>   (3.236-241, *author's italics*)

Given the Reformation understanding of divine utterance, Christ's
verbal offering equals the Crucifixion, and so Milton is able to
finesse a full-scale narrative account of the life and death of
Jesus. The equation of word and deed also removes any taint
of theopaschitism[16] (the heresy that considered the atonement
to be an intratrinitarian transaction), because this divine col-
loquy, properly understood, is an incursion into history.

In Book III, the catechetical dialogue emphasizes the noetic
character of God's speech, that is, its power to convey concepts
and information. Always, the information conveyed is the same:
a report of an historical event and an interpretation of its ben-
eficial results—the Son had "ransom'd" man. God's speech,
however, was more than a simultaneous enactment and report.
According to Reformation thought, all God's utterances (of giv-
ing law, threatening, commanding, and creating) were assimi-
lated to the promissory, as if they were subordinate clauses of
a single sentence. Unlike God's speech in Creation, God's "lit-

[15] Malcolm Mackenzie Ross, *Poetry and Dogma*, 1954; reprint New York, Octagon, 1969, p. 188.

[16] See Boyd Berry, who says in *Process of Speech: Puritan Religious Writing and Paradise Lost*, Baltimore, Johns Hopkins University Press, 1976, p. 56, that the Son's "humiliation and exaltation are outside of time. . . . It is the eternal Son who humiliates himself here, not a Jesus on the cross in time, blood and sweat."

erary" (scriptural) speech did not work *ex opere operato*, but "federally." To use seventeenth-century parlance, the promise had to be "challenged."[17] Only when a locution is interpreted as promissory—when the promiser is judged to have goodwill and the power to carry out his promise, and when the promise is accepted as offered—can it be said to take effect. This "federal" structure of God's promise figures prominently in even the strictest Calvinist practice. Despite Calvin's view that man cannot by himself have faith in God or do good of any sort, the *Institutes* exhorts the reader to believe the biblical promise (and "bridle" his animal passions) *as though* the choice and motive power were entirely his. Indeed Calvin often falls into a hortatory vein, as in the following:

> Let that target ["evangelical perfection"] be set before our eyes at which we are earnestly to aim. Let that goal be appointed toward which we should strive and struggle. For it is not lawful for you to divide things with God in such a manner that you undertake part of those things which are enjoined upon you by his Word . . . . For in the first place, he everywhere commends integrity as the chief part of worshipping him.
>
> (*Inst.* 3.6.5)

Calvin is aware that his rhetorical habits appear to be at odds with his theology, and his opponents indeed argued that his position made exhortation pointless, if not deceptive. He is, therefore, at some pains to explain *The meaning of exhortation*: the Spirit works both man's belief and man's good deeds, but God's word is the *instrument* used to rouse man's desire; man never knows whom God's promise may move, but nonetheless

---

[17] See, for example, "The Relapse," in *Silex Scintillans*:
>   But he that with his bloud, (a price too deere,)
>   My scores did pay,
>   Bid me, by vertue from him, *chalenge here*
>   The brightest day.

(*The Works of Henry Vaughan*, Oxford, Clarendon, 1957, p. 433, ll. 21-24, author's italics)

is *commanded* to preach the word and exhort the faithful to persevere (*Inst.* 2.5.5). Owing to this large suasive element in the *Institutes*, there was less change in verbal habits among English puritans than one might expect when belief in predestination declined during the seventeenth century.

In the divine dialogue of Book III the hortatory element is muted as the noetic fullness of the Primal Promise is set forth. In the dialogue God makes promises for man's life in time ("I will renew/His lapsed powers" [3.175-176]), for his demise ("Death his death's wound shall then receive" [252]), and for all of human history ("and from her ashes spring/New Heav'n and Earth" [334-335]). The amplitude of this dialogue, as it thrice runs over the course of salvation history in a doctrinal rondo is a conspicuous contrast to the succinctness of divine conversation in classical epic. The grand redundancy of Milton's God is in part a demonstration that his word does not inhere in any particular verbal formulation, but it is also the strategy of a wise pedagogue. Repetition is useful if a conceptual grasp of the Promise must be coincident with, if not prerequisite to, any "challenge" of it. One had to grasp a complex trinity of literary modes—narrative, generalization, and promise, not merely *mythos* and *logos*.[18] The report of the Son's death had to be assimilated to its metaphysical effects, which in turn became a promissory appeal reaching out its hand to the hearer. These relationships were by no means simple and had to be hammered into consciousness. It is not surprising that Calvin routinely speaks of God as the Schoolmaster and Christians as God's "schollers,"[19] nor that after the Reformation, learning the catechism began to eclipse baptism as the rite of initiation into the Kingdom of God, the teacher in consequence eventually being elevated above the scholar.

In direct contrast to the noetic character of God's word was

[18] U. Milo Kaufmann, *"The Pilgrim's Progress" and Traditions in Puritan Meditation*, New Haven, Yale University Press, 1966, p. 45.

[19] *Sermons of Master John Calvin, upon the Booke of Job* translated out of French by Arthur Golding, London, 1574, p. 679, hereafter cited as *Sermons on Job*; *TT*, p. 182.

its dramatic character. Regardless of the verbal formulation used, God's words always were to be construed as direct address. Luther, with an eye on Hebrew idiom, concluded that God "spoke no impersonal words" (*LW* 16.25). God had talked with the patriarchs concerning the concrete circumstances of their lives, and his address did not stop with them but continued in what may be called "apostolic address": God's speeches were directed over the shoulders of the patriarchs, as it were, to men of faith in later ages.[20] The force of God's speech in Hebrew carried over into Luther's biblical theology. He took for granted that general statements of doctrine also were addressed to particular men. From Luther to Milton, little distinction of value was made between God's counsel to Abraham and a generalized statement of doctrine drawn therefrom.[21] One was as much God's word as the other. As a schoolboy, Milton had learned, by making metrical versions of the Psalms, that human words were easily interchangeable, even expendable, before God's word, which remained efficacious through translation and paraphrase.

As self-contained as the divine dialogue in Book III may appear, its promissory character gives it the force of direct address. Or to use the idiom of Milton's prose, many "heavenly privileges [are] reacht out to us by the Gospell" (*YP* 1.749). That God might "speak" directly to a man from a doctrinal statement as surely as from a "dramatic" speech to Abraham is demonstrated by the catechetical colloquy. As Father and Son

[20] *LW* 26.226; *LW* 3.38. Cf. *CD*, p. 575: "The Holy Scriptures were not written merely for particular occasions as the Papists teach. They were written for the use of the church throughout all succeeding ages, not only under the law but also under the gospel."

[21] Paul Althaus, *The Theology of Martin Luther*, trans. Robert C. Schultz, Philadelphia, Fortress Press, 1966, p. 53. Cf. *LW* 3.28-29: "Now because Abraham is not alone but has the promise of descendants, and his descendants are of the promise, that is, believe the promise, Paul transfers the promise from Abraham's physical seed to the believers among the Gentiles. Since the entire outcome depends on the fact that Abraham believed God and this was reckoned to him for righteousness, . . . Paul constructs this universal proposition: that everyone who believes the promise as Abraham did is an heir of the eternal kingdom and righteous."

bend their attention to the problem of Satan's approach to the
Garden, God seems to be making an appeal *through* time to the
narrator and reader, as much as to the Son. Although the cat-
echetical properties of the dialogue militate against a sense of
drama, there is a rhetorically generated sense of sequence, if
not crisis. First comes the judgment, then its closure of grace,
which the Son announces as if commenting upon an event:
"Father, thy word is past, man shall find grace" (3.227). Very
early in the Father's commentary comes an oblique evangelical
appeal:

> The rest shall hear me call, and oft be *warn'd*
> Thir sinful state, and to appease *betimes*
> Th' incensed Deity, *while offer'd grace*
> *Invites* . . .
> (3.185-188, *author's italics*)

The references to time, the shifting of tenses ("invites," "shall
oft be warn'd"), and then a few lines later an indirect invitation
(*if they will hear* . . .)—all seem to urge immediate response.
Even when the Father utters a warning, it is an implied invi-
tation:

> *This* my long sufferance and *my day of grace*
> *They who neglect and scorn, shall never taste*. . . .
> (3.198-199, *author's italics*)

The divine speaker momentarily has forgotten Satan's advance
on Eden and seems to be speaking to the common reader, an
impression fortified when the father then suddenly recalls, "But
yet all is not done; Man disobeying . . ." (203), and so returns
to the problem at hand—finding a remedy for sin.

No matter how dull the language, no matter how proposi-
tional its character, God's speech holds incipient drama. This
drama, only implied in Book III, is given its full bent in Book
V. Milton takes great care to make the Primal Decree a grand
occasion, even to the extent of inventing a celestial "Time"
(5.580) that simulates the linearity of human experience and
enhances our perception of God's speech as an *event*. Milton

locates the Primal Decree in heavenly *history* as having been uttered the day that "Heav'n's great Year" began (583), and he particularizes the setting as an assembly of "Innumerable" angels in circumambient formation before the shadowed throne of God (584-599). Nevertheless, God's proclamation is likely to strike one as the sheer assertion of authority and therefore as essentially nondramatic. Does not this proclamation rule out all the stresses and strains, gives-and-takes that we call drama? Does not the "totalism" of the authoritarian voice preempt drama entirely? Let us look again at the Primal Word in its entirety, for it comes complete with its own explication, God himself pointing out the "dramatic" properties of his speech:

> Hear all ye Angels, Progeny of Light,
> Thrones, Dominations, Princedoms, Virtues, Powers,
> Hear my Decree, which unrevok't shall stand.
> This day I have begot whom I declare
> My only Son, and on this holy Hill
> Him have anointed, whom ye now behold
> At my right hand; your Head I him appoint;
> And by my Self have sworn to him shall *bow*
> All knees in Heav'n, and shall confess him Lord:
> Under his great Vice-gerent Reign abide
> United as one individual Soul
> For ever happy: *him who disobeys*
> *Mee disobeys*, breaks union, and that day
> Cast out from God and blessed vision, *falls*
> *Into utter darkness*, deep ingulft, his place
> Ordain'd without redemption, without end.
>
> (5.600-615, *author's italics*)

The Prime Decree itself indicates that there are two kinds of response: one can "bow" the knee, or one can disobey. There was no third choice. God's words, it was presumed, were never spoken without effect, since they always left the metaphysical status of the hearer changed: either he was unresponsive, and so damned, or he was granted grace in the "hearing." There was no such thing as casual reading of Scripture or casual attendance at a sermon. This principle obtained beyond the initial access of grace; with subsequent hearing, one's heart was hardened more or one grew in grace and understanding.

Empson is right when he finds God's pronouncement deliberately provocative, but he fails to understand that in Milton's tradition God's words were assumed to be pugnacious and combative. Luther stressed this point in his debate with Erasmus. Deploring the reluctance of the great humanist to take dogmatic stands, he claimed assertions to be the very stuff of Christianity: "Why, the Holy Spirit is given them from heaven" and takes the initiative "as if he would provoke a fight" (*LW* 33.21). Luther liked to cite what he called his "Achillean texts"—Romans 7:14ff. and Galatians 5:16ff.—in order to emphasize that the proclamation of God's word was so profoundly disturbing that it turned the world upside down.[22] Unlike the oracles of ancient epic, which were certified by some wondrous sign, God's words were certified by creaturely resistance and antagonism: "As soon as the Word of God appears, the devil becomes angry" (*LW* 26.455). One important function of the war in heaven is that it serves as validation for the Primal Text. The celestial war reifies a rhetorical commonplace from Reformation commentary, much in the way that *Antony and Cleopatra* crystallizes on an epic scale the commonplaces about love and war found in Elizabethan sonnets. The following is typical of the war imagery in Calvin's commentary:

> Even so it is with us when we . . . pluck ourselves from his [God's] hand, & become stubborne against him; for then is there warre proclaymed on our side. We defie God with our mouth nogher [*sic*] do we send a herrault to defie him.[23]

---

[22] *LW* 33.288. Cf. Calvin, *Commentary on the . . . Psalms*, I, 12: "Nor is it at all wonderful, or unusual, if the world begin to rage as soon as a throne is erected for Christ."

[23] John Calvin, *Sermons on Job*, p. 706; "There is always a battle with the Word of God" (*LW* 16.10).

This crisis-bearing property sharply distinguishes God's words from Platonic ideas. MacCaffrey makes the attractive suggestion that God's style in Book III is a "Platonic" language, and Fish agrees that a Platonic esthetic governs the colloquies of Milton's heaven.[24] The suggestion is attractive, first, because it accounts for the lexical qualities of God's speech and, second, because the Reformers themselves sometimes speak of doctrine in ways that make it appear similar to Platonic universals. Calvin extols "the completely heavenly character of . . . doctrine, savoring of nothing earthly" and admires "the beautiful agreement of all the parts with one another" (*Inst.* 1.8.3). Luther likened doctrine to a mathematical point in order to emphasize its unity and its status as an *a priori* (*LW* 27.37). He was very anxious to establish the independence of doctrine from human experience. "Doctrine belongs to God . . . . Life belongs to us," was his famous formulation of the point (*LW* 27.37). One could let the latter go, along with goods and kindred if need be, but doctrine was to be clung to for dear life. Though doctrine was transcendent and eternal like Platonic ideas, and roughly analogous as the "cause" of the physical world, it behaved quite differently toward man. No Platonic idea was ever presumed to "speak" to a man, much less initiate a conversation or promise him anything. Though Reformation commentary routinely treats heaven as the upper metaphysical story of the universe, its distance from earth was closed—not by a Platonic eros located in man, nor by a rational ascent from the physical world via a ladder of increasing abstraction, nor by a chasteness of life that earns a mystical glimpse of the intelligibles—but by God's (continual) action. In other words, the operation of the Holy Spirit was responsible for closure between heaven, God's doctrine, and man—a closure that was sometimes described as a divine condescension, sometimes as an elevation of man to heaven.

In either case, God's word was never glimpsed as a pure

[24] Isabel G. MacCaffrey, "The Theme of *Paradise Lost*, Book III," in *New Essays on Paradise Lost*, ed. Thomas Kranidas, Berkeley, University of California Press, 1971, p. 72; Stanley Fish, *Surprised by Sin: The Reader in "Paradise Lost*," Berkeley, University of California Press, 1971, p. 88.

intelligible. It was not "heard" at all until applied to some palpable heart. This principle is strictly observed in *Paradise Lost*: before the narrator in Book III presents the quasi-systematic survey of doctrine from Mount Sion, he confesses that it is the locus of his real life:

> but chief
> Thee *Sion* and the flow'ry Brooks beneath
> That wash thy hallow'd feet, and warbling flow,
> Nightly I visit.
>
> (3.29-32)

We then observe how the exquisite pain of the man isolated in "ever-during dark" (3.45) gives way to expansive joy as he listens to God's system of divinity and then loses himself in the corporate "we" of the angel choir who repeat it.[25] In human terms this is a mighty victory over depression and loss, but in Reformation terms, it demonstrates the performative power of God's words when they take hold in the human heart. In such cases, God's speech was bonded to the concrete just as intimately as in Creation. Luther explains:

> The soul which clings to them [the promises of God] with a firm faith will be so closely united with them and altogether absorbed by them that it not only will share in all their power but will be saturated and intoxicated by them. If a touch of Christ healed, how much more will this most tender spiritual touch, this absorbing of the Word, communicate to the soul all things that belong to the Word.
> . . .
> Just as the heated iron glows like fire because of the union of fire with it, so the Word imparts its qualities to the soul.
>
> (*LW* 31.349)

---

[25] Cf. 3.372 and 413. Louis L. Martz, *The Paradise Within*, New Haven, Yale University Press, 1964, p. 109.

Despite the systematizing bent of the Protestant scholastics, among whom Milton belongs by virtue of his tract, *Christian Doctrine*, something of the Hebrew understanding of *dabar* with its almost palpable force still clung to the notion of God's speech. God's words conveyed an overbearing strength of will and communicated his purpose with marvelous exactitude, but revealed nothing about his essence or being. While human language is wont to say something more, or less than intended, or something beside the point, the Creation shows God's words "Answering his great Idea" exactly (7.557). Everything besides God's *purpose*, however, remained dark. Milton's God demurely dwells in the "unapproachable light" called for by I Timothy 6:16, the verse that the Reformers took as the mandate for their antiphilosophical stance (*CD*, p. 133).

As regards expressive function, however, there was virtually no analogy between divine and human speech. One normally assumes that words express the experience of the speaker, if only in oblique ways. Wittgenstein's famous sentence that if a lion were to speak we could not understand him because we have not a lion's experience is apropos of the "natural" mistake that readers make about God's speech in *Paradise Lost*. A vast gulf separates God's speech from Satan's because his words do not imply a familiar psychic life as do those of Satan and Adam. Milton is adamant that the human metaphors by which God presents himself in Scripture cannot be construed as a key to God's experience (*CD*, pp. 133-134). Luther voiced similar warnings and thought that the human metaphors in the scriptural presentation of God were important mainly as prefiguration of the Incarnation (*LW* 4.133). They might pique curiosity in unwonted directions, but such curiosity was to be resisted. The question of what God was doing before the Creation was an old chestnut by the fifth century, but Luther liked to repeat it (along with St. Augustine's smart reply that God was making a hell for people who asked that question) because it gave him occasion to point out the boundaries of revelation (*LW* 1.10-11). One was not to ask questions about God on points that he

112

himself had not disclosed in Scripture—hence ontological description or any philosophical consideration of God's nature was ruled out. One was not to go *beyond* the words of God into realms of idle speculation. God's verbal (that is, biblical) speech was both the medium and limit of revelation.

Adam carefully observes these distinctions in his intimate talk with the Father in Book VIII. He asks for a wife on the grounds that to be solitary is to be unhappy. Tolerant and avuncular, God teases Adam for thinking that pleasure has to be social:

> What think'st thou then of mee and this my State,
> Seem I to thee sufficiently possest
> Of happiness, or not? Who am alone
> From all Eternity . . . ?
>
> (8.403-406)

God is posing a hermeneutic test for Adam by invoking an analogy between divine and human experience, as if a language of "experience" were common to them. But Adam, with his prelapsarian acuity, blocks this analogy. He begins very tactfully—

> To attain
> The highth and depth of thy Eternal ways
> All human thoughts come short, Supreme of
> things . . . .
>
> (8.412-414)

He then proceeds to enumerate the ways in which God is incomparable, making clear that he understands the ground rules according to which the conversation is taking place:

> Thou in thy secrecy although alone,
> Best with thyself accompanied, seek'st not
> Social communication, yet so pleas'd,
> Canst *raise* thy Creature to what highth thou wilt
> Of Union or Communion, deifi'd;
> I by conversing cannot these [animals] erect

From prone . . . .

(8.427-433, *author's italics*)

Adam correctly observes that conversation with God is an asymmetrical affair, involving two styles of apprehension and two kinds of language: God admits that he does not need human speech to know Adam—"I, ere thou spak'st,/Knew it not good for Man to be alone" (8.444-445)—and Adam understands that God must "raise" (430) man's apprehension to supernatural pitch if communication is to take place.

Again, the tone of God's speech was not to be derived from its lexical character. Doctrine might be conveyed in a stately and austere manner or in a plain and homely one, but the real tone was always tender and intimate. As Calvin says, God "lisps" and "prattles" to us in Scripture.[26] Properly understood, God's word was a children's story, as George Herbert dramatized in a poem like "Even-song."[27] The tone of Milton's God in the Edenic colloquy just discussed represents Milton's climactic revelation of divine love—and God's true and constant tone.[28]

Paradise Lost, however, is a long time arriving at this scene of paternal intimacy and love, and during the course of the epic God speaks in several other tonal registers. His first speech in Book III is harsh and mean-spirited and remains the most persistent problem in *Paradise Lost*, despite Stanley Fish's contention that it is intended to be purely scientific and denotative language.[29] It is doubtful that a reader ever existed who could read the following speech of the Almighty as clinical data:

So will fall
Hee and his faithless Progeny: whose fault?

[26] John Calvin, *Commentary on the Gospel According to John*, trans. William Pringle, Edinburgh, Calvin Translation Society, 1847, I, 119.

[27] *The Works of George Herbert*, ed. F. E. Hutchinson, Oxford, Clarendon, 1959, pp. 63-64.

[28] "God hides his eternal goodness and mercy under eternal wrath" (*LW* 33.62).

[29] " 'Ingrate' is not a judgment, but a scientific notation with the *emotional* value of an X or a Y" (*Surprised by Sin*, p. 65).

Whose but his own? ingrate, he had of mee
All he could have; I made him just and right,
Sufficient to have stood, though free to fall. . . .
Freely they stood who stood, and fell who fell.
(3.95-99; 102)

This wrathful speech, and God's changing "faces" throughout
the epic, embody an important Protestant principle: *fides facet
personem*—faith "creates" man and concomitantly his percep-
tion of God.[30] No psychological relativism obtains here. The
Almighty was understood to be "always one," so that it was
man's faith that was variable. Luther observes, "God becomes
God and changes in accordance with the change in our feeling
toward Him" (*LW* 9.67). Calvin similarly explains that the word
"*Wrath*, an human affection, after the manner of the Scripture,
is put for the revengement of God; because God, when he
punisheth, seemeth (in our opinion) to be angry. Therefore it
doth not signify any motion in God, but only hath respect unto
the sense of the sinner being punished."[31] In *Samson Agonistes*,
for example, it is a mark of the hero's despair that he thinks
God has turned his face and abandoned the erstwhile champion.
In a similar way the changing faces of God in *Paradise Lost*
gauge the faith of the narrator and the putative reader.[32] The

[30] "For as the conscience is, so is God" (*LW* 9.130); "Look how much our
faith increaseth in us, and how much we have profited in this knowledge, by
so much the righteousness of God, together with them, is augmented in us;
and, after a sort, the possession thereof is established. As soon as we do taste
of the gospel, we see the countenance of God, but afar off, favourable and
pleasant towards us: the more that the knowledge of piety groweth in us, as
it were by coming nearer, we behold the grace of God more clearly and more
familiarly" (Calvin, *Commentary on . . . Romans*, p. 22).

[31] Ibid., p. 25.

[32] For the relation of the narrator to his fable, see Martz, *The Paradise Within*,
pp. 105-116; Anne Davidson Ferry, *Milton's Epic Voice*, Cambridge, Harvard
University Press, 1963; Jackson Cope, *The Metaphoric Structure of "Paradise
Lost,"* Baltimore, Johns Hopkins University Press, 1962, pp. 149-164; William
G. Riggs, *The Christian Poet in "Paradise Lost,"* Berkeley, University of Cal-
ifornia Press, 1972; and Stein, *The Art of Presence: The Poet and Paradise
Lost*, Berkeley, University of California Press, 1977.

115

angry voice of God in Book III, which has elicited so many critical attempts to justify or ameliorate its tone, belongs not to God as he *is* but to God as the sinner perceives him. Milton had learned from Dante, as well as from the Reformers, that from the perspective of Hell, God is an unspeakable menace.[33] As Milton's narrator has just emerged from Hell, it is little wonder that the vision of God that he first presents is one assimilated to the viewpoint of the dungeon just escaped. The tone of icy wrath, even of defensiveness,[34] matches perfectly the "image" of the unnamed and threatening deity to whom Satan directed *his* wrath in the opening books.

The "development" of God's character thus measures the jagged course of the narrator's religious experience, which goes from deep rebellion and hatred through clarity, understanding, admiration, and finally to familial love and intimacy. Each stage in the narrator's experiential journey is marked by a change in God's tone, the initial wrath being almost immediately dispelled when the Father turns a complacent glance upon the Son (3.168-169). Thereafter, and for most of the colloquy in Book III, the neutral tone of noetic transmission presides. In Book V, however, the tone has become one of grand and ceremonial authority, and the Prime Decree (600-615) seems to correspond to the narrator's (and possibly the reader's) growing grasp of doctrine. Calvin, at least, explained that the "begetting" of Psalm 2:6-7 "ought to be understood as referring to men's *understanding*" of God's promise.[35] In Book VIII, God speaks as an artist and shows a "face" particularly appealing to the post-Romantic reader. Even if his doctrinal grasp has not grown in accord with the economy of the epic, the reader most likely will respond to God's esthetic power—his shaping of incom-

[33] In *Inferno* 6.96, Christ is *la nimica podesta* (the "enemy judge," the "hostile power") because the damned know goodness only as wrath and judgment.

[34] Gary D. Hamilton, "Milton's Defensive God: A Reappraisal," *Studies in Philology*, 69 (1972), 87-100.

[35] John Calvin, *Commentary on the . . . Psalms*, I, 17 (*author's italics*).

patible elements so that they conglobe into the simplest sig-
nificant shape:

> Thus far extend, thus far thy bounds,
> This be thy just Circumference, O World.
> Thus God the Heav'n created, thus the Earth,
> Matter unform'd and void: Darkness profound
> Cover'd th' Abyss: but on the wat'ry calm
> His brooding wings the Spirit of God outspread,
> And vital virtue infus'd, and vital warmth
> Throughout the fluid Mass, but downward purg'd
> The black tartareous cold Infernal dregs
> Adverse to life; then founded, then conglob'd
> Like things to like, the rest to several place
> Disparted, and between spun out the Air,
> And Earth self-balanc't on her Centre hung.
>
> (7.230-242)

In Books VII and VIII, God's voice becomes markedly more
intimate and tender, as he discloses his presence to newborn
Adam and as he draws Eve away from her narcissistic lake
towards wedded life. If there is a flaw in Milton's portrayal of
God, it is not in the harsh retributive voice of Book III, but in
the attempt in Book VIII to present God as a teasing uncle.
Clearly Milton intended to show a loving and playful parent
drawing out his son in Socratic fashion and delighting in a son
who, though born but the day before, has become a prodigy at
making doctrinal distinctions. Unfortunately, God's tender
playfulness never manages to be anything but ponderous. He
seems strangely inept at the business of intimacy and is rather
like an elephant cavorting with a "Lithe Proboscis." In partic-
ular, God's irony on the subject of women proves leaden:

> A nice and subtle happiness I see
> Thou to thyself proposest, in the choice
> Of thy Associates, *Adam*, ...
>
> (8.399-401)

117

Whatever the degree of poetic success, Milton's God is presented as gradually, if not steadily, becoming nearer and dearer. This changing apprehension of God embodies a fundamentally Protestant understanding of the working of grace. The Thomistic concept of grace as an infused *habitus* emphasized just as strongly as did Luther's doctrine that grace was the gift of God. Luther either misunderstood the Thomistic concept or was attacking later nominalistic distortions of it. Nonetheless, there was a real divergence in the psychological interpretation of the working of grace. In the Catholic view, grace, though a gift, was located *in* the human soul, either in its potentialities or, as St. Thomas taught, in the *essentia animae* that underlies the potentialities. Luther, on the other hand, located grace in the category of *relation* and employed the concept of "the person" in a way not thus used before in the doctrine of grace.[36] According to him, grace does not alter something *in* man, but altered the *situation*. In the "hearing" of faith there occurred a change in man's standing in the sight of God. Man still understood himself as a sinner, but saw God as gracious and merciful despite that fact. Whereas Thomistic grace may be described as "organic" in its working, Reformation grace is "dramatic." It does not manifest itself in the rational unfolding of the potentialities of a seed, as it were, but in sudden and extreme shifts in rapport between two "persons"—a shift experienced by man as a changed perception of God. To have faith, said Luther, is

> to regard [God] as truthful, wise, righteous, merciful, and almighty, in short, to acknowledge Him as the Author and Donor of every good. Reason does not do this, but faith does. It consummates the Deity; and, if I may put it this way, it is the creator of the Deity, not in the substance of God but in us.
>
> (*LW* 26.227)

[36] Gerhard Ebeling, *Luther: An Introduction to His Thought*, trans. R. A. Wilson, Philadelphia, Fortress Press, 1970, p. 156; see also pp. 141-174.

More important than the deterioration of Satan as a character in *Paradise Lost* is the "creation of the Deity," as his face is carefully redrawn during the course of Books I-VIII. The same pattern is repeated more concisely in the sentencing and re-habilitation of Adam in Book X, and also in Books XI and XII, where only one-half of this perceptual drama is shown. In these last two books the reader cannot "see" God unless (like Adam) he credits the grand extraliterary properties of God's speech demonstrated in the preceding books.

III

Wherever the Word of God is preached, there is Zion.

(*LW* 16.53)

Luther never explored the relation of God's words to human language in any systematic way. In the main, he relied upon the epithets and images of the Old Testament itself. God's word, for example, was never empty (Deuteronomy 32:47), could break rocks like a hammer (Jeremiah 23:29), and furnished food to a starving man (Jeremiah 15:16). Frequently, Luther uses clothing metaphors for God's word, as when he likens the promise within Scripture to the Christ Child in swaddling clothes, or when he speaks of David as presenting God "dressed and clothed in His Word and promises" (*LW* 12.312). The imagery of wrapping and packaging, however, is not designed to suggest a Platonic separation between *res* and *verba* but to emphasize the act of discovery—"the sense of finding" that was so important in the literary experience of the Reformation—or to emphasize that the "name God must be understood in a relative sense" as the God who is worshiped and adored rather than God in his essence and naked majesty (*LW* 3.117). In any event, the apparent Platonism of such imagery was far outweighed by the impressive array of instrumental images in Luther's commentary—God's word is a flail, an iron rod, a threshing hook, a wine-press, a two-edged sword. Luther subordinated the noetic aspect of God's speech, "which signifieth and presenteth something," to its performative aspect, which functions as "an instrument through which the Holie Ghost worketh . . . righteousness or justification" (*TT*, p. 12). The event-making, crisis-bearing property of God's word cuts across any static view of language, both that which assumes a separation and that which assumes a fusion of *res* and *verba*. Sometimes speaking as if God's promise were to be distinguished from the lexical "creature" that bears it, sometimes speaking as if the scriptural form

120

The Verbum Reale

of the promise were itself an "invisible" to be opposed to all sensory experience,[37] Luther consistently gives his attention to the moment when the *viva vox Christi* flames forth from some human presentation of God's promise. Whether *in, with, by, through,* or *under* the verbal sign, Christ was assumed to be present. This literary experience became for Luther a *de facto* sacrament, even though he never relinquished the idea of the Real Presence on the Communion altar.

Calvin analyzed and codified the behavior of words in Luther's "verbal" sacrament. He is quite explicit about the role of figuration in his theology. On the one hand, he attacks the Catholics for being "literalists" and on the other defends himself against the label "tropist," which Joachim of Westphal, the most active of his Lutheran critics, had thrust upon him (*Inst.* 4.17.20-21). In defense, he pled literary analysis: "We have explained the sacramental phraseology," he said, "according to the common usage of Scripture" (*Inst.* 4.17.21). Indeed, Calvin often adverts to metonymy to explain a problematic passage in Scripture. The examples that he gives vary in their structure of figuration, but most of them could be termed metonymy according to the loose taxonomy of Renaissance tropes:

"the lamb is the passover" [Exodus 12:11]—part for the whole

"the sacrifices of the law are expiations" [Leviticus 17:11; Hebrews 9:22]—cause for effect

"the rock from which water flowed in the desert [was Christ]" [Exodus 17:16]—effect for cause

"the Ark of the Covenant is called God and God's face" [Psalm 84:8; 42:3]—adjacency of ownership

[37] Sometimes Luther treats "the spoken Word itself" as a "visible sign" and lists it with Baptism, the Eucharist, and "other visible forms" (*LW* 3.109). More often he treats the Promise as "invisible" (*LW* 12.35) and not "subject to the senses" (*LW* 16.65). His usage seems to depend upon whether he is considering the danger of idolatry from immersion in sensuous experience and from "worshiping God through the creatures" (*LW* 16.262) or whether he is stressing the "objectivity" and givenness of God's word as an act of deliverance (*LW* 1.309).

121

"the dove, the Holy Spirit" [Matthew 3:6]—temporal contiguity.

(*Inst.* 4.17.21).

The common principle in all these figures is that of contiguity—temporal, causative, or proprietary. Spatial metonymy, though, is conspicuously missing. Calvin's brilliant achievement is to invoke the almost subliminal experience of figurative transfer as a sudden leap and to use it to describe the motions of faith.

Holy Communion, as Calvin explained it, is a ritual repetition of Christ's promise—that is, of the benefits deriving from the Crucifixion (*Inst.* 4.17.39). Considered as speech, Holy Communion is a paradox of tropes, comprised of figures of analogy and contiguity, but *not* of identity. Calvin did not believe that the elements of bread and wine became Christ's body. In his eyes, they are merely rhetorical appositives and "have the same office as the Word of God: to offer and set forth Christ to us" (*Inst.* 4.14.17). The bread and wine are a "figure" adapted to our small capacity for the purpose of explaining man's union with Christ. Calvin claimed that "this very familiar comparison penetrates into even the dullest minds: just as bread and wine sustain physical life, so are souls fed by Christ" (*Inst.* 4.17.1). Coincident with the metaphor was a metonymy, a figure of speech, Calvin emphasized, that is "commonly used in Scripture when mysteries are under discussion" (*Inst.* 4.17.21). The bread has a close "affinity" to the reality it represents, indeed such a "closeness" to the flesh of Christ that "transition from one to the other is easy" (*Inst.* 4.17.21). This "easy transition" is nothing less than a cosmic leap because, in Calvin's view, the Son's body remains in the Empyrean till Judgment Day. There is in every celebration of Holy Communion an ascent: "*Christ* [is] *not brought down to us; we are lifted up to him*" (*Inst.* 4.17.31). Sacramental action is thus a tropological event, and heaven and earth are joined by metonymy. Bread, wine, and verbal promise are alike metonymic to the thing promised and share the mysterious action of God's figures, which, Calvin observed, are different from the figures of speech constructed

122

by men in that they represent, not "things absent," but "things present" (*Inst.* 4.17.21). The Communion bread stands for Christ's body, to which it is "*so to speak* attached" (*Inst.* 4.17.5, *author's italics*). Calvin stops short of asserting a necessary contiguity between sign and spiritual signification, however. What bridges the slight gap between bread and the heavenly Christ is the secret working of the Spirit. Aware of criticism that he was making the Son subject to the rules of grammar, Calvin always stressed the mystery of this cosmic leap with remarks like "I ask you whether it is from physics we have learned that Christ feeds our souls *from heaven* with his flesh" (*Inst.* 4.17.24, *author's italics*).

Calvin's identification of God's presence with the action of tropes held important consequences for literary history and for the history of consciousness because the play of the Spirit in reading Scripture is the same as the work of the Spirit in Communion. The promise of the Lord's Supper can be contemplated at any time, and the tropological mystery of Communion can occur just as well in the solitude of one's chamber as in divine service. The action of the Spirit is not tied to place or priestly authority or to concrete objects, but instead to language. Though the bread and wine are appositive to the verbal promise, even in Communion they are not interchangeable, as the bread and wine lack clarity without the words (*Inst.* 4.17.39). Apart from these objects divinely designated for an emphatic function as "seals," language is the sole instrument connecting God and man, according to Calvin.

The verbal and psychological structure of Calvin's communion, if not his precise doctrinal formulation, came to dominate the devotional and literary practices of the English puritans in general and of Milton in particular. Of course the notion of *spiritually* ingesting a *physical* body that was located a cosmos away[38] was never firmly grasped by the English puritans, but

[38] If there is a confusing mixture of spirit and matter in the war in heaven, as Dr. Johnson objected, it scarcely would have fazed a Calvinist who understood the transaction described in the *Institutes* as taking place in the Lord's Supper: "if we are lifted up to heaven with our eyes and minds, to seek Christ there

the notion that a mental ascent was effected by divine "figures" conferred a remarkable numinosity upon the tropes of Scripture and, in effect, turned reading the Bible and meditating upon it into a homemade sacrament. For instance, Calvin recommends such a mental ascent in his meditation upon Colossians 3:1:

> If we are the members of Christ, we must ascend into heaven, because he, on being raised up from the dead, was *received up into heaven* (Mark 16:19,) that he might draw us up with him. Now, we *seek those things which are above*, when in our minds [*de coeur et esprit*] we are truly sojourners in this world, and are not bound to it. . . . Let us therefore bear in mind that *that* is a true and holy *thinking* as to Christ, which forthwith bears us up into heaven, that we may there adore him, and that our minds may dwell with him.[39]

This well could be a prescription for the dangerous journey that Milton's narrator makes to the Empyrean in *Paradise Lost*,[40] a journey that has the same structure as Calvin's sacrament and the same structure as his meditation upon Scripture, because both effect a mental ascent into God's presence via words.[41] For Luther, as well, "contemplation" was a mental ascent achieved while concentrating upon Scripture or doctrine. To set aside God's word and wait for extraordinary illumination, he held,

---

in the glory of his Kingdom, as the symbols [bread and wine and verbal promise] invite us to him in his wholeness, so under the symbol of bread we shall be fed by his body, under the symbol of wine we shall separately drink his blood, to enjoy him at last in his wholeness" (*Inst.* 4.17.18).

[39] John Calvin, *Commentaries on the Epistles of Paul the Apostle to the Philippians, Colossians, and Thessalonians*, trans. John Pringle, Edinburgh, Calvin Translation Society, 1851, pp. 205-206.

[40] William Kerrigan sees the narrator's flight above the Aonian Mount as a presumptuous wish "to participate in . . . the private motions of God" (*The Prophetic Milton*, Charlottesville, University Press of Virginia, 1974, p. 127).

[41] In Calvin's Communion, the experiential mark of God's presence—and evidence that the sacramental metonymy of the promise had taken effect—was a mental ascent: *The presence is known when our minds are lifted up to heaven* (*Inst.* 4.17.18).

was a "desire to ascend into heaven without ladders" (*LW* 3.275). The contemplative life of the Reformation was a "literary" one, as demonstrated by the narrator in Milton's epic when he ascends to heaven by courtesy of the tropological properties of language—and the presence of the Spirit. The narrator claims that he is taught by the heavenly Muse "up to reascend" (3.19-20), and, instantaneously, he is borne aloft where the promise he contemplates is adjacent to all that is promised. His flight to the upper reaches dramatizes the Protestant mystery of "promissory possession"—the man of faith has verbal visiting rights to heaven, but does not abide there yet.

The coterminous reality of present and future kingdom could fit no available syntax,[42] and the Reformers dealt with the paradoxes of Christian doctrine by assuming that pleats or tucks occur in the syntactical chain whenever faith is being discussed. For example, in Colossians 1:5, which treats "the hope that is laid up for you in heaven," Calvin says that

> an instance of *metonymy* [occurs] in the use of the term *hope*, as it is taken for the thing hoped for. For the hope that is in our hearts is the glory which we hope for in heaven. At the same time, when he says, that there is a *hope* that is *laid up for us in heaven*, he means, that believers ought to feel assured as to the promise of eternal felicity, equally as though they had already a treasure laid up in a particular place.[43]

Colossians 1:5 thus has the structure of a figurative conundrum and demonstrates how faith, formally considered, is a mastery of complex tropological relations. The passage contains the catachresis "is laid up," which Calvin explicates as a latent treasury metaphor, and it also contains metonymy. The words articulating hope touch, or virtually touch, the object of hope and thereby make the heart adjacent to heaven.

The belief that words could have transcendental reach through

[42] George Steiner, *After Babel*, New York, Oxford University Press, 1975, p. 151.

[43] John Calvin, *Commentaries on . . . Colossians*, p. 139.

metonymy underlies the devotional practices of the English puritans, including Milton, who also thought an "affinity" obtained between a sign and the thing signified (CD, p. 555). In consequence, puritan writing is much more figurative than often supposed because discursive language treating divine matters may be metonymy. Puritan texts therefore become very fluid, their shape shifting as metonymy is discovered in verbiage seemingly barren of figuration, or as a metaphor is suddenly seen in its metonymic aspect. The coincidence of metaphor and metonymy often makes alternate routes available by which to arrive at a "correct" reading; everything depends upon whether the Spirit chooses to move along the metaphoric or metonymic axis. Milton, in *Paradise Lost*, takes pains to ensure the hermeneutic fluidity, now leaning heavily toward one axis, now toward the other, but committing himself absolutely to neither. Raphael announces the metaphoric axis when he suggests that heaven and earth are alike: "What if Earth/Be but the shadow of Heav'n . . . ?" (5.574-575). And so we are invited to explore the resemblances between the plight of men and angels. The narrator, on the other hand, relies upon the metonymic axis for his ascent to the Empyrean and invites us to see the connection between the language of promise, heaven, and a particular human existence. Any reading of *Paradise Lost* will take advantage of both lines of figurative sight and will result in a unique pattern of discovery as the reader alternates between the two figurative axes.

Most readers have ignored one axis to the exclusion of the other and have made Milton's heaven either too mystical or too mundane. Kerrigan, for example, misses the metaphor in the medium and objects that the narrator wishes to relate a full, unmediated vision without the decorous cover of a dream.[44] He is unaware that Milton is only dramatizing the Reformation topos that in Christian doctrine we see the face of God (*LW* 22.157). T. S. Eliot, on the other hand, missed the metonymy

[44] "The narrator of *Paradise Lost* claims to write unpremeditated verse, see mystical visions, and nightly to experience prophetic dreams" (*The Prophetic Milton*, p. 5).

in the celestial recital of doctrine and objected to the static quality of heaven and the boredom of "large rooms insufficiently furnished with *heavy* conversation." Properly understood, however, the colloquy in Book III is intrinsically dynamic, at the same time impressing divine purpose upon history and lifting men up to heaven for metaphysical recreation. If, as the Calvinist sacrament assumes, one can "go" to heaven merely by hearing, saying, or meditating upon God's promise, then doctrine is not leaden but quick as light.

Even in Milton's hands, doctrine is lexically impotent to convey its power to connect heaven and earth. But this is as it should be if persuasion is presumed to come, not by the technology of rhetoric, but by the "operation" of the Holy Spirit. It was Calvin's genius to track the motions of the Spirit along the precise but "viewless" paths of metonymy and metaphor, because words themselves bear no outward mark of alteration when they are discovered to be figurative. In Milton's tradition, discovering a clear and relevant meaning in a dark biblical text was understood as the work of the Spirit. The most frequent way of discovering clarity and relevance was to perceive that one of the words or phrases was actually a trope. Hence discovery of figuration became a sign of the Holy Spirit's presence. That the presence of metonymy, or the play of the Spirit, has so often been missed in the verbal fabric of Milton's heaven is but one example of the difficulty in reading what the puritans wrote. Only a mastery of puritan experience (or what we can recover of it by, say, reading their biblical commentary) can tell us where the tropes are. As Luther was wont to explain, God gives both the words and the experience by which they are understood (*LW* 3.67, 69). Those who claim that Milton preoccupied himself with "the cosmic vision, traced out the mind of God," and did not properly attend to history or the temporal processes of speech,[45] overlook the tropes and fail to understand

---

[45] Berry, *Process of Speech*, p. 33, cf. pp. 9-10; Ross, *Poetry and Dogma*, p. 220; Kerrigan, *The Prophetic Milton*, p. 263.

127

that it is precisely by the figurative processes of speech that Milton's "absolute" vision connects with present occasion.

Just as the tropological reach of doctrinal statement cannot be inferred from the text itself, so doctrinal statement gives little intimation of its affective riches. Only the attitudes and responses of interpretants, that is, only the testimonies of "hearers" reveal the *pathos* of doctrinal statement. For Luther, doctrine was clearly a movable feast and its proclamation a celebratory occasion; we find him breaking into a dance of participles when he speaks of his "delight" in doctrinal assertion, in the "adhering, affirming, confessing, maintaining, and an invincible persevering" in the word of God (*LW* 33.19-20). As improbable as it may seem, doctrine was the focus of Reformation eros. Just as Luther (and David in Psalm 119) yearns and sighs for the word of God (*LW* 31.345-346), so Milton's narrator, when poised for flight to the upper regions, confides that he is "Smit with the love of sacred Song" (3.29)—song that is repetition of the doctrinal outline uttered by the Father and Son. The case of the narrator in Book III demonstrates that, formally speaking, faith is a dramatic tautology: God speaks and man repeats.

If language with its metonymic reach is the link between heaven and earth, it is also the link between remote points in history—between the Incarnation and the present. From St. Augustine to Thomas Hobbes, Christian doctrine was presumed to be an indivisible whole. In the seventeenth century this understanding, together with wide general interest in doctrinal matters, allowed a writer to invoke the whole by a single tenet. The Crucifixion, in Milton's tradition, often was invoked metonymically by its effects. In part, this was owing to the Reformers' position that the Crucifixion could not be repeated, though its effects could be repeated infinitely. Partly it was a catechetical matter; crediting a scriptural report of the Crucifixion might be easy enough, but grasping the promissory import of the event with respect to oneself was a more stubborn matter, and so there could scarcely be too much repetition. Luther, for example, recommends that scenic presentation of the Crucifixion for its own sake be replaced by lucid exposition of its effects:

> Now there are not a few who preach Christ and read about him that they may move men's affections to sympathy with Christ, to anger against the Jews, and such childish and effeminate nonsense. Rather ought Christ to be preached to the end that faith in him may be established that he may not only be Christ, but be Christ for you and me, and that what is said of him and is denoted in his name may be effectual in us. Such faith is produced and preserved in us *by preaching why Christ came, what he brought and bestowed, what benefit it is to us to accept him.*
>
> (*LW* 31.357, *author's italics*)

This is exactly Milton's emphasis in the résumé of history in Books XI and XII. It is not that Milton fails to emphasize the Incarnation, but that he gives no detailed narrative account of it. Michael actually mentions the death of Christ at least four-teen times between lines 398 and 430 of Book XII, all of which amounts to considerable rhetorical emphasis, but his interest is to explain the metaphysical mechanics that make his death promissory. He alludes therefore to the death of Christ by such phrases as "penalty of death" (12.398) or as "ransom paid" (12.424) or as fulfillment of "the Law" (12.404). Once the metaphysical exchange is understood, the unique historical event could be invoked innumerable times as (promissory) speech. Michael himself demonstrates:

> He shall endure by coming in the Flesh
> To a reproachful life and cursed death,
> *Proclaiming Life to all who shall believe.*
> (12.405-407)

> to death condemn'd
> A shameful and accurst, nail'd to the Cross
> By his own Nation, slain *for bringing Life;*
> (12.412-414)

Milton and the Science of the Saints

        [Christ] Man from death redeems,
His death for Man, *as many as offer'd Life*
Neglect not, *and the benefit embrace*
By Faith not void of works.
                    (12.424-427, *author's italics*)

The verbal formulations are varied and inconsequential, but these undistinguished lines all are presumed to have enormous epiphanic potential. In the event that the word "life" is understood as metonymic to the quality of life promised, a sacramental transaction will have taken place.

This shift in emphasis from the moment of the Crucifixion to its ever-ongoing results did not always mean a shift to the discursive mode. Sometimes it yielded narrative elaboration or the invention of mythic equivalents. Calvin offers a precedent and perhaps even the model for Milton's mythic revision of Calvary. Calvin's explanation in the *Institutes* of "expiatory sacrifice" concludes thus:

> Yet we must not understand that he fell under a curse that overwhelmed him; rather—in taking the curse upon himself—he crushed, broke, and scattered its whole force. Hence faith apprehends an acquittal in the condemnation of Christ, a blessing in his curse. Paul with good reason, therefore, magnificently proclaims the triumph that Christ obtained for himself on the cross, *as if the cross, which was full of shame, had been changed into a triumphal chariot!*
> *(Inst.* 2.16.6, *author's italics)*

On several such occasions, Calvin remarks that the cross, rightly perceived, is a "triumphal car"; but perhaps the liveliest exposition of the point occurs in his commentary on Colossians 2:15, the verse that Milton was to use as a proof-text for deploying his angels in ranks: "And having spoiled principalities and powers, [Christ] made a shew of them openly, triumphing over them in it" (*CD*, p. 349). Calvin remarks that there is "no

130

doubt [that by 'principalities'] he means devils," and further concludes:

> For as [St. Paul] had previously compared the cross to a signal trophy or show of triumph, in which Christ led about his enemies, so he now also compares it to a triumphal car, in which he shewed himself conspicuously to view [*En grande magnificence*]. For although in the cross there is nothing but curse, it was, nevertheless, swallowed up by the power of God in such a way, that it has put on, as it were, a new nature. For there is no tribunal so magnificent, no throne so stately, no show of triumph so distinguished, no chariot so elevated, as is the gibbet on which Christ has subdued death and the devil, the prince of death; nay more, has utterly trodden them under his feet.[46]

This passage explains one way in which Milton includes the Crucifixion in his epic—as a mythic metonym suggested by Scripture. As is nearly always the case with divine figures, no single trope provides adequate analysis. Calvin insisted that the word "chariot" was a designation for the *cross*, because it was too mean a word to apply to Christ himself (p. 190). If we follow Calvin's line of thought, the final event in Book VI of *Paradise Lost* is not precisely metonymy but metaphor: the Son "ascends" the Father's chariot as a metaphorical substitution for "ascending" the cross. Calvin emphasized that the Crucifixion, properly perceived, was *itself* a victory, not that it re-sulted in a victory. In Book VI, this vision of faith is made a narrative fact when the Crucifixion is presented as a Triumph of Life scattering the host of Satan before it to the edge of doom.

As with the changing face of Milton's God, the emphasis here is upon the perceptual transformation wrought by the eye of faith. The "poetic" vision of faith is a figurative one and in the case of Milton is usually traceable to some trope or verbal idiosyncrasy in Scripture. The Son's chariot in Book VI, for ex-

---

[46] *Commentaries . . . on Colossians*, pp. 190-191.

ample, not only elaborates a suggested metaphor from the New Testament, but also sums up those moments in the Old Testament when the word "salvation" is used for "victory" (as in I Samuel 14:45), a point that Luther was prompt to note and make use of in his evangelical appropriation of Hebrew history (*LW* 16.129).

When Milton suppresses a narrative account of Christ's death, be it by metaphor or by metonymy, he makes its tacit presence all the stronger. Or so it would seem to puritan cognoscenti, because the power of both metaphor and metonymy depends upon an ingrained knowledge of the matter treated. The power of metaphor in Book VI depends upon the reader's knowing what event should stand at the center of a Christian epic and what the central work of the Son consisted of; otherwise a substitution will not be perceived. And it will help if he is familiar with the biblical vocabulary available for metaphoric substitution. In like manner, the power of metonymy depends upon knowing the whole story very well—upon knowing what is next to what. Though the Crucifixion is not given narrative treatment in *Paradise Lost*, it is connected to every point of doctrine that is dramatized and so, for example, it is evoked metonymically by its human cause (the Fall) and by its effects (the recoveries of the hero and the blind scop). If in addition one considers that, besides the Messiah's Chariot in Book VI, there is also the Son's verbal (and enactive) offer to die in Book III, the Son's prevenient gesture of cloaking Adam and Eve's guilt in Book X, and finally the discursive account of the Crucifixion supplied by Michael in Book XII, then it does appear that "the sacrifice of the Son is an overwhelming concern of *Paradise Lost*."[47] Milton brilliantly solves the problem that had

---

[47] William B. Hunter, Jr., "Milton on the Exaltation of the Son: The War in Heaven in *Paradise Lost*," *ELH*, 36 (1969), 231. Though Hunter stops short of finding the onslaught of the Son's chariot as a version of the Crucifixion *qua* event, he argues that Milton recalls the Resurrection throughout the narrative of the celestial war. Most commentators have followed Joseph H. Summers in seeing the victory of Christ's chariot as an anticipation of the Last Judgment (*The Muse's Method*, Cambridge, Harvard University Press, 1962,

eluded him in *Comus*. In the epic he leaves no question of his doctrinal orientation—indeed he hardly could have been more explicit—yet he manages to hide the Crucifixion in plain sight when he presents the cross in its "new nature" as the vehicle of victory.

p. 135) or as a coincidence of the beginning and the end (Michael Fixler, *Milton and the Four Kingdoms of God*, London, Faber and Faber, 1965, p. 227). Fixler argues that the kingdom established by the Son's victory is also "a form of worship" (p. 228), and Stella P. Revard notes that the "coming of Christ in a chariot of victory was a popular image in the sermons of the seventeenth century" and that the chariot was "a symbol of succor for the present world," as well as for the Last Judgment and the world to come (*The War in Heaven*, Ithaca, Cornell University Press, 1980, pp. 124, 126).

✦ 5 ✦
The Garden of Reason

─────────── I ───────────

Since the beginning of the world, God has dealt
with all the saints through His Word.

(*LW* 12.170)

The body of Christ is mystically one, so it
follows that the communion of his members
must be mystic . . . : it includes people from
many remote countries, and from all ages since
the creation of the world.

(*CD*, p. 500)

Milton's Garden is innocent of the kind of doctrinal formula
that fills heaven, but nonetheless takes its shape from Refor-
mation doctrine, particularly Luther's evangelical "opening" of
the Old Testament and his *de facto* institution of a verbal sac-
rament. Hitherto exegesis had valued the Old Testament mainly
for the typology it contained. The Old Dispensation was a dark
and barbaric era that was of little intrinsic interest as history,
however useful it might be as a contrast to the New Dispen-
sation. MacCallum, Madsen, and Lewalski have reminded us
that, for all the Reformers said about the literal level, they were

135

still using some typology in their exegesis.[1] The Reformers' hermeneutic, which Milton inherited, was a highly paradoxical one, however, and typology comprised but one-half the paradox. The notion that history sweeps qualitatively on from shadowy types toward the Truth of the Incarnation is held in balance with the notion that all times are equal before the word of God. To ignore either half of the paradox will seriously skew a reading of *Paradise Lost*, because Milton balances temporal stress and counter-stress with the same intricacy that he does metrical stress. The typological perspective is unquestionably important in the epic, particularly in the war in heaven and in Michael's recital of history in Books XI and XII, but it is minimally useful when applied to the story of Adam and Eve.

The Garden scenes take their shape from Luther's evangelical exposition of the Old Testament and from his view that God's Promise constitutes an inner scripture. Like medieval exegetes, he found the Messianic prophecies of the Old Testament to be dark, but held that the New Testament had presented in daylight the Christ who *was* hidden there—the tense is important—in various oracles. Christ's own use of Scripture, like that of the apostles', had "opened" the oracles and revealed once and for all the "eternal New Testament" in them.[2] In consequence, the Old Testament became useful in the narrative *present* for pious

---

[1] Hugh MacCallum, "Milton and Figurative Interpretation of the Bible," *University of Toronto Quarterly*, 31 (1962), 397-415; Madsen, *From Shadowy Types to Truth*, New Haven, Yale University Press, 1968; and Barbara Kiefer Lewalski, *Milton's Brief Epic*, Providence, Brown University Press, 1966.

[2] Typical of Luther's comments is the following: "Therefore also Luke, in his last chapter [24:45], says that Christ opened the minds of the apostles to understand the Scriptures. And Christ, in John 10 [:9,3], declares that he is the door by which one must enter, and whoever enters by him, to him the gate-keeper (the Holy Spirit) opens in order that he might find pasture and blessedness. Thus it is ultimately true that the gospel itself is our guide and instructor in the Scriptures" (*LW* 25.123): and "Moses points out the difference between the New and the Old Testament. The New Testament is the older, promised from the beginning of the world, yes, 'before the times of the world,' as Paul says to Titus (1:2)" (*LW* 9.63).

exhortation. The patriarchs "were the first Christians," to whom "were promised and entrusted the oracles of God" as Romans 3:2 had declared (*LW* 9.215). Moses in his first book had taught not only "whence sin and death came," but also "whence help is to come for the driving out of sin and death," namely by " 'the seed of the woman,' Christ [who was] promised to Adam and Abraham . . . [and] throughout the Scriptures from the beginning" (*LW* 25.237). Luther's emphasis is upon how the patriarchs responded to God's oracles in their own day and generation: "Genesis, therefore, is made up almost entirely of illustrations of faith and unbelief, and the fruits that faith and unbelief bear. It is an exceedingly evangelical book" (*LW* 25.237).

Luther's concept of the "eternal New Testament," which is virtually the same as Calvin's perpetual sense of the Scripture (*Inst.* 2.11.10), became the key that "opened" the Old Testament and transformed the stories of the ancient Israelites into accounts of "Christian" experience. It mattered little that the form that the Promise took was oblique or couched in dark imagery, because the clarity of the Promise was no longer a question. Man's response, however, was still a matter of the same consequence. Luther explains:

> If Adam, Noah, and the other patriarchs had lived at the time of Abraham, who received the new promise, it would have been necessary for them to believe that Christ would be of the seed of Abraham or they would have lost God who promised the seed.
>
> If Abraham had lived at the time of David, it would have been necessary for him to believe that Christ would be of the lineage of David, or he would have believed in vain in the seed of the woman.
>
> If David had lived at the time of John the Baptist, it would have been necessary for him to believe in Jesus, the seed of his descendant, Mary, or he would have perished.
>
> If John the Baptist had lived after the resurrection of Christ, no, rather in his own time, and would have believed

that Christ would come or had not yet come, he would have been damned.

(*LW* 34.304)

Calvin also claims that the covenant that God made with the patriarchs differs only in "outward form and manner" from that of the post-Advent era: it is really "the same doctrine" (*Inst.* 2.11.13: cf. *CD*, p. 126). He shares Luther's paradoxical hermeneutic, in that he finds Christ "shadowed" or prefigured in certain Old Testament personages, but does not find the sole or even the primary significance of the Old Testament to lie in its types and shadows (*Inst.* 2.9.2). Calvin's stress upon the interpretative element in the patriarchs' experience is even greater, for he thinks that they saw through the dark oracles given them. "The saints testify in their own words," he said, citing Psalm 142:5, that they read the promise of immortality in the promise of temporal blessing (*Inst.* 2.11.2). Men of the Old Testament continued to believe in God's promised blessing at the end of their lives, when there was no hope of earthly fulfillment, and this fact was also evidence of how they read God's oracles (*Inst.* 2.10.13). In sum, Calvin agrees with St. Augustine, whose influence is evident throughout the *Institutes*, that though the patriarchs lived under an obscurer dispensation, they nevertheless "believed especially in the mediator" (*Inst.* 2.11.10).

Milton stands firmly in this tradition because he too holds that such men in the Old Testament as Abraham, Noah, and David gained salvation for believing whatever God spoke to them (*CD*, p. 475). Like Luther, Milton holds that Genesis is a Gospel book because Genesis 3:15 records the *protevangelium*—that is, the first promise of Christ—or, as Milton called it, the first announcement of God's covenant of grace.[3] In *Par-*

---

[3] *CD*, p. 515. John M. Steadman, "Adam and the Prophesied Redeemer (*Paradise Lost*, XII, 359-623)," *SP*, 56 (1959), 214-225, and C. A. Patrides, "The 'Protevangelium' in Renaissance Theology and *Paradise Lost*," *SEL*, 3 (1963), 19-30, discuss the *protevangelium* with respect to Michael's explication of it in the last two books of Milton's epic and cite numerous Renaissance references to Adam's Christian faith and hope. Patrides thinks the attempt to make Adam not only the first Christian, but "the first Protestant," was an

adise Lost the *protevangelium* is rendered thus—"[Eve's] Seed shall bruise [the serpent's] head" (10.181). Accordingly, Adam and Eve are presented as the first Christians, whose "literary" experience with God's speech is of more importance than their role as first types.

Milton's decision to write an epic about Old Testament "Christians" was perhaps his most important esthetic choice. That he chose Adam and Eve in particular allowed him to moot the controversy over predestination, because even Calvin affirmed that Adam and Eve had free choice before the Fall (*Inst.* 1.15.8). Perhaps even more important, writing about Old Testament "Christians" introduced an element of indirection that was poetically enhancing yet not incompatible with his doctrine of *claritas*. The assumption that the Old Testament had been "opened"—that it was a narrative *à clef*—provided Milton with what one might call "evangelical irony," and with a suitable poetic cover for bald doctrine. The Old Testament provided him with puritan "saints' legends" of great pith and power, in which God speaks directly to the patriarchs in sentences of high dramatic concentration. Needless to say, God's call, "Where *art* thou?" to Adam hiding in the Garden (Genesis 3:9) conveys divine displeasure and judgment more immediately than a dozen Pauline generalities about law and sin. Likewise, the *protevangelium*, with its vivid oracular imagery, comes as a response by God to a particular couple and is more compelling than any possible discourse on the meaning of the Incarnation and the Crucifixion. Hovering in the background, however—or more precisely, hovering above in Mt. Sion—is a Pauline discourse that holds the interpretive key to the Garden scenes. Epiphanies will occur in the course of reading *Paradise Lost*, when a referential spark is perceived to connect the heavenly excursus with the earthly narrative. The doctrinal colloquy of Book III, for example, shows not only how the actions of the first couple set in motion the sweep of history that eventuates in the Incarnation, but also how the benefits of that blessed event accrue

---

attempt to counter the charge that Protestantism was a "new religion" (p. 29).

to them. Because the verbal Promise of Christ was understood to work backward and forward in time, Adam and Eve are included when the Almighty promises grace to those who "hear me call" and further promises, "for I will clear thir senses dark,/What may suffice" (3.185, 188-189).

The "sacramental" potential of God's promise was considered to be just as great in its Old Testament versions as in the explicit ones of the New. Luther's most eloquent discussion of the mysterious connection between the words of promise and that which is promised occurs in his Old Testament commentary. He assumed that the Father and Son were related as speaker to speech, and this natural analogy, rather than the abstract doctrine of the *Logos*, informs his exegesis.[4] He believed, further, that Christ was present in the Old Testament, not merely in a proleptic or symbolic way, but in his own person, speaking whatever was there promised. For example, Luther claims of Psalm 109, "David composed this psalm about Christ, who speaks the entire psalm in the first person against Judas, His betrayer" (*LW* 14.257). In like manner, Luther believed that "the Son of God himself spoke in the first prophecy . . . to Adam."[5] Milton seems to have the same understanding of Christ's presence in the Old Testament because, contrary to the Genesis account, Milton has the Son descend to the Garden and speak the *protevangelium* to Adam in Book X. 179-181. Though Milton may not have been drawing specifically upon Luther, he demonstrates the sacramental connection that the Reformers invariably make between Christ and the verbal promise about him.

Insofar as Milton's narrator, who from time to time apostrophizes the epic characters, is audience to his own epic, he displays the relation of the reader to the scriptural "gest" that Reformation hermeneutics recommends. The narrator empathizes with Adam and Eve's experience, which is more important

---

[4] *TT*, p. 181. For a discussion of this point, see Heinrich Bornkamm, *Luther and the Old Testament*, trans. Eric W. and Ruth C. Gritsch, Philadelphia, Fortress Press, 1969, pp. 200-201.

[5] *TT*, no. 5800, cited by Bornkamm in *Luther and the Old Testament*, p. 201.

to him than their involuntary service as typological symbols of the New Dispensation. As Calvin explains,

> It was also his will *to testify to all ages*, that whosoever desired to worship God aright, and to be deemed members of the Church, *must pursue no other course than that which is here prescribed.* But as this is the commencement of faith, to know that there is one only true God whom we worship, so it is no common *confirmation* of this faith that *we are companions of the Patriarchs*; for since they possessed Christ as the pledge of their salvation when he had not yet appeared, so we retain the God who formerly manifested himself to them.[6]

"Companion of the Patriarchs" well describes the relation of the reader in this tradition to Old Testament characters. As the patriarchs shared religious experience with Christians in any age, God's Spirit might speak simultaneously to both from within the same story. What God might speak—warning, judgment, reassurance, consolation, or the conferral of initial grace—depended of course upon the motions of the Spirit in each case. Luther and Calvin identify with favorite Old Testament characters and find that patriarchal experience "spoke" to them. Luther, for example, found in David's deep depressions and in Jonah's stubborn reluctance to preach, a "mirror" of his own situation, the one story offering him hope and consolation and the other, judgment and rebuke. Even Calvin, who is usually reticent, confesses in his preface to the Psalms, "[In] considering the whole course of the life of David, it seemed to me that by his own footsteps he showed me the way, and from this I have *experienced no small consolation.*"[7] Calvin goes on to explain that he too was plucked from obscurity by God's call (Farel's summons to Geneva) and was thrust into a post of political leadership only to be beleaguered by enemies (notably the Anabaptists) in later years. It was heartening to see that persecution

---

[6] John Calvin, *Commentaries on . . . Genesis*, I, 66 *(author's italics)*. Cf. *LW* 1.224.

[7] John Calvin, *Commentary on the . . . Psalms*, I, xliv *(author's italics)*.

and distress befell God's most eminent servants and that this distress did not necessarily betoken God's displeasure. It was not so much that Luther considered the Bible to be predicting in detail the events of his life or that Calvin thought of himself as David *forma perfectior*,[8] but rather that the Reformers expected God to speak to them *through* the accounts of the patriarchs and to speak variously at various times.

Concern for the audience of Scripture was one of the new emphases of Reformation exegesis, as one might expect when Holy Writ was understood to be a "sacramental" vehicle through which the Spirit might speak in daily acts of refreshment and guidance. In this "literary" theology, meaning was *not* presumed to be permanently fixed in the order of creation and in the order of history. Instead, meaning came under the aegis of the Holy Spirit, who made application and reference where he pleased, who made biblical story and promise intimately topical to a given reader. Though still in use, typology had lost the unchallenged support of natural theology and no longer enjoyed the status of a norm,[9] becoming only *one* of the routes of meaning that the Spirit might take. New metaphorical and allusive uses of biblical motifs appear side by side with traditional typology in the seventeenth century and give lyric poetry much of its excitement and vigor. Of more importance to *Paradise Lost*, however, is the way in which traditional typology loses ontological precedence to the historical sense (cf. *CD*, p. 581), at times being relegated to the status of rhetorical flourish beside

---

[8] See Barbara Kiefer Lewalski, *Donne's "Anniversaries,"* pp. 160-161; see also the chapter "Donne's Poetic Symbolism and Protestant Hermeneutics," pp. 142-173. *Protestant Poetics*, p. 130; see especially two chapters, "The Biblical Symbolic Mode: Typology and the Religious Lyric," pp. 111-144, and "Art and the Sacred Subject: Sermon Theory, Biblical Personae, and Protestant Poetics," pp. 213-250.

[9] Lewalski accurately observes that typology perseveres in the exegesis of Protestants but seems to assume that it still has the force of a norm. Cf. *Donne's "Anniversaries,"* p. 154, and *Protestant Poetics*, p. 117: "The characteristic Protestant approach takes the Bible . . . as a complex literary work whose full literal meaning is revealed only by careful attention to its poetic texture and to its *pervasive symbolic mode*—typology" (*author's italics*).

the narrator's immersion in the radical "present" of the Old Testament fable being probed.

At the very least, this focus upon the perseverance of God's oracle provides a strong counterweight to the onward temporal thrust of the typological perspective and emphasizes a community of lived experience that spans two dispensations. Luther thought that both he and the men of the Old Testament belonged to the same community of "saints," Calvin thought himself a "companion" of the patriarchs, and Milton felt that he shared the "mystic" communion of the Church that began in Eden (CD, p. 500). In The Pilgrim's Progress, both Lot's wife and David had traveled the same evangelical road as Christian, though the first was a cautionary witness and the second a model of faith. The experience of both "spoke" to him, in warning and in encouragement, just at the appropriate moment, but Pilgrim's own experience is unique, different in its course even from his companions Faithful and Hopeful. More important than the patterns (or types) of experience that Bunyan presents is the way in which the experience of other "saints" is made mysteriously and suddenly apposite to Pilgrim's spiritual condition of the moment.

It is possible of course to assimilate Protestant exegesis entirely to typology of one kind or another,[10] but to do so is to ignore the heart of Protestant hermeneutics: the sacramental power of God's promise, its central place in Scripture and pious

[10] Lewalski attempts to account for Protestant emphasis upon the religious experience of the patriarchs by making adjustments in the classical scheme of typology. She claims that Protestants considered Old Testament men to be types that find their fulfillment or antitype in the latterday Christian (Donne's "Anniversaries," pp. 160-161). She makes further adjustment in the classical scheme when she introduces the category of "correlative types" to deal with instances in which perfection or apocalyptic fulfillment is obviously not at issue. She sees "correlative types" as "recapitulating the situation of Israel of old . . . in that they await afar off the millennial antitypical fulfillment of all types" (Protestant Poetics, pp. 130-131). Her conclusion is that Protestants shifted the antitypical fulfillment of the Bible from the incarnate Christ to the contemporary Christian, thereby locating the subject of the Bible in the self (Donne's "Anniversaries," p. 160; Protestant Poetics, p. 137).

143

experience, and the Spirit's role in making the promise heard. Even when Tyndale embraces the recurrent patterns in the religious life of the Old Testament, he sees man's reception of God's oracle as the crux of human experience. Moreover, he expects God's promise to slice perpendicularly through all parallels of experience and address the reader directly:

> As it was with their true prophets, so shall it be with ours until the world's end. As they had ever among them false prophets and true, and as their false persecuted the true, and moved the princes to slay them, so shall it be with us until the end of the world. As there was among them but a few true-hearted to God, so shall it be among us; and as their idolatry was, so shall ours be, until the end of the world. *All mercy that is shewed there is a promise unto thee, if thou turn to God.*[11]

Milton of course chose the story that contained the sacramental Promise in its aboriginal form, the story of the patriarch whose case or state would fit everyone. No doubt he intended his retelling of the Genesis story to have full "apostolic address," and Stanley Fish has shown how *Paradise Lost* is constructed for evangelical purposes so as to elicit a pattern of alternating identification with and rejection of the characters, in order to convict the reader of sin. Fish, however, argues that "the terminal point of the reader's education" comes when the reader acknowledges an identification with Adam's decision to fall, but condemns it.[12] Rather, Milton's strategy depends upon the reader's identifying with Adam right up to the moment when he grasps the meaning of the *protevangelium*. According to Reformation hermeneutics, there is always the possibility

[11] "Prologues by William Tyndale Shewing the Use of the Scripture, Which He Wrote before the Five Books of Moses," *Doctrinal Treatises and Introductions to Different Portions of the Holy Scriptures*, ed. Henry Walter, Cambridge, Cambridge University Press, 1848, pp. 404-405 (*author's italics*), cited hereafter as *Doctrinal Treatises*.

[12] *Surprised by Sin: The Reader in "Paradise Lost,"* Berkeley, University of California Press, 1967, p. 271.

that a sacramental promise in the Old Testament may quicken
the reader of any age. As Tyndale put it, "The scripture is that
wherewith God draweth us to him."[13]

The stylistic power of the Old Testament, as Luther admits,
varies considerably, from the moving taciturnity of Abraham
on the way to Mount Moriah to passages that are repetitious
and dulling. Nevertheless, one is to listen to them, or rather to
listen for the *viva vox Christi*, that might issue forth from an
undistinguished passage. The expectation was that the voice of
the Lord *bricht durch wies feuer*, coming forth from the text
with the burning efficacy of a sharp instrument or a hammer,
and lodging in the reader's heart like a burning coal.[14] Calvin
has very much the same understanding, except that he uses
different rhetoric and is wont to describe the phenomenon as
the internal testimony of the Holy Spirit, "by whose effort the
promise of salvation penetrates into our minds, a promise that
would otherwise only strike the air and beat upon our ears"
(*Inst.* 3.1.4).

Literary devices of emphasis, then, could not of themselves
bring about a "sacramental" grasp, but self-indulgent verbiage
could obscure the promise. God's "word" never could be sat-
isfactorily replaced by any symbolic object, not even by such
biblical ones as mirrors, lanterns, flails, and two-handed swords,
which metaphorically describe its extraliterary properties. The
exercise of literary invention in all other areas, however, was
strongly recommended, even enjoined (cf. Chapter 3). Accord-
ingly, Milton makes God's word, in the earliest biblical for-
mulation of the Law and the Gospel, the center of his Garden
narrative, while summoning all the riches of his experience to
give substance to Adam and Eve's religious experience. Milton's
considerable literary experience furnished him with a rich vo-
cabulary of incident and description, as scholarly notes over
three centuries have attested. The use of his own intimate ex-
perience is more difficult to assess, but a reader coming to the

---

[13] Tyndale, "The Obedience of a Christian Man," *Doctrinal Treatises*, p. 317.

[14] "Revisions: Protocoll zum Psalter" (1531), *WA, Die Deutsche Bibel*, III,
20.

scene in Book X in which Eve prostrates herself before Adam may, for example, recall Mary Powell's penitent return to her husband. The political experience that the poet wove into his epic also is tantalizing, but even more elusive, no doubt because marriage in the seventeenth century was regarded as both a little state and a little church and because the facts of Milton's biography are easier to master than the political configurations of the period. Christopher Hill thinks that Milton's description of the foul distrust and alienation after the Fall is a deliberate description of the state of English politics in the 1660s.[15] It is not necessary, however, to identify the exact experiences that Milton used in his poetic commentary on Genesis in order to see that the narrative is inwrought with them and that Milton followed Luther's advice (and example) by filling in the interstices of scriptural narrative with his own experience—as an act both of private devotion and public witness. The dimension of personal allusion exerts a pressure upon the reader to concentrate upon the psychological texture of the narrative and thus to follow the narrative present to the end of the poem. Secondary typological reference is by no means precluded because typology in Milton's hands becomes the hermeneutic axis coordinate to that of realistic narrative and thereby plays its part in making Milton's text a highly changeable one. But if the Eden story is allowed to dissolve into typological symbolism at the end of Book X, Milton's narrative theodicy will be lost and the epic structure irretrievably warped. To be sure, Milton's "Life of Adam and Eve" adumbrates the whole course of salvation history, but the poet emphasizes how salvation history— as verbal report and verbal promise—figures in the *consciousness* of the first couple. The Garden scenes are a *mimesis* of what the Reformers understood to be the essential "Christian" experience. From the first conscious moments of Adam and Eve, through their Fall and Redemption, to their exit as wayfarers in the wilderness, their experience is both formed and measured by God's speech.

[15] Christopher Hill, *Milton and the English Revolution*, New York, Viking, 1978, p. 377.

─────────── II ───────────

For not to irksome toil, but to delight
He made us, and delight to Reason join'd.
(9.242-244)

Where there is no higher word to guide us,
we are right in following our reason.
(LW 3.323)

One of the triumphs of Milton's invention is the way in which
he dramatizes the formation of psychic life and shows that it,
no less than organic life, is constituted by God's speech. As if
to demonstrate the inadequacy of natural theology,[16] Adam's
waking query of the world yields no important answers, no
reply from Creation about who had made it all. The answer
comes from "A shape Divine," for even in Paradise God is
"seen" and known as a guiding voice. In a single verbal inter-
change, Milton demonstrates the principle that Calvin had built
into the structure of the Institutes: knowledge of self and knowl-
edge of God are inextricably intertwined. Adam learns the iden-
tity of his "great Maker" and at the same time learns his own
identity when it is verbally conferred upon him. Like any pu-
ritan, he receives a very specific identity from God's "calling":

> thy Mansion wants thee, Adam, rise,
> First Man, of Men innumerable ordain'd
> First Father, . . .
> (8.296-298)

Falling to his feet "Submiss" (8.316), Adam assumes at once
the proper posture before God's voice.

At the beginning of psychic life stands God's word, not as an

[16] See Hugh MacCallum, "Most Perfect Hero: The Role of the Son in Milton's
Theodicy," in Paradise Lost: A Tercentenary Tribute, ed. Balachandra Rajan,
Toronto, University of Toronto Press, 1969, p. 86; and Madsen, From Shadowy
Types to Truth, p. 143.

Augustinian faculty or light of Reason, but as a word having
the specifically literary character that it does in Reformation
commentary. Milton thereby suggests that man possesses a
sensus divinitatis,[17] an innate knowledge of God impressed upon
him by divine speech during his earliest hours in the Garden.
His Adam differs in this respect from Thomistic man, whose
knowledge of God is predicated upon his sense experience and
for whom the natural world is an important avenue to God.
According to this view, man cannot know even what is divinely
revealed without his use of images from the the natural world.[18]
Reformation man, by contrast, is equipped from the outset with
an innate knowledge of God that facilitates his independence
from nature when it later becomes unreliable. This assumption
goes to the heart of Milton's biblical faith and underlies his
larger poetic strategies: his version of the temptation calls in
question the analogical value of sense experience, and his version
of the Fall breaks and discards the Analogy of Being. Though
Milton, like Raphael, makes abundant use of sensuous analogy,
especially in the first two-thirds of the epic, he invests much
more in the oracular possibilities of speech *qua* speech.

Similarly, at the dawn of Eve's consciousness stands a form-
ative encounter with divine words, which are all the more nec-
essary because in her case the created world is not just inartic-
ulate but already misleading. In a mirroring lake she meets her
own shape, which pleases her "with answering looks/Of sym-
pathy and love" (4.464-465). The incident poignantly demon-
strates the Reformers' view that God's word—far from being
the repressive instrument that the Romantic tradition consid-
ered it—is an objective and liberating reality that takes us *extra
nos* (*LW* 26.387). Eve admits that she indeed would have re-
mained entangled forever in her own glances, had not a voice
warned:

> What there thou seest fair Creature is thyself,
> With thee it comes and goes: but follow me. . . .
> (4.468-469)

[17] *Inst.* 1.3.3. Cf. *PR* 4.352.
[18] St. Thomas Aquinas, *Summa Theologica*, trans. Fathers of the English
Dominican Province, New York, Benziger, 1947, I, Ia.89. I.

And follow the voice she does, thereby becoming properly oriented to reality—which is to say, she finds a husband. The mysterious voice leads Eve to a love object who is "no shadow" (470), and in solemn tones the voice pronounces her identity— "Mother of the human Race" (475)—an identity that is given final definition by Adam's first words to her:

> Whom thou fli'st, of him thou art,
> His flesh, his bone; to give thee being I lent
> Out of my side to thee, nearest my heart
> Substantial Life, to have thee by my side
> Henceforth an individual solace dear.
> (4.482-486)

In *Paradise Lost*, Adam appears as the image of God primarily because he too is a speaker, but his mode of verbal authority differs from that of the Almighty: God commands, but Adam must entreat. In the world of *Paradise Lost*, Adam's words are presumed to be the principle of a sound marriage, just as God's are the principle of a sound mind, and Milton takes care to show the basic soundness of Adam's mind in his reaction to news of an evil intruder. So firmly has Adam internalized the word given him and the relations implied thereby, so clearly is it the premise of his mental world, that the mere possibility of disobeying God strikes him as irrational. To Raphael he objects:

> Can we want obedience then
> To him, or possibly his love desert
> Who form'd us from the dust, and plac'd us here
> Full to the utmost measure of what bliss
> Human desires can seek or apprehend?
> (5.514-518)

Adam has accepted as axiomatic the divine right of God's voice to command. He judges the arbitrary and irrational prohibition of the Tree of Life, not on its merits, but on its authorship. Difficulty will arise, not over the question of authority per se, as in the case of Satan, but over the discreet and limited way in which God exercises his authority. Things would have been much easier if more had been commanded. The precise and limited nature of the "law" given to Adam and Eve is a fact of the Genesis story, but Milton goes out of his way to stress it. Just as in the case of psychological life, it is the divine voice that gives civil life its definition. The civil realm is to fill the "negative space" outside God's prohibition, a space in which Milton's invention plays freely as it imagines the quality of life in Eden with its spontaneous religion and its charming "governmental" problems. Despite Milton's originality of detail, he draws the boundaries for the *regnum fidei* and the *regnum rationis* in the Garden just where Luther saw them in the fallen world of history.

The Reformers, by no means the irrationalists that they have sometimes been painted, considered Reason to be the highest human power, and they referred to it in their commentary as a synecdoche for, and often the apex of, the flesh (*LW* 26.216). To live according to the flesh (or Reason) was to live in a human fashion. Like other human powers, they considered it to have been created pure. Even in the fallen world, Reason quite properly exercised itself in the realms of politics, business, and domestic life. It is little wonder then that, one tree excepted, Milton's earthly paradise is a veritable Garden of Reason. To the surprise of many a first reader, the narrator hails wedded love because it "hath his seat/In Reason" (8.590-591), by which Milton may intend to distinguish conscious desire for the good from the tyranny of instinct as Dante does (cf. *Purgatorio* 17.127-128); but Adam seems to have something else in mind. In arguing for a mate in Book VIII he pleads above all for psychological congruence, for a partner "fit to participate/All rational delight" (390-391). This definition of love is surprising only from the point of view of a Romantic tradition, which makes love directly proportionate to its irrationality—to the inappropriateness of its love object (for example, a Montague or an Othello) or to the inappropriateness of its conclusion (say, the unattainability of Laura or the death of Tristan). Milton condemns passional misfit, especially the irrationality of Petrarchan frustration (4.769-770) and hails the "wedded" love in Paradise because, after no more impediment than brief amorous delay, it finds its "solution sweet," as Keats would have said.

The government of the Garden, like domestic relations, is the province of Reason, a point that Eve grasps as well as Adam. When the Serpent brings her to the foot of the cursed tree, she exclaims, "Serpent, we might have spar'd our coming hither" (9.647), and then explains that God's word is different from all other objects of their experience, being the one thing in their environment that is not subject to their Reason. Of God's "irrational" prohibition, she says,

> God so commanded, and left that Command
> Sole Daughter of his voice; *the rest*, we live
> Law to ourselves, *our Reason is our Law*.
> (9.652-654, *author's italics*)

The Reformers' disjunction between God's word and Reason is thus built into the fabric of Edenic life; and trouble first arises in Paradise, not because Eve fails in piety, but because she is not hermeneutically astute enough to keep from confusing the *regnum rationis* and the *regnum fidei*.

In his account of Eve's proto-sin—the departure from her spouse's side against advice—Milton seems to have drawn heavily upon his own experiences, not the least agonizing of which was his role as ineffectual counselor to the English nation. The language of Book IX teases us with the possibility of political reference, and Christopher Hill believes that Milton is assigning blame for the failed Revolution. Hill suggests that Adam personifies the regenerate Parliamentarians of the 1650s,[19] but Adam appears very close to Milton's own persona, and seems to telescope the political experience of several decades. Adam's initial position, for example, is one that Milton had long held on the separation of religious and civil affairs, one that he had communicated to Cromwell in no uncertain terms: "You should not suffer the two powers, the ecclesiastical and the civil, which

---

[19] *Milton and the English Revolution*, p. 377.

are so totally distinct, to commit whoredom together" (*CE* 8.235). Though Eve can articulate the principle of the separation of the kingdoms well enough, her *applicatio* leaves much to be desired. To be fair to Eve (and to the epic), one must acknowledge Eve's paradoxical place in the scheme of things: she is equal to Adam in the democracy of grace and original righteousness,[20] but below him in the hierarchy of creation. Milton takes the severe view that woman becomes subject to man at Creation (*CE* 4.76, *PL* 4.295-299), rather than at the Fall or at "marriage." He explicitly notes that Eve is not, like Adam, formed for "contemplative" and higher mental operations.[21] In his tracts Milton had argued that in both marriage and in government one should hearken to one's natural superior. However distasteful his view now, we should take his hierarchical protocol into account in the Garden scenes, where it is assumed to belong to the structure of Creation and to partake of original goodness, and where its harshness is mitigated by the egalitarian tenderness of mutual (though different) needs.

Eve has no great trouble espousing the hierarchical principle ("so God ordains,/God is thy Law, thou mine" [4.636-637]),

[20] Anthony C. Yu, in "Life in the Garden: Freedom and the Image of God in *Paradise Lost*," *Journal of Religion*, 60 (July 1980), 247-271, reminds us that Luther and Calvin stress Adam and Eve's equality in original righteousness and in the reception of grace.

[21] See Yu, pp. 265-268, for a review of the way in which reason and mental functioning have predominated in historic definitions of the *imago dei*. Since Milton pointedly makes Eve the image of God in the second degree (*CE* 4.76) with inferior "contemplative" faculties, the logical suspicion that Eve suffers from some moral bias of nature will linger so long as the *imago dei* is understood largely in terms of *ratio* or *mens*. Yu readily concedes the "difference in endowments" between Adam and Eve—especially her "tendency to reason incorrectly" (p. 250). Perhaps for this reason, Yu argues that Milton anticipates Bonhoeffer in taking Adam and Eve together, in their free and loving relationship, as the *imago dei* (p. 259). It is simpler, however, to accept the *paradox* that Eve is somewhat intellectually inferior to her spouse, but that in Milton's view faith and frowardness do not depend upon sheer mental acuity. As Yu correctly observes, Adam's superior "contemplative" faculties in no way prevent his Fall.

152

and she listens rapt to Adam's *mundarum explicatio* as he gives the creatures their correct classifications and explains some elementary operations of the universe. His hermeneutic superiority is evident by the way in which he can dissolve apparent inconsistencies in the Second Scripture. In his answer to Eve's question about the superfluous light of the stars (4.657-658), he gives explanations both metaphysical and practical (4.660-688), and Eve rests content in his account of stellar influence, of the coming and going of spiritual creatures, and of the danger of universal Night. (On a simpler point, Eve needs no instruction and spontaneously joins him in interpreting the silent praise of Nature in a morning hymn [5.136-208])

Just as readily, Eve accepts Adam's explication of their charter to the Garden. Standing to Eve as a minister to a congregation of one, he patiently spells out the implications of God's Edenic grace. The terms of their lease are favorable, thinks Adam, and show "the regard of Heav'n on all [our] ways" (4.620), just as the work and responsibility for the Garden imply their "Dignity" (619). So much Eve accepts, but she does have a quarrel with Adam about the most reasonable way to care for the Garden. Adam's view is reminiscent of Milton and other naïve revolutionaries from the 1640s: the way to maintain paradise is simple and self-evident. With the first approach of morning light, says Adam, they are to be at their pleasant labor, "to reform/Yon flow'ry Arbors . . ./With branches overgrown" (4.625-627). Eve, who bears more than a little resemblance to the English Vulgar over whom Milton finally despaired, will not accept this sensible arrangement. The narrator tells us that "much thir work outgrew/The hands' dispatch of two Gard'ning so wide" (9.202-203), and, given such luxuriance, Eve thinks working *a deux* is not efficient. No doubt aware of the problem posed by Adam's "Commotion strange" (8.531), she urges that they divide in order to conquer the rank growth. What could be more reasonable? Milton here seems to be following in the footsteps of Luther, who identified Eve's primal sin with the exercise of her Reason and who, when in an allegorical mood,

153

assimilated Eve to a type for Reason rather than for Passion, as was usual in medieval commentary.[22] Milton goes a bit further and makes Eve's proto-sin a specifically interpretive offense. She first violates God's word in a lefthanded way. Her proto-sin (for she is still officially sinless) is that of "adding to the word."[23]

From God's initial charter of grace—the *unmerited* gift of the Garden (4.418)—Eve infers a law: thou shalt work unremittingly from dawn to dark and leave no twig unturned. If such were God's command, she would be entirely right to insist upon working separately. But no such command has been given. When she insists that they must work separately and unremittingly lest "th' hour of Supper [come] unearn'd" (9.225), she introduces a mercantile element into the theological equation. This mentality was a particular target for the Reformers: Reason was dangerous when it insisted upon setting up a reciprocity between man and God, when it sought to balance accounts, to become even with God. In political terms, Eve in effect is invoking divine sanction for *her way* of governing the Garden. To "add to the word" was to make a law out of the liberty of grace, to take what Scripture offered as counsel for a dread command, or to make an extrabiblical commandment out of whole cloth. Eve adds to God's charter for Eden with no hesitation whatever and seems to have "itching eares . . . , as if the divine Scripture wanted a supplement, and were to be eek't out" (*YP* 1.626). She adds to the Edenic word, moreover, in a way that thoroughly confuses the civil and spiritual realms.

---

[22] "For just as Satan disturbed Eve in Paradise by injecting the question (Gen. 3:2) why and with what intention God forbade the eating of the fruit, so our reason hampers and deceives us too" (*LW* 3.282). Typical of the way in which Luther links women with offensive reason is his comment, "Reason, as Paul requires of women in the church (I Cor. 14:34), should say nothing but keep silence" (*LW* 12.54).

[23] *LW* 9.51. See Calvin's sermon on Galatians 5:6-10: "Wee muste holde our owne, and not suffer any thing to bee added to Gods pure worde" (pp. 247-248). Milton characteristically cites Deuteronomy 4:2 and Revelation 22:18-19 to support this injunction—see *Of True Religion* (*CE* 6.166), and *CD*, p. 591.

Adam's position is that God has given them wide latitude, that he

> *requires*
> From us *no other service* than to keep
> This one, this easy charge, of all the Trees
> In Paradise that bear delicious fruit
> So various, not to taste that only Tree
> Of Knowledge, planted by the Tree of Life . . . .
>
> (4.419-424, *author's italics*)

In the absence of divine *commands* regarding the upkeep of Eden, Adam argues for the ready and easy way to maintain paradise. To continue their leisurely pace of work with its admixture of "sweet intercourse/Of looks and smiles" (9.238-239), he claims, is the most rational way to proceed. And, he pointedly reminds Eve, "smiles from Reason flow" (9.239). He naturally wants his work lightened by continual amorous parley, and he might have said, as Milton did of his own proposal for perpetual Parliament in 1659,

> The way propounded is plane, easie and open before us; without intricacies, without the introducement of new or obsolete forms, or terms, or exotic models; idea's [*sic*] that would effect nothing, but with a number of new injunctions to manacle the native liberty of mankinde; turning all vertue into prescription, servitude, and necessitie, to the great impairing and frustrating of Christian libertie: I say again, this way lies free and smooth before us; is not tangl'd with inconveniencies; invents no new incumbrances; requires no perilous, no injurious alteration or circumscription . . . .
>
> (CE 6.133)

Eve, however, returns again to the magnitude of their task, stressing that the undergrowth has become "wild" and the yield of fruit "enormous," as though there were a divine command to keep Paradise swept clean at all times. The garden debate thus focuses upon an issue over which there was much contro-

155

versy and some bloodshed in Milton's day: how far does God's scriptural word apply—or where does it cease to apply—in the secular realm? Adam's position is that the secular garden is to be administered according to man's reasonable choice. God had not "so strictly" commanded them to work the Garden (9.235). They need only clear an area "as wide/As we need walk" (9.245-246). Despite all Adam can say, Eve ironically puts their native ("Christian") liberty into "narrow circuit strait'n'd" (9.323) when she insists on her freedom of movement and her self-devised imperative for perfect household economy. Eve thus falls under Milton's proscription in *Of Civil Power*, where he declares that "the only heretic" is someone who adds to the word (*CE* 6.166).

In 1659, just before or perhaps during the time that Milton was writing *Paradise Lost*, the return of Charles II seemed imminent. The Restoration, Milton reckoned, would surely confound the religious and civil realms: the church would be re-established, returning the land to slavery of conscience. Aware that his own arguments for the reasonable (and secular) way to govern the nation were being ignored, Milton was tempted in *The Readie and Easie Way* to advocate compelling the English people "to retain their liberty"—*compelling* them to institute an annual parliament instead of recalling a king. In a similar way, Adam toys with the idea of compelling Eve to remain in the liberty of his company, since he foresees the dangers of Satan persuading in secret. Christopher Hill thinks Milton is blaming Adam and the revolutionary leaders because they failed to act upon their foresight,[24] but Milton in *The Readie and Easie Way*, like Adam in dispute with Eve, sadly concedes that to compel is to destroy. In his epic, he seems to intimate that Eve and the English nation are at fault; they should have listened to a natural superior. Here as elsewhere in his poetry, Milton's apparent antifeminism is intertwined with and hard to distinguish from his rage at the political perversity of his countrymen in the 1660s. When left to themselves, Eve and the English

[24] *Milton and the English Revolution*, p. 379.

156

people do not think clearly, and so confuse the kingdoms. Adam and Milton understood with painful clarity that God's word obtained *as command* only in the inner kingdom.

Since what disobeys (superior) reason is not long free, there inevitably follows destruction of the respective gardens. As the cautionary case of Eve demonstrated, bad hermeneutics meant bad politics.

------------------ III ------------------

Oh, Thou, that dear and happy Isle
The Garden of the World ere while, . . .
What luckless Apple did we tast,
To make us Mortal, and The Wast?
                    (Marvell, "Upon Appleton House,"
                              ll. 321-322, 327-328)

The Divel . . . is readie to tear the Word
out of our hearts.
                                        (*TT*, p. 7)

The temptation scene that follows upon Eve's departure from connubial safety brings together, with great dramatic clarity, the mighty opposites animating Milton's poem. There is a battle for the mind and heart of Eve, a contest between the words of God and almost everything that goes under the rubric of "experience." Satan opposes God's word with a full arsenal of emotional appeal, Reason, chop-logic, whimsy, surprise, sensuous allure, and celestial gossip. At first blush, the conflict would seem to be unbalanced and unfair. How, one wonders, could mere *remembered* words hold their own against the grand immediacy of the elegant, darting Satan? How could the simplicity of God's prohibition prevail against the bewildering multiplicity of the Arch Fiend's rhetorical sallies? To put the question thus, however, is to treat God's speech as ordinary language. While Satan's speech is allied with the familiar faces of experience, God's words were presumed to carry ontological weight. The contest for Eve's allegiance seems less biased in favor of Satan when we remember that God's speech has molded her consciousness and has the privileged status of an *a priori* and that God's word, if clung to, held the power to triumph over the most sensational "experience."

Milton's temptation scene is very rich and does not lend itself to easy schematization, but it proceeds through a series of baleful illuminations. The first of these is a literal eye-opener. Eve meets something new under the sun—a freak in the Garden:

> What may this mean? Language of Man pronounc't
> By Tongue of Brute, and human sense exprest?
>
> (9.553-554)

It may be pointless to ask what Adam would have made of the phenomenon of the talking snake as it is to ask why Romeo and Juliet did not elope to Padua, the question being very much beside the plot; but the interpretive acuity that Adam showed in labeling the beasts according to their natures would have enabled him to see the verbal serpent as a fraud, not a "miracle" (562). Yet, for all Eve's amazement, she is not immediately gulled and resists Satan's first onslaught (495-646). When she is shown the miracle fruit, she is still skeptical—"*The credit of whose virtue rest with thee,*/Wondrous indeed, *if* cause of such effects" (649-650, *author's italics*). She correctly assumes that the reptile's testimony, since it conflicts with God's words, must be false, and she emphasizes the point by repeating the divine prohibition. As the Lady in *Comus* knew, this is the proper way to handle temptation. Eve then dismisses Satan's Iago-like "Indeed?" by repeating God's prohibition, the second time *verbatim*: "Ye shall not eat/Thereof, nor shall ye touch it, lest ye die" (662-663).

The bravura performance that Satan then rouses himself to is almost comic in its fecundity, but the fecundity works admirably to obscure the basic hermeneutic issue of the scene. In various and inconsistent ways, which Milton criticism has minutely analyzed, Satan invites Eve to measure God's words by human experience and human reason, rather than the other way round. When he represents himself as a reptile with an adventurous history, Eve is confronted with a simulation of the fallen world and its choices. Satan's impersonation presents her with a situation in which nature and experience do not give *prima facie* support to God's words. Her fatal error is not that of mistaking a fallen angel for a brazen reptile, nor that of reasoning from empirical evidence, true or false. The conflict

159

in *Paradise Lost* is never simply one of sensuous versus verbal experience, for the sensuous components of the temptation are themselves verbally mediated. Eve's mistake is that she believes the words of a creature against those of the Creator. Had Satan actually been a freakish snake, the issue would have been the same because Book IX essentially is a logomachy.

Once given orientation by the divine voice, Eve had found the natural world to be trustworthy; all her wondering examination of nature handily confirmed the authority of the divine voice. But now the experience of meeting a beautiful reptile, who happens to be wittier and much more attentive than Raphael, has to be discounted if Eve is to credit the divine voice who "educated" her. (Adam has a similar problem squaring his perception of Eve's loveliness, which seems "so absolute," with his knowledge based on a colloquy with God that she is only an "occasional" creature [8.528-556]). Such a discount of experience, however, is the demand of faith. Instead of repeating God's prohibition in the face of counter-evidence as before, Eve undertakes to dissolve the cognitive dissonance between her new experience and her previous experience with God's word. She asks which position is good and reasonable, not which speaker is to be trusted. She does not ask: who is the Serpent that he contradicts God? As soon as she tries to determine for herself whether the forbidden fruit enhances life or destroys it, *ratio* is well on the way to undermining *obedientia*. That Eve does not yet know experientially what "death" means does not really distinguish her from Reformation believers, who were asked to trust God's words even though their "existential" meaning was not entirely clear. Even if the nature of the punishment promised is unknown, the *proscription* is sufficiently clear to Eve. That she makes such elaborate use of her mental powers in *Paradise Lost* and that she so badly needs a reason-induced illumination before she will reach for the fruit, marks her as a conspicuously Reformation Eve (cf. *LW* 3.282). She may take up various lines of thought suggested by Satan, but in the final soliloquy she follows a primrose path of logic on her own. The serpent "hath eat'n and lives" (764), she muses, accepting his verbal self-presentation utterly. "What fear I then," she poses the question, "Of God or Death, of Law or Penalty?" (773, 775). Her conclusion—"To reach, and feed at once" (779)— comes as a syllogistic illumination with the gratifying force of logical necessity. Adam, in his turn, sees more clearly the scope of the loss involved in breaking God's prohibition and hence is all the more desperate in grasping for an illumination that will allow him to dismiss it. With his superior mind, he has no trouble arriving at one of his own:

> Nor can I think that God, Creator wise,
> Though threat'ning, will in earnest so destroy
> Us his prime Creatures, dignifi'd so high,
> Set over all his Works, which in our Fall,
> For us created, needs with us must fail,
> Dependent made; so God shall uncreate,
> Be frustrate, do, undo, and labor lose . . . .
>
> (9.938-944)

If so, Adam concludes, 'tis "Not well conceiv'd of God" (945). The climactic point of his auto-temptation is his "seeing" that God's decree is irrational and hence invalid. Only then does he take the plunge into sin, when it appears to him that self-preservation is the law of nature (he and Eve are "One Flesh" [959] and he cannot lose her) and that being faithful to the bond of the "flesh" is perfectly natural and rational (9.952-959).

Eve's third illumination is the artificial one following the ingestion of the forbidden fruit. It comes as a grand mystical experience confirming her "rational" conclusions. She feels "hight'n'd as with Wine" (793), feels herself rising in the Chain of Being, rapidly maturing toward Godhead (803-804), and having access to the secrets of the universe. To the Tree, she gratefully cries, "Thou op'n'st Wisdom's way" (809); to Adam, she rhapsodizes that she feels "Life/Augmented, op'n'd Eyes, new Hopes, new Joys" (984-985, *author's italics*). Adam's artificial illumination from the "sciential sap" is similar, but goes beyond the perception of an expanded self to a heightened perception of his sexual partner. Eve appears to him more alluring than

161

the day he "wedded" her (1029-1033), and, under the sway of "concupiscence," he seizes her wrist, exulting:

> if such pleasure be
> In things to us forbidden, it might be wish'd,
> For this one Tree had been forbidden ten.
> (9.1024-1026)

With this salute, Adam turns to lovemaking as to an apotheosis of experience, the idolatry of which Milton suggests by the telling use of "Seal":

> There they thir fill of Love and Love's disport
> Took largely, of thir mutual guilt the Seal.
> (1042-1043)

Here "Seal" suggests the sexual imagery that John Donne favored as well as an inversion of Calvin's Communion, in which the visible analogy to God's verbal Promise was termed a "seal." Adam's lascivious onslaught upon Eve, whose virginal allure seems miraculously restored, provides a visible analogy to (and metonymy of) the violation of God's command, a deed characterized as a defloration (901).

The final illumination in Book IX is the first painful one, but it is the only one so far that is true. The first couple awake to find

> *thir Eyes how op'n'd, and thir minds*
> *How dark'n'd;* innocence, that as a veil
> Had shadow'd them from knowing ill, was gone . . . .
> (1053-1055, *author's italics*)

The content of this illumination—"Good lost, and Evil got" (1072)—is true as far as it goes, but Adam and Eve's doleful vision of a ruined present and a deteriorating future simply represents the highest illumination that "experience" can give. It is not, however, as Milton shows in Book X, all there is to see.

―――――――――― IV ――――――――――

What revelation sees is grace: what reason sees
is nature.
(Northrop Frye, *The Return of Eden*, p. 97)

I will clear thir senses dark,
What may suffice.
(*PL* 3.188-189)

Adam's rehabilitation from the Fall is accomplished by a rad-
ically different kind of illumination—and not through the
prompting of Eve's love—the common assumption from Till-
yard onward.[25] A medieval hermeneutic often is imposed upon

[25] The assumption seems to be that there is a clear connection between Eve's
love and Adam's rehabilitation. E.M.W. Tillyard, in his classic essay "The
Crisis of *Paradise Lost*," asserts that a "common-place trickle of pure human
sympathy" from Eve brings with it "the first touch of regeneration" (*Studies
in Milton*, London, Chatto and Windus, 1956, p. 43). Arnold Stein notes a
shift in Book X from the ethos of obedience to the ethos of love, in which man
comes to love of God through a creaturely love (*Answerable Style*, Minneapolis,
University of Minnesota Press, 1953, p. 118). "It is finally Eve who points
Adam in the right direction," says Stanley Fish, "by suing for *his* forgiveness"
(*Surprised by Sin*, p. 273). Joseph H. Summers makes an eloquent case for a
typological reading in which Eve, because of her gratuitous offer to take all the
punishment upon herself, stands as a mirror of the Redeemer (*The Muse's
Method*, Cambridge, Harvard University Press, 1962, pp. 177-178, 183). More
recently, J. Douglas Canfield has argued that Eve's penitence and her "com-
passionate attempt to assuage Adam's 'fierce passion' " elicits humility from
Adam, and because of their repentance, they "have earned the right to under-
stand fully the Promise" ("Blessed are the Merciful: The Understanding of the
Promise in *Paradise Lost*," *Milton Quarterly* 7, 1973, 42, 45). Anthony C. Yu
in "Life in the Garden: Freedom and the Image of God in *Paradise Lost*," p.
271, calls Eve "the true heroine of the Christian epic" because she "overcomes
his estrangement from her and God by breaking the hardshell of his self-
centeredness." Yu goes on to add that "the love which brings about such a
powerful reversal" precedes prevenient grace and "has no other immediate
source than the mystery of the human depth." Like all the foregoing inter-

163

Book X, which makes the Crucifixion, as typologically repre-sented by Eve's reconciling gestures, the climactic moment in the book. But a reading that centers on the typological value of Adam and Eve's reunion, like any reading that focuses mainly upon the achievement of domestic peace, usurps the religious significance of the narrative *present*—or at least tends to distract from the moment when the first couple are themselves recon-ciled to God. In Milton's tradition, the primary focus rests upon the narrative present, *within* which the Crucifixion is invoked metonymically.

In any case, a close look at Book X shows that Eve's love has only incidental bearing upon Adam's return to faith. As the book begins, Adam and Eve are locked into a perfectly reciprocal hostility. Whereas before, Adam had been superior, the couple now seems equally matched as to mental agility in finding out ever-fresh blame. Whatever the role of Reason before or during the Fall, it now serves the additional function of calibrating the *crassa peccata* of the other. Thus engaged, their Reason cannot help them because it has become part of the problem, for their charmed circle of mutual complaint can be broken only from the outside. As in the case of newborn Eve, deliverance comes from a divine voice, or more precisely from the *memory* of a divine oracle and its reinterpretation. Though there can be little doubt about the providential disposition of the reconciliation scene, it proceeds in a deceptively natural way. Every step of Adam's progress from despair to faith seems explicable in hu-man terms—except one.

At the beginning, Eve is sitting quite apart while Adam speaks in grand soliloquy and makes a blasphemous apostrophe of cre-

pretations, Yu's reading assumes that *deliberate* acts of human love can induce repentance and grace—a view that, however attractive, appears sentimental in the light of Milton's "theology of the word." This is not to deny that Eve, like Dalila, is a providential stimulus that jolts Adam from his obsessive recital of wrongs, but rather to assert that according to this tradition grace is understood to be radically discontinuous with human effort: God mysteriously orders the minutiae of (domestic) history so as to work repentance and faith *despite*, and yet through, human motions of despair.

ation. It is a speech that inevitably calls to mind the anthem
that had celebrated their wedding night:

> O Woods, O Fountains, Hillocks, Dales, and Bow'rs,
> With other echo late I taught your Shades
> To answer, and resound far other Song.
>
> (10.860-862)

Eve's response is to approach Adam with "Soft words" (865
Is she touched with sentimental remorse, or is this a trickle
pure human sympathy? The context is at best clouded. Milto
emphasizes Eve's despair; she appears "Desolate where she sat
(864). Apparently she is just as miserable as Adam, though les
articulate. Her "Soft words" seem as much an expression o
her own need as of gratuitous love.

To this first assay, Adam responds with something close to
total rejection: "Out of my sight, thou Serpent," and there
follows an extended vilification of all women to come in history
at the end of which "He . . . from her turn'd" (909, author'
italics). What follows has been seen by Summers as "the em
bodiment of humility and uncalculating love," a veritable
Christlike gesture;[26] but Eve's plea here is far from disinter-
ested. She is reaching out to Adam, terrified at the prospect of
total isolation. As Adam turns his back on her and starts away,
she reminds him that she literally has no place to go—

> forlorn of thee,
> Whither shall I betake me, where subsist?
>
> (10.921-922)

There is something of a wail in her "Forsake me not thus,
Adam" (914, Milton's emphasis), and she wildly pours forth
her misery at having sinned against both her God and her
demigod. Before she is done, she is rashly promising to take
"the sentence" all upon herself (934). Her wild offer expresses
the ultimate in vulnerability: she will risk anything rather than
be left totally alone. Because her offer is an unconsidered and

[26] Summers, The Muse's Method, p. 183.

165

almost instinctive gesture of self-preservation, it happens to be brilliantly, if unconsciously, manipulative.

In any case, Adam melts, gently explaining to Eve why her simplistic remedy will not work. And so they are reconciled. They even have a special tender rapport as they face a long day's dying together. We begin to sense a restorative movement afoot, mainly because things are visibly returning to the *status quo ante*. Adam is no longer prostrate, but again standing "God-like erect," and it is tempting to conclude that there is a causal connection between the couple's renewed love and their reconciliation with the Almighty. It is important to note, however, that even if we grant Eve the purest love for Adam, she is still estranged from God. Her very next word points, not in the direction of faith, but in the direction of despair: she proposes suicide.

With almost prelapsarian tenderness, Adam begins to explain why a love-death will not work either:

> *Eve*, thy contempt of life and pleasure seems
> To argue in thee something more sublime
> And excellent than what thy mind contemns;
> But . . .
>
> (10.1013-1016)

In the process of trying to be tactful to Eve, the words of Christ's sentence fortuitously occur to Adam:

> such acts
> Of contumacy will provoke the Highest
> To make death in us live: Then let us seek
> Some safer resolution, which methinks
> I have in view, *calling to mind with heed*
> *Part of our Sentence, that thy Seed shall bruise*
> *The Serpent's head*; piteous amends, unless
> Be meant, whom I conjecture, our grand Foe
> *Satan*, who in the Serpent hath contriv'd
> Against us this deceit: to crush his head
> Would be revenge indeed; which will be lost

By death brought on ourselves, or childless days . . . .
(10.1026-1037, *author's italics*)

The *instant de passage* from despair to faith is precisely the
moment when Adam recalls Christ's words of judgment and
perceives the *promise* in them. The moment changes every-
thing; there is now a reason for loving and living and having
children. Once Adam sees the promise, he begins to see promise
everywhere. The joy of children is promised in childbed pain.
The sweat of his brow promises a labor that is sustaining. Though
Adam's "literary" insight may in itself seem like a rather mild
"Eureka!" it is nevertheless monumental. It lets Adam choose
to live.

Here Milton dramatizes the Reformation view that Adam is
not merely a type of Christ, but the first believer, the Church
actually beginning in the Garden of Eden. Luther, for example,
exhorts:

> Look at Adam and Eve. They are full of sin and death.
> And yet, because they *hear the promise* concerning the
> Seed who will crush the serpent's head, *they have the same
> hope we have,* namely, that death will be taken away, that
> sin will be abolished, and that righteousness, life, peace,
> etc., will be restored. In this hope our first parents live and
> die, and because of this hope they are truly holy and right-
> eous.[27]

---

[27] *LW* 1.197. This is a point that Luther never tires of reiterating; for example,
"Such a promise was given to Adam after his fall, when God spoke to the
serpent [Gen. 3:1], 'I will put enmity between you and the woman, and between
your seed and her seed; he shall bruise your head, and you shall bruise his
heel.' [Genesis 3:15]. In these words, however obscurely, God promises help
to human nature, namely, that by a woman the devil shall again be overcome.
This promise of God sustained Adam and Eve and all their children until the
time of Noah. They believed in it, and by this faith they were saved; otherwise
they would have despaired" (*LW* 35.83); and "This first comfort, this source
of all mercy and fountainhead of all promises [Genesis 3:15], our first parents
and their descendants learned with the utmost care. They saw that without this
promise procreation would indeed continue to go on among people as well as
among the other living beings, but that it would be nothing else than a pro-

Similarly, Calvin claims that

> all the pious who have since lived were sustained by *the very same promise of salvation* by which Adam was first raised from the fall.[28]

In *Paradise Lost*, Adam's sudden memory and reinterpretation of his sentence epitomizes the Protestant experience of a sacramental encounter with Scripture. Luther's famous struggle to understand Romans 1:17 stands as the model for many puritan "literary" experiences to come in the seventeenth century. He tells of anxiously pondering the following:

> For therein is the righteousness of God revealed from faith to faith: as it is written, The just shall live by faith.

At first, the single word "righteousness" was a stumbling block for him. He read "the righteousness of God" in a philosophical way as the "formal" righteousness that is manifest in punishing the wicked. Luther "raged" over such an impossible God—"As if, indeed, it is not enough, that miserable sinners, eternally lost through original sin, are crushed by every kind of calamity by the law of the decalogue, without having God add pain to pain by the gospel and also by the gospel threatening us with

---

creation to death. And so that gift which was given by God to our nature is here made greater, nay, even made sacred; for there is hope of a procreation through which the head of Satan would be crushed, not only to break his tyranny but also to gain eternal life for our nature, which was surrendered to death because of sin. For here Moses is no longer dealing with a natural serpent; he is speaking of the devil, whose head is death and sin. And so Christ says in John 8:44 that the devil is a murderer and the father of lies. Therefore when his power has been crushed, that is, when sin and death have been destroyed by Christ, what is there to prevent us children of God from being saved? *"In this manner Adam and Eve understood this text* . . . . And through the hope based on this promise they will also rise up to eternal life on the Last Day" (*LW* 1.191, author's italics).

[28] Calvin, *Commentaries . . . on Genesis*, I, 65 (*author's italics*). Important studies of the exegetical tradition by Arnold Williams, *The Common Expositor*, Chapel Hill, University of North Carolina Press, 1948, and by J. M. Evans, *Paradise Lost and the Genesis Tradition*, Oxford, Clarendon, 1968, focus almost entirely upon events leading up to the Fall, as if Milton's story ended there.

his righteousness and wrath!" (*LW* 34.337). Then, in a sudden flash, he understood the "righteousness" of God in Romans 1:17 as the gratuitous giving of faith. It was all a matter of God's bounty, not his just wrath. Luther describes his new insight thus:

> Here I felt that I was altogether born again and *had entered paradise itself through open gates.* There a totally other face of the entire Scripture showed itself to me . . . .
>
> And I extolled my sweetest word with a love as great as the hatred with which I had before hated the word "righteousness of God." *Thus that place in Paul was for me truly the gate to paradise.*[29]

Calvin puts the matter similarly in one of his sermons:

> God openeth to us the door of paradise when we hear the promises that are made to us in His name. It is as much as if He reached out His hand visibly, and received us for His children.[30]

The grand moment toward which *Paradise Lost* is moving is thus the moment when the gates of Paradise swing open to Adam and he *hears* the promise in the *protevangelium* (10.1028-1038), as distinct from the moment when Christ first pronounces it some 850 lines earlier (10.179-182).

Adam's rehabilitation by delayed insight is much like Christian's escape from the Dungeon of Despair in *Pilgrim's Progress*. Christian strays from the King's Highway and is captured by a Giant who furnishes him with all sorts of deadly instruments and urges him to commit suicide. Christian is almost persuaded to take deadly steps when suddenly he remembers that in his pocket he has had the Key of Promise with him all along. Now remembering it, he draws it out, finds that it turns the lock,

---

[29] (*LW* 34.337). See also *LW* 33.92: " 'The opening of thy words gives light; it imparts understanding to the simple.' Here the words of God are represented as a kind of door, or an opening, which is plain for all to see and even illuminates the simple."

[30] Calvin, *The Mystery of Godliness*, p. 122.

and so he is immediately released from the Dungeon of Despair to fare forward on his way to the Celestial City. Such delay in grasping God's promise is a conspicuously Reformation touch, for both Calvin and Luther insisted that God's verbal promise did not work *ex opere operato*, but as the Spirit chose. Though it is sometimes said that the religious life of the puritans adhered to a rigid pattern and was utterly predictable,[31] such a view leaves out of account the mystery that pervaded life simply because the timing of the Spirit would not be calculated. One could never tell when a passage of Scripture would be "activated," as it were. A chief role of the Holy Spirit was that of remembrancer, "of bringing to mind what he had taught by mouth" (*Inst.* 3.1.4). Both Reformers found the Holy Spirit operating in the "literary" experience of the patriarchs, Pentecost notwithstanding. Luther says, "It is clear from [Genesis 3:20] that after Adam had received the Holy Spirit, he had become marvelously enlightened, and that he believed and also understood the saying concerning the woman's Seed" (*LW* 1.220); and Calvin concludes that God illumined the patriarchs when they embraced God's word, not by the "general mode of communication which is diffused through heaven and earth and all the creatures of the world," but by "that special mode which both illumines the souls of the pious into knowledge of God and, in a sense, joins them to him. Adam, Abel, Noah, Abraham, and the other patriarchs cleaved to God by such illumination of the Word" (*Inst.* 2.10.7).

In the setting of a realistic narrative, Adam's "opening"—as the Quakers were wont to call such an experience"[32]—may

[31] U. Milo Kaufmann, *"The Pilgrim's Progress" and Traditions in Puritan Meditation*, New Haven, Yale University Press, 1966, p. 45.

[32] Hugh Barbour, *The Quakers in Puritan England*, New Haven, Yale University Press, 1964, p. 26. The idea of the "opening" is of course much older than the Quaker term and probably derives from the account of Luke 24, in which the resurrected Christ returns and explicates Scripture for his awestruck disciples: "And he said unto them, These are the words which I spake unto you, while I was yet with you, that all things must be fulfilled, which were written in the law of Moses, and in the prophets, and in the psalms, concerning me. Then *opened* he their understanding, that they might understand the

appear to be ordinary insight, because Milton does provide some narrative preparation. Eve's love may have no bearing on Adam's salvation, but she plays an inadvertent role as a stimulus to memory. She mentions returning to the place of sentence (10.934), and once she has dropped the matter of "the sentence" into the conversational air, it remains there in the periphery of the discourse. She also provides Adam with the stimulus of a wrong answer that needs correction, but this fact does not really explain how Adam hits upon the referent for "Serpent," how he connects the Serpent with the Grand Enemy of cosmic wars that Raphael had warned of. Adam's sudden grasp of the oracular sentence simply constitutes a great interpretive leap.

Someone familiar with Calvin's doctrine of the Spirit would not have to wait until Book XI to hear the Almighty explain that Adam's lucky insight is due to God's "motions" in him (11.2-6, 22-27, 91). Nor would the absence of anything ecstatic be surprising because Milton is temperamentally closer to Calvin on the question of the Spirit than to the more colorful experimentalists of the period. It is Sin and Death who base their actions upon vague "subjective" promptings and journey to earth because they feel drawn by a mystic "sympathy" with Satan (10.243-263), while Adam's restoration hinges upon the "objective" matter of Christ's words. For Calvin, the sheer fact of belief—the enlightened grasp of Scripture—was certification of the Spirit's presence.

It may be that *mimesis* of a literary experience does not itself

---

scriptures" (Luke 24:44-45). One could argue that St. Augustine's account of his conversion in the *Confessions*, Bk. VIII, Ch. xii (in which he tells how mysterious singing in the garden urged him to take up the Scripture and read, and how his eyes then lit upon Rom. 13:13: "Walk honestly as in the day, . . . not in chambering and wantonness"), is the prototype of the "opening" in the evangelical tradition. It seems, however, that Luther provides the pattern of "literary" experience for the English puritans. The Quaker term "opening" is useful and not inappropriate in a discussion of Milton, since the Quaker Thomas Ellwood was known to be a frequenter of Milton's household during the poet's later years. William Riley Parker speculated that toward the end of his life, Milton's faith in the "inner light" was very close to the Quaker position (*Milton*, Oxford, Clarendon, 1968, II, 1058, n.12).

make for a compelling literary experience because critics have often found an esthetic falling off after Book IX. It also may be that Milton deliberately underplays Adam's "literary" experience since he includes none of the emblematic touches, like the fading garland and the groaning earth, that earlier he had used for the Fall. Milton may have intended the scene as a pious test (or opportunity), presuming that the "natural" reader would respond to the affecting reconciliation between man and woman, while the reader with "the eyes of faith" would perceive the sacramental nature of Adam's grasp of the Promise—and hear the *viva vox Christi* along with him. Tillyard remarked upon the contrast between the noisy works of Satan (witness Pandemonium) and the quiet works of God, who "hushes chaos into peace before creation."[33] God's work of re-creation, one might say, is accomplished by a whisper of "literary" interpretation. At least, to see Adam's "opening" in Book X as the grand climax of the epic requires that, for the nonce, one adopt certain extraliterary assumptions: one must perceive the special weight and metonymic reach of the divine Promise, understand the *protevangelium* as the Bible in epitome, and expect the (verbal) gate to Paradise to open at the motion of the Spirit.

Milton, though, does not abdicate his vocation as poet and renounce all persuasive strategies just because the Holy Spirit is needed. The poet provides an oblique gloss on Adam's "opening" by bringing the epic tradition to bear upon the scene. Book X invokes a parallel incident in *Aeneid 7*—one that has no equivalent in Homer—and thereby manages to suggest the doctrinal weight of Adam's "opening" and something of its metaphysical mechanics. In *Aeneid 7* the Trojans, having newly landed in Italy, treat themselves to an outdoor feast. They pile up the fruit of the field on flat rounds of bread, and Iulus playfully remarks, "We are eating our tables" (*heus, etiam mensas consumimus* [*Aen.* 7.116]). Aeneas instantly stops him, for he recognizes that a dire oracle given him by his father[34]

[33] Tillyard, *Studies in Milton*, p. 34.
[34] Vergil nods here. Actually Celaeno the Harpy gave Aeneas the oracle (*Aen.* 3.250-257).

172

has found a fortunate fulfillment. The oracle had foretold that the Trojans would not found their destined city until they became so hungry as to eat their tables. Aeneas, struck by the power of God (*stupefactus numine*), grasps the solution of the oracle and joyfully cries, *hic domus, haec patria est* (*Aen.* 7.119, 122). He takes the solution of the oracle to be a signal that he has arrived in his promised land, and so the scene ends, just as it does for Adam and Eve, with prayer and sacrifice.

The strikingly different ways in which Vergil's and Milton's gods signal their approval of the rites offered measures the distance between the two poets. The sacrifices of Adam and Eve, of course, are the sighs and groans of contrite hearts. They do not receive divine commendation by a triple peal of thunder as Aeneas does (7.141-143), but rather by a sense of something understood. Adam tries to explain:

> Methought I saw him placable and mild,
> Bending his ear; persuasion in me grew
> That I was heard with favor; *peace return'd*
> *Home to my Breast, and to my memory*
> *His promise, that thy Seed shall bruise our Foe;*
> Which then not minded in dismay, yet now
> Assures me that the bitterness of death
> Is past, and we shall live.
>
> (11.151-158, *author's italics*)

Jupiter may rule his universe by noisy blasts, but Milton's God rules the inner man almost imperceptibly: a remembered promise is his thunder.

Here, as throughout *Paradise Lost*, Milton seems to be transposing the action of ancient epic into a verbal register. If the scene of Adam's return to faith in Book X alludes to *Aeneid* 7.107-147, Milton thereby emphasizes the role of God's Spirit in the solution of the oracle, and suggests that Adam has received a decisive, saving revelation—that with the grasp of God's oracle he has entered *his* promised land. For Adam, however, the oracle is both the gate through which he enters the promised land as well as its definition and substance, because the "Paradise

Within" is constituted by a literary grasp of God's promise, that is, by faith. It should be stressed that solving the oracle marks only the entry and that in both epics the moment of arrival is more compelling than the process of taking possession. Just as Aeneas has many hard battles ahead before he will secure the site of Rome, so Adam has the long, hard catechetical battles ahead in Books XI and XII before he will be in firm possession of his promised land.

❖ 6 ❖
The Portable Paradise

―――――――――― I ――――――――――

For our chiefest felicitie is that God draw
neere unto us, and we unto him. And how
shall this be done . . . and by what meanes?
It is done when he is present with us by meanes
of his worde.
(Calvin, *Sermons on Job*, pp. 375-376)

When Dante arrives at the Earthly Paradise atop Mount Pur-
gatory, he meets something resembling a Corpus Christi proces-
sion—he sees a veiled Beatrice drawn in a car by a Gryffon,
preceded and followed by a file of white-robed elders repre-
senting the books of the Bible. The parade presents the entire
span of sacred history, the central point of which is the Incar-
nation (figured by the two-natured Gryffon) and the Host (fig-
ured by a veiled Beatrice). In much the same way, the last two
books of *Paradise Lost* present the puritan "sacrament" set
within biblical history as the *sine qua non* of earthly paradise.
Neither the puritan sacrament nor the puritan view of history
can be represented satisfactorily as spectacle or, indeed, as any
visual image. The breaking of the Analogy of Being is a con-
sequence of the Fall that Milton's Adam must confront and
understand.[1]

――――――――――

[1] For Milton's rejection of natural theology, see Robert L. Entzminger, "Mi-

175

At the beginning of Book XI, there is already a disjunction between the visible and the spiritual. Adam cannot see the "glorious Apparition" of heavenly bands now alighting in Paradise (11.203-211), and so his first question to the armed "Man" (11.239) who approaches him is quite wrongheaded: "In yonder nether World where shall I seek/His bright appearances, or footstep trace?" (11.328-329). The answer is nowhere, for "God áttributes to place/No sanctity" (11.836-837). Nor can anything important about God be discerned from the face of things now fallen, what with roses growing thorns, beasts turning predatory, and all the air darkening. Even the Apollonian beauty of human flesh, corrupt now and subject to death, cannot be read as the image of God because, says the Angel Michael, God either withdrew his image from human flesh after the Fall (11.515-516), or man himself effaced the divine image by intemperance and other kinds of self-abuse (11.522). The angel nevertheless declares that God is present in the world and proceeds to show how God's presence is located in the dynamic processes of speech. If Paradise is defined by God's presence and if words are the privileged way by which God makes himself present to man, then Adam's Paradise Within is a mind and heart well furnished with biblical theology. No static, sensuous picture can adequately define such a paradise, much less its acquisition.

Adam himself must learn, first of all, about the supremacy of the verbal over the visual. The tableaux seem designed to demonstrate Calvin's view that "mute visions are cold."[2] The burning bush, for example, would not have been efficacious had not God at the same time spoken to Moses. Whenever God spoke to men by signs, he always added an accompanying word. Even with Adam's lucky guess that what happens to Abel is "death," and even with his recognition that the rainbow must be a good sign, he does not find the dumb shows intelligible

---

chael's Options and Milton's Poetry: *Paradise Lost* XI and XII," *ELR*, 9 (Spring 1978), 197-211.

[2] Calvin, *Commentaries on the First Book of Moses*, trans. John King, Edinburgh, Calvin Translation Society, 1950, II, 114.

without the attendant Spirit's explanations; often they are quite misleading. It is possible to see Adam's "bodily" vision in Book XI as a "symbol for the restoration of man's marred faculties of reason" that enable him to be "guided by the Law of Nature,"[3] but it is more probable that the dumb shows demonstrate the inadequacy of human reason operating apart from the guidance of the Spirit. For example, Adam's estimate of the bevy of fair women he sees dancing is:

> Here Nature seems fulfill'd in all her ends.
> (11.602)

Michael rejects this estimation, "though to Nature seeming meet" (11.604), and counterposes another standard of judgment. The reasons of the Spirit—"conformity divine" (11.606)— take their referential authority from no thing visible and clash with human reason operating from the premises of sense perception and desire.

Many of the sights presented to Adam seem designed to make him turn away from the raw data of history and seek the comfort and discrimination of words. The sight of his great-grandchildren and their world destroyed by the Flood returns Adam, reasonably enough, to the despair that he voiced in Book X: "Why is life giv'n/To be thus wrested from us? rather why/Obtruded on us thus" (11.502-504)? The Masque of Death, shown with its hundred variants of mortality also drives Adam to rely upon the Spirit's words, since his own verbal effusion— "O sight/Of terror, foul and ugly to behold,/Horrid to think, how horrible . . . !" (11.463-465)—cannot compass or palliate the horror. He turns again and again to Michael with some variant of "unfold, Celestial Guide" (11.785). Adam does not really "see" the dumb shows until the Angel's verbal account has been interposed, like a theatrical scrim, between his pupil and the visible vision. Although Michael's visions from the beginning have a "literary" component, it is a mark of his

---

[3] Barbara K. Lewalski, "Structure and the Symbolism of Vision in Michael's Prophecy, *Paradise Lost*, Books XI and XII," *PQ*, 42 (1963), 31.

spiritual growth that the Angel can dispense with the spectacle entirely and move on to a purely "literary" presentation in Book XII.

Dante earns his Earthly Paradise by dint of laborious penance as he slowly works his way up to the summit of the Purgatorial Mount, but in *Paradise Lost* Adam has only to be willing to follow the Spirit's lead, and almost immediately he is brought to the Mount of Speculation. The Angel, whose eyedrops pierce "Ev'n to the inmost seat of mental sight" (11.418), represents either the Holy Spirit or a heaven-sent preacher, much like Bunyan's Evangelist. Although Adam does not "earn" Paradise in a moral sense, he does earn it in an experiential sense. The final books of *Paradise Lost* take considerable esthetic risk to save Adam from being "a heretick in the truth" (*YP* 2.543)— that is, one who has knowledge of words only or who believes "by a Deputy."[4] Books XI and XII are a *mimesis* of the protracted "literary" experience that comprises "explicit faith," a faith confirmed "by attentive study of the Scriptures & full perswasion of heart" (*CE* 6.177). Milton's undertaking here is a difficult one because it reverses the common assumption that reading and study comprise experience of a secondary or derivative kind. The study of Scripture was for Milton the staff of life, not an idle occupation of children gathering pebbles by the seashore (cf. *PR* 4.330). Everything important here and hereafter, he thought, depended upon certain "motions" of consciousness in response to Holy Writ, and upon the permanent acquisition of a "literary" cast of mind. As in New Criticism, the relation between text and reader was held to be inviolable; one was to puzzle and search out the meaning without the intervention of any "arbiters," save the Spirit (*CD*, p. 124). Adam, with his absolutely "virgin mind,"[5] stands as the pro-

[4] *CE* 6.175-176. Milton's abhorrence of implicit faith is a constant theme in his prose; see especially *CD*, pp. 118-124, 203-204.

[5] For an account of Adam's education in Book XI as a defloration, see F. T. Prince, "On the Last Two Books of *Paradise Lost*," *Essays and Studies*, n.s. 11 (1958), p. 236.

totype of the evangelical Christian who studies Scripture in all "newness of life."

That Milton, like the New Critics, was more indebted to tradition than he perceived, or that reading any text with a "virgin mind" may be an impossibility is not at issue, nor is the degree to which the central tenet of Reformation doctrine prevailed amidst the proliferation of subsidiary ones. Sometimes Milton's emphasis upon the individual character of scriptural apprehension is mistaken for a claim to possess a "fresh" revelation and present *Paradise Lost* as a Third Testament that completes Scripture.[6] Nothing could be further from Milton's understanding. In *Christian Doctrine*, for example, he claims that he does *not* accept any of the systems of divinity he has read (ones that in fact are very close in form and substance to his own tract). Yet he also claims, "I do not teach anything new" (*CD*, p. 127). In Milton's eyes, "innovation" or "something new" meant something extrascriptural. Accordingly, Michael's presentation includes no historical events beyond those mentioned in the Bible, not even the Reformation. In shape, however, Michael's history conforms to the Reformers' hermeneutic, and the Old Testament figures treated—Abel, Enoch, Noah—correspond to the selection and emphasis of Hebrews 11:1-7.[7] Michael's history is thus one that has been "opened" by New Testament verses, so that the patriarchs appear as "heroes of faith" in their own right, not just as typological precursors of the New Dispensation.

In the process of working out his own explicit faith, Milton had written his tract *Christian Doctrine*, and the outcome of Adam's encounter with "Scripture" also will be a catechetical utterance. Although Milton's tract is merely the map of one man's Paradise Within, Books XI and XII of Milton's epic show Adam slowly building his paradise. His experience with Michael's word does not proceed with the rational smoothness of

---

[6] Kerrigan, *The Prophetic Milton*, Charlottesville, University Press of Virginia, 1974, p. 264.

[7] Summers, *The Muse's Method*, Cambridge, Harvard University Press, 1962, p. 198.

a Ramian diagram, but has all the affective vicissitudes of a learning curve. The poet's task in these last books is to demonstrate that real learning has taken place. He must show that Adam not only has understood God's word, but embraces it "with full perswasion of heart." Again, this is a difficult task, for a certain mystery always surrounds any verbal learning. Wittgenstein was to puzzle over exactly when one "understood" the meaning of a sentence, but Luther anticipated his conclusion that it took place when a sentence "meshes with life."[8] One could not understand God's words, Luther said, unless one had the "experience" to match them: suffering

> doth rightly expound and declare the Word, as the Prophet *Isaiah* saith: *Vexatio dat intellectum*, grief and sorrow teacheth how to mark the Word. And *Ecclesiasticus* saith: *Non tentatus qualia scit?* What knoweth hee, that is without tribulation and temptation? No man (said *Luther*) understandeth the Scriptures, except hee bee acquainteth with the Cross.
>
> (*TT*, p. 24)

Adam's little stock of experience by now already includes disobedience, guilt, anger, despair, sudden "literary" insight, reconciliation, and joy. These experiences are called into play as he encounters Michael's "Scripture." Adam's emotional engagement with it becomes precisely that recommended by Reformation hermeneutics, which sees reading Scripture as, among other things, an exercise in self-analysis.

For Adam, Scripture is first of all a mirror of man (*LW* 2.208-209). To read accounts of great murderers, defectors, traitors, and backsliders is to see oneself writ plain, to see that one belongs to the tribe of Cain—of Adam. To read and weep over one's spiritual kindred, as Adam repeatedly does, accords with Reformation piety, in which repentance follows faith and becomes a lifelong activity (see *CD*, p. 469). Perhaps the most

---

[8] Ludwig Wittgenstein, *Philosophical Grammar*, trans. Anthony Kenny and ed. Rush Rhees, Berkeley, University of California Press, 1974, p. 66.

touching moment comes when Adam understands how his own life "meshes" (metonymically) with that of the farmer who "Groan'd out his Soul with gushing blood effus'd" (11.447). The irony of intention almost overwhelms Adam because he had not meant murder when he chose to be "faithful" to Eve.

That Adam is now "heart-strook," now revived, now felled by a "sudd'n damp," now heartened by the promissory Angel, does much to convince us that Adam is really coming to understand divine words, and in no superficial way. The affective shape of Adam's education is that outlined by Luther, who thought that the times of Law and Promise, though very far apart historically, appeared in nearly every book of the Bible, and that within a human heart they might be conjoined within a single hour (LW 26.301, 339-340):[9]

> This is Scripture's way: first to terrify, to reveal sins, to bring on the recognition of oneself, to humble hearts. Then, when they have been driven to despair, its second office follows, namely the buoying up and consolation of consciences, the promises. This is how the Holy Spirit teaches. Satan, on the other hand, worms his way in by means of sweet speeches and flattering words. . . .
>
> (LW 16.6)

This quotidian alternation of Law and Grace is Adam's experience in Books XI and XII. Adam's responses in Book XI, as Summers has pointed out, err on the side of terror and despair, while those in Book XII err on the side of elation.[10] From this hermeneutic wobbling, this interpretive "drunkenness," Adam finally arrives at a point of emotional poise when he can relate his "sum of knowledge" without being either unduly spirited or dispirited. In the rhetoric of Reformation commentary, Adam achieves "soberness" when he neither loves nor hates life, but loves the word and "walks in it." Adam's education is a long

---

[9] Jason P. Rosenblatt, "Adam's Pisgah Vision: Paradise Lost, Books XI and XII," ELH, 39 (1972), 66-86, traces Adam's experience of Law and Grace in his shifting identification with Moses; see especially p. 81.

[10] Summers, The Muse's Method, pp. 93, 196-197.

and patient process, and nothing shows more clearly the temperamental distance between Milton and the ranting sects of his time than the way in which the *paideia* of the last two books[11] of *Paradise Lost* is balanced against the false *paideia* of the first two. Both Adam and the devils must learn to live a postlapsarian existence. While Satan's theatrical words *raise* the fallen angels in one great awakening ("They heard, and were abasht, and up they sprung" like locusts [1.331]), Michael rears a sinking Adam over and over again with tender words. For every little repetition of the Fall, the Spirit patiently repeats the gesture of the Almighty, who with his voice had first raised Adam to conscious life (8.296).

Taken as a whole, the last two books of Milton's epic provide a phenomenology of faith that complements the essential paradigm of Adam's "opening" in Book X. The initial "opening" relates to the *paideia* of these books as "entrance" to "building." It was important to Milton to show that faith was not a steady state, but one of fluctuating growth in which "subsequent grace" repeats with variations the paradigm of "prevenient grace":[12] Adam is to exclaim over and over again in these last books about his "eyes' true opening" as he moves toward fuller understanding of Michael's "Scripture." It is not that Adam has yet to gain a saving faith, but that he is continually being "confirm'd" in it (11.355). He steadily increases his knowledge of God's word, whose depths one could never plumb completely.

[11] Irene Samuel, "*Paradise Lost*," *Critical Approaches to Six Major English Works: "Beowulf" through "Paradise Lost*," ed. R. M. Lumiansky and Herschel Baker, Philadelphia, University of Pennsylvania Press, 1968, p. 225. Cf. George Williamson, "The Education of Adam," *MP*, 61 (1963), 96-109.

[12] *LW* 9, 86. Luther borrows St. Augustine's distinction between "prevenient" or healing grace and "subsequent" or strengthening grace; he characteristically insists that prevenient grace is "that by which we were chosen, called, and justified before we have done any work at all," while subsequent grace comes through experience and works, and brings us "certainty."

————————— II —————————

What is the world without the word, but even
hell, and the very kingdome of Satan?
(Luther, *Gradual Psalms*, p. 46)

Let no man think (said *Luther*) that hee hath
tasted of the Scriptures, except hee had gov-
erned one hundred years in the Church with
the Prophets, with *John* Baptist, and with the
Apostles. To conclude, It was a work of great
wonder rightly to understand God's Word.
(*TT*, p. 6)

The final books of *Paradise Lost* raise the question of how history, with all its dark cataclysms, can be said to be "God's word." Granted that Books XI and XII present the outline of salvation history that Milton considered to be "predestinated," the concrete existence of men does not seem to be improved or ameliorated. From the perspective of someone living within it, history appears to give Satan the last word.

The unambiguous verbal style of the last books belies the radical ambiguity of history considered as a text, because it presents a number of interlocking patterns—cyclic, progressive, degenerative, and perennial—that may be read and integrated in a variety of ways. Because the Reformers' God is known in the "category of relation," sorting out the patterns of history and God's connection to it becomes an important "literary" task for the man of faith. Biblical narrative, according to the Reformers, is both a mirror of the world *and* a mirror of God (*LW* 2.208-209). Michael's narrative presents an unblinking view of human affairs. It is a world notable for "The brazen Throat of War," "luxury and riot," "Rape or Adultery" (11.713-717)—a world where good men go without their reward. Adam's out-cry, "Is Piety thus and pure Devotion paid?" (11.452), is a question that will return until he has generalized it into a maxim about history as the "burd'n of many Ages" (11.767). Isabel MacCaffrey has shown how compulsive repetition is characteristic of both history and Hell.[13] To see this is an important part of Adam's education—to see that "the tenor of Man's woe/Holds on the same" (11.632-633).

The penultimate lesson that Milton's Adam must learn is not to place his faith in history, and yet not to despair because he is immersed in it. Bad as history is—and it is one of the achievements of recent criticism to note the ways in which Milton's history recreates the world of the opening books[14]—it includes something that sharply differentiates it from Hell, God's oracle. In Hell, God's speech, even in redacted form, is absent. There, cut adrift from the Reality-principle of Milton's universe, the devils can change at will, but never grow. Even after they collide with Reality, imaged as a grand war chariot, they are none the wiser. History, on the other hand, is never out of touch with the Reality-principle and, in a sense, "contains" it. Amidst all the dispiriting data there comes God's promise that all will be well, that "Faith approv'd/Lose no reward" (11.458-459). If we remember that this promise is *not* ordinary language, but a sacramental offer with the power of the universe behind it, any attempt to weigh it quantitatively against all the dispiriting data becomes absurd, and other patterns appear in the carpet besides the demonic one.

Amidst the cycles of degeneration there emerges a single constant: the availability of God's oracle. In each era there comes a man who "utter[s] odious Truth" (11.704). First ap-

[13] *Paradise Lost as Myth,* Cambridge, Harvard University Press, 1959, pp. 119-120.

[14] John B. Broadbent, *Some Graver Subject,* London, Chatto and Windus, 1960, p. 274; Madsen, "The Idea of Nature in Milton's Poetry," *Three Studies in the Renaissance: Sidney, Jonson, Milton,* 1958, reprint Hamden, Conn., Archon, 1969, p. 267; Martz, *The Paradise Within,* New Haven, Yale University Press, 1964, p. 151; and Stein, "The Paradise Within and the Paradise Without," *MLQ,* 26 (1965), 599.

pears the man whom Luther called the "saint of saints in that first world" (*LW* 1.344), a man

> Of middle Age . . . rising, eminent
> In wise deport, spake much of Right and Wrong,
> Of Justice, of Religion, Truth, and Peace,
> And Judgment from above. . . .
>
> (11.665-668)

To be sure, Enoch would have been killed on the spot, had not heaven provided a covering cloud, but God's word had been made available in a dark and dangerous age, and his spokesman had been protected.

God's word is the constant in history, but its expression traces a progressive pattern. Milton adroitly coordinates Adam's spiritual growth with the increasing clarity of God's promise in the course of history.[15] When Adam in Book X suddenly grasps that his sentence is promissory, he becomes reconciled to the Father (11.46-47), even though his understanding of the *protevangelium* is rudimentary. He grasps the promise of victory, but does not know the referents of such key terms in the oracle as "Seed," "the Woman," and "bruise." Adam gains light on these matters by degrees. After Enoch's version of "Religion, Truth, and Peace," another age brings a slightly more evangelical Noah, who "preach'd/Conversion and Repentance" to his people (11.723-724). With Abraham, the word is specifically delineated as "promise" (12.137), and God then also promises an unfolding explication ("whereof to thee anon/Plainlier shall be reveal'd" [12.150-151]). Book XII is then given over to further explication of the *protevangelium*, showing that God's word gives history its structure, as it goes from promise to promise, from hope to hope. The verbal formulations vary and change

---

[15] See John M. Steadman, "Adam and the Prophesied Redeemer," *Paradise Lost*, XII, pp. 214-225; C. A. Patrides, "The 'Protevangelium' in Renaissance Theology and *Paradise Lost*," *SEL*, 3(1963), pp. 214-215; Lewalski, "Structure and the Symbolism of Vision in Michael's Prophecy, *Paradise Lost*, Books XI and XII," pp. 25-35.

with the advancing years, but the Promise itself is shown to be always the same:

> the like shall sing
> All Prophecy, That of the Royal Stock
> Of *David* (so I name this King) shall rise
> A Son, the Woman's Seed to thee foretold,
> Foretold to *Abraham*, as in whom shall trust
> All Nations, and to Kings foretold, of Kings
> The last, for of his Reign shall be no end.
>
> (12.324-330)

Toward the end of the narrative, Adam comes to identify "the Woman" as Mary and bursts into a magnificat (12.378-382), to identify "the Seed" as the Son of God and exclaim over Him with participatory paternal joy (12.381-382), and to identify the "capital bruise" with the defeat of the Serpent (12.383). Just how much Adam understands of the last point is not clear (it will take Milton himself another epic to explain).

The main axes of Reformation hermeneutics stand out boldly in these final books. The onward rush of time going from "shadowy Types to Truth" (12.303) is poised against the identity and perseverance of God's verbal Promise. Milton notes the traditional typological roles of Enoch, Moses, David, and Joshua (as suggested in most cases by Pauline epistles), but he places equal importance upon their role as carrier of God's verbal message to their *own* generations. In this "opened" version of history, Christ presides over all times by means of his oracle. If each promissory oracle is understood to be potentially sacramental and mysteriously connected with the divine "presence," then Michael's roll call of Old Testament "preachers" amounts to a constant evangelical focus. Just as Christian's journey in *Pilgrim's Progress* takes him through a veritable minefield of pits and holes that could take one straight to Hell, so Michael's historical narrative (like the entire epic) is studded with variants of the sacramental Promise that lead Adam and the reader repeatedly to "the verbal gate to heaven."

History, in Milton's account, is a journey *through* the word,

186

purposefully going in the direction of greater and greater clarity until it reaches a climax of clarity in the Incarnation. After the triumph of clarity follows a triumph of dissemination as the word spreads beyond a single nation. Michael's narrative becomes clotted at this point (12.446-458), and it appears that universal proclamation of the word is the earthly manifestation of Christ's victory, which, in mythical description is a rising in triumph through the air to cast Satan down in "Chains." Michael is so anxious to get on to the world's great period that he is not clear about the implied connection between the triumph of preaching and the establishment of the Son's Kingdom. Once he has reported the Son's resumption of his exalted seat, it is but a short doctrinal step to the end of the world, when Christ shall "reward/His faithful" and receive them into bliss (12.461-462). Michael's first account paints history as progressive—as a glorious and rapid triumph of the word.

Adam will finally accept this interpretation of history, but Milton takes great pains here to distinguish between rote acceptance and explicit faith. Adam's resistance is important in showing that he acquires a *theologia pectoris*, rather than a "speculated divinitie." From the outset he occasionally had balked at the angel's explanations, showing a mild sense of injured merit over the way in which the image of God "once/So goodly and erect" (11.508-509) had been effaced by disease and death. At one point he is close to rejecting the Spirit's revelation as officious: "Let no man seek/Henceforth to be foretold what shall befall/Him or his Children" (11.770-772). His integrity as a pupil, though, is most striking when he questions Michael about his rapid summary of history. It is partly by such searching questions and partly by his empathetic tears that Adam "earns" his Paradise Within.

Michael's revised version of the end of history dwells upon the worsening of the world that goes on at the same time that there is an ever-widening proclamation of the word. Michael's first version is not false; it simply takes two narrations to show the irreconcilable cleavage between the way of the *world* and the way of the *word*. Here the "fissure" that Martz has noted between Michael's doctrinal abstractions and the concrete woes of the world becomes painfully pronounced,[16] for Michael now presents the most devastating indictment that, given Milton's theology, could be made of history. Hitherto, there have been corrupt ages with corrupt men and corrupt institutions, all followed by cataclysms of judgment, but the word itself always had been shielded from destruction. Now Michael begins to tell how, late in history, the word itself will be threatened:

> Wolves shall succeed for teachers, grievous Wolves,
> Who all the sacred mysteries of Heav'n
> To thir own vile advantages shall turn
> Of lucre and ambition, and the truth
> With superstitions and traditions *taint* . . . .
> (12.508-512, *author's italics*)

History is then no longer a conflict between the just man, who is God's spokesman, and a corrupt people who will not listen. The very conditions for "hearing" will have been corrupted: "Spiritual laws by carnal power shall [be] force[d]/On every conscience" (12.521-522). Milton gives no precise clues as to the date of this latter day, but by the time he is writing his epic, the heady days in England when one could hear an unlicensed preacher at a conventicle are past. Royal and Erastian forcers of conscience had been restored. Even in such dark times, though, God's word is available, "Left only in those written Records pure,/Though not but by the Spirit understood" (12.513-514). In lieu of one prophetic spokesman, God would provide a Faithful Comforter for the dark days when

> Truth shall retire
> Bestuck with sland'rous darts, and works of Faith
> Rarely be found: so shall the World go on,
> To good malignant, to bad men benign,
> Under her own weight groaning, till the day
> Appear of respiration to the just . . . .
> (12.535-540)

[16] Martz, *The Paradise Within*, p. 151.

The final pattern to be observed in Milton's version of history, then, is the one that, through all the little cycles of degeneration and renewal, traces a large arc downward.[17] The world tends toward its destruction, while the word marches toward its final triumph. Milton thus puts the question of faith in its harshest possible light. Not only does he pile up concrete woes as counter-evidence, but the angelic messenger himself becomes dejected over how the endgame of history is to be played out. Michael is a rather jaded minister who announces the gift of the Comforter (12.486), but says less and less about "inward consolations" (495) as he goes on. He is virtually cheerless as he reaches—or rather sinks toward—the final period of history, when all renewals and reformations from Noah onward grind down, yielding Satan's "perverted World" (547). Michael can manage only a bare mention, a mere notation, of "Joy and eternal Bliss" (551). It is as if he has lost faith in history—but no matter, history is not faith's proper object. The Angel himself has just observed that men stand by "Thir own Faith not another's" (528). It is Adam's response that counts, and he compliments the Angel—rather curiously it has seemed to most readers—on the pithiness of his narrative:

> How soon hath thy prediction, Seer blest,
> Measur'd this transient World, the Race of time,
> Till time stand fixt. . . .
>
> (12.553-555)

The disjunction between Adam's tone and Michael's establishes Adam's faith as very much his own, because it cannot be attributed to contagion of mood or to the virtuosity of his teacher.

The difficulty here is that the common reader, accustomed to ordinary literary persuasion, tends to identify with the Angel and finds it unaccountable that Adam should seize upon a per-

---

[17] For the Augustinian character of Milton's history, see C. A. Patrides, *The Grand Design of God: The Literary Form of the Christian View of History*, London, Routledge & Kegan Paul, 1972, pp. 16-19, and Michael Cavanagh, "A Meeting of Epic and History: Books XI and XII of Paradise Lost," *ELH*, 38 (1971), 206-222.

functory line and exult over the final disposition of history. But
this brings us to the heart of the Protestant mystery. As in the
case of Adam's initial access of faith, he must embrace divine
words without any "literary" reason at all, with full awareness
that "no eye can reach" eternity (12.556). In each of Milton's
major works, the moment when "objective" words become part
of the hero's "subjectivity" leaves a hiatus in the narrative,
because such change is owed to a secret agency. Fish contends
that the religious desideratum of the puritans is mute genu-
flection,[18] but faith for the puritans, like love in Shakespearean
comedy, is terribly verbal. Indeed, one mark of man's resto-
ration, though not in itself a conclusive one, was the gift of
words: "God every morning raines down new expressions into
our hearts" and, for a "variety of Circumstances," gives a "var-
ietie of words" (YP 3.505). If Adam's confession here is lamely
platitudinous and somewhat less exuberant than the anthems
sung by the narrator and the angels round the throne of God,
it nevertheless comes unprompted and unforced. Hence it carries
weight as evidence that God's promise, to use Michael's term,
has been "engraved" upon his heart:

> Greatly instructed I shall hence depart,
> Greatly in peace of thought, and have my fill
> Of knowledge, what this Vessel can contain;
> Beyond which was my folly to aspire.
> Henceforth I learn, that to obey is best,
> And love with fear the only God, to walk
> As in his presence, ever to observe
> His providence, and on him sole depend . . . .
> (12.557-564)

The sheer length of Adam's education, which otherwise is an
esthetic drawback, now becomes persuasive. Because we have
seen Adam respond to the Angel's presentations and have been
convinced of his emotional honesty thus far, as he alternately
becomes overelated and then dejected, we tend to accept the

---

[18] *Surprised by Sin*, p. 291.

probity of his emotions now. Because we have watched him repeatedly resist and then submit to Michael's explanations on many small points, we can accept the ease with which he accepts the whole now. Wittgenstein remarked that the moment of real understanding, whether of number series or melodies, comes when one can say, "Now I know how to go on."[19] Adam has reached this point. He knows how the pattern of history will run: that God's word will always be available, if only on the written page; that the course of history, despite periodic renewals, will be degenerative; but that the word marches toward its triumph at the end of time, when the faithful receive their promise in full. Adam also knows how to go on, in the sense of "how to live," because he has "seen" the key term and the way in which it informs history seriatim. Adam sees the Incarnation as the hermeneutic key to history because it "opens" the oracle in each age and because it exemplifies the secret work of a *deus absconditus* concealed under a contrary (*LW* 3.318). Each dark occurrence, like the Flood, may be overturned to show that the disaster is hooded providence. Milton even seems to suggest that God had arranged a special period of darkness to be the setting of the Incarnation. In sharp contrast to the Nativity Ode, in which Milton took history as a pathetic fallacy and made the civil peace of the first century into a compliment for the Christ Child, he now shows how the surface of history stands in ironic relation to divine activity. Michael thus describes the state of politics in Israel just before the advent of the Prince of Peace:

> But first among the Priests dissension springs,
> Men who attend the Altar, and should most
> Endeavor Peace; thir strife pollution brings
> Upon the Temple itself: at last they seize
> The Sceptre, and regard not *David's* Sons,
> Then lose it to a stranger, *that* the true
> Anointed King *Messiah might be born*

[19] Wittgenstein, *Philosophical Grammar*, p. 80.

Barr'd of his right. . . .

(12.353-360, *author's italics*)

Adam grasps the Angel's point that history is a mirror of God insofar as it shows political (and intellectual) powers continually being overturned. He swears to observe God's providence in all such revolutions, to see good

Still overcoming evil, and by small
Accomplishing great things, by things deem'd weak
Subverting worldly strong, and worldly wise
By simply meek . . . .

(12.566-569)

Accordingly, Adam acquires a dynamic template—not a static one—by which he will perceive and master future experience. Under any dire occurrence he will look for God at work. Milton does not appear to be forecasting the overthrow of any particular government in the expectation that a better one will replace it. Rather, he seems to be suggesting that no civil regime is ultimate. It is impossible to conclude whether or not Milton thought he was living in the last downward spiral of history or in just another evil age (like Nimrod's) that the Almighty would plough under. Either way, man's spiritual dilemma was the same, and Milton could omit mention of the Reformation because it was no special case, but belonged to the perennial texture of history.[20]

[20] Christopher Hill claims that Milton does not mention the Reformation in *Paradise Lost* because he considered the true reformers to be English ones—"Wyclif and his Lollard successors, the humble Marian martyrs and the persecuted sectaries" (*Milton and the English Revolution*, New York, Viking, 1978, pp. 85-86). But it appears that Milton considered "reformation" to be a recurrent feature of history: "Speedy and vehement were the *Reformations* of all the good kings of *Judea*" (YP 1.602); Scripture gives accounts of Reformation "and Antiquity to boot" (YP 1.602, 570).

As Christ says: "The kingdom of God is within you" (Luke 17:21). It is as if He were saying: "Outside of you is exile. Outside of you is everything which is seen and touched, but within you is everything which is believed only by faith."

(*LW* 26.282-283)

Milton's main concern in the last books is to describe the psycho-intellectual template that is to be Everyman's defensive armor for the battle of the wilderness. Michael's narrative becomes a part of Adam's experience in much the same way that *King Lear*, or any compelling literary work, becomes part of a reader's history, identity, and conceptual framework—except that the process is both more intense and more programmatic. He is acquiring the verbal structures for patience, and in the process of internalization,[21] Michael's narrative undergoes an abstraction into sentences of great integrative and mnemonic value. The Reformers liked to speak of the biblical narrative as a "glass" that holds up before one's eyes the dark passions of men, the degenerative movements of history, and the incomparably bright promises of God—all arranged in triumphant configuration. In Milton's universe there can be no question of a Romantic marriage of Heaven and Hell, because in the long view evil is only a beauty spot. Just as Satan appears from a distance to be a sun spot on a golden globe (3.588-590), so in Books XI and XII the abstract or conceptual language distances history and arranges it into a simple configuration that is intelligible at a glance: history is bracketed by the Son.

In Hell, where any connection to Reality is lacking, the devils see things in "dimensions like themselves," whichever way they

[21] See Northrop Frye, *The Return of Eden*, Toronto, University of Toronto Press, 1965, p. 111: "There is nothing to be done with this objectionable creature [Milton's God] except swallow him."

fly (1.793). Their bloated sense of self accounts for the overwhelming scale of things physical and moral, just as it does for the sense that time has bogged down in the sloughs of immediacy. In Milton's history, on the other hand, God's word provides a plumbline, a "yardstick" by which to take the measure of each age (CD, p. 120); and so history, when compassed by divine words, appears much smaller than Hell. Arnold Stein says that the language of these books is like that of a bad dream remembered in which "the surface of things dominates, clear, cold, and hard."[22] It is exactly the language needed to cut history down to size, to tame it by miniaturizing it, so that it can be folded into consciousness like a winter's tale. An enormous theological irony attends these graceless general sentences of the final books. They are potentially the most powerful and subversive of all "things deem'd weak" because they are potential vehicles of grace and metonyms to heaven. Of such unprepossessing catechetical materials is the Paradise Within constructed.

Adam's inner paradise is "happier far," not because it brings a headier affect or a lighter mood—and certainly not because it is impervious to disaster and historical change—but because it offers him a "sober certainty of waking bliss." Milton's tradition prized multileveled, paradoxical awareness and scorned ecstatic experience involving dissociation from the body or loss of the awareness of being historically rooted in the world. Adam's interior paradise is to be "happier far" because it is to be more *knowing* than the old one. In Eden, Adam and Eve are "happier than [they] know" (8.282), but at the end of *Paradise Lost* they know more than their "happiness" in the wilderness. The consciousness of Adam and Eve has acquired a "literary" dimension by the end of Book XII. They know that reading events alone yields despair, and so they are prepared to read them instead through the "Spectacles of Scripture." Or, as Calvin put it on another occasion, God's word is the "thread" that leads man through the labyrinth of history (*Inst.* 1.6.3).

[22] Arnold Stein, "The Paradise Within and the Paradise Without," p. 599.

Finally, words connect the Paradise Within to the world that it transcends and distinguish it from a quietist interiority. Adam's inner Paradise is not a Stoic retreat from which to watch the rest of the world go by. It may appear to be a mental universe that is poetically generated, or a refuge that is quite out of phase with the world, but it is linked with the world by an imperative to participate in it. The attendant Spirit's parting admonition to Adam is to add deeds to what he knows (12.581-582). Adam knows that he has been called "To life prolong'd and promis'd Race" (11.331). His faith meets its final test on the question of action, on whether he will choose to enter the wilderness of history and obey his "call" to begin the human race, now that he knows it is to produce both murderers and divine spokesmen, both mighty hunters and a Messiah. Adam sees the radical ambiguity of history and yet, prompted by the Spirit, interprets history as promissory all the same, in both the long and (more difficult) short run. So he chooses to set out. In so doing, Adam masters what the tradition from Luther to Kierkegaard considered the most difficult task of faith—accepting the risk of moral evil. For Dante, the Earthly Paradise was the point at which, all sins having been expiated, man ascends effortlessly to the Empyrean. For Milton, however, the earthly paradise marks no cessation of effort or of sin. Adam descends the Mount of Speculation into the nether world equipped with a set of emotionally charged verbal structures that comprise his paradise. It is a paradise that is neither a *terminus a quo* nor a *terminus ad quem*, but a traveling paradise.

The paradoxes multiply within each other like the wheels of cherubim. Adam chooses to participate in history (understood as God's word), but he is to carry God's word (understood as a doctrinal abstract drawn from the narrative of biblical history) in his heart as a guide to life in history. The reflexive possibilities of these last two books, like those of *Paradise Lost* in general, stem from the underlying extralinguistic unity of Christian doctrine, from the assumption that God's word constitutes the sum of reality. Because any formulation in human language is partial, repeated formulation is useful, and there are a vast number of permutations and combinations in which doctrinal matter, paradoxical in itself, may be joined and rejoined. In consequence, Milton's epic has virtually unlimited possibilities for doctrinal discovery. *Paradise Lost* greatly surpasses its epic rivals in regard to reflexiveness. For example, just as Aeneas weeps at Dido's banquet over his own story, Milton's hero weeps over his own story but is also restored by it. A.S.P. Woodhouse commented long ago that Michael's tableaux, with their genre scenes, resembled the panels on Achilles' shield,[23] and Milton may have expected the epic tradition to suggest the latent image of a shield in Books XI and XII. It is more helpful, however, to see Michael's set pieces as reminiscent of the shield of Aeneas, which was inscribed with the history of Augustan Rome. Milton then appears to have transposed into the arena of consciousness the grand Vergilian moment when Aeneas takes up his shield and his destiny (*attollens umero famamque et fata nepotum* [*Aen.* 8.731]). When Adam internalizes the Angel's story, he too shoulders his destiny—but in an important psychological sense, Adam's storied destiny is also to be his shield.

Images, even latent ones supplied by a reader, may be helpful in explicating one aspect or another of Milton's new paradise, but no single image can define it adequately. Milton, for example, calls the repentant prayers of Adam and Eve the "first fruits" of the new paradise (11.22), but he never develops the metaphor. The image of the garden, like all visual images, is radically incommensurate with Milton's verbal paradise. No visual image can begin to convey the complexity of its shape-shifting contours, the richness of its contents, the activity by which it shapes perceptions and affections, or impels to action— much less the way it "touches" heaven. Only an exhaustive account of the dynamic processes of speech, the psychological leverage of myth, and the integrative uses of abstraction can account for such complexity, a temporal complexity almost as great as that of consciousness itself. It is little wonder that the

[23] A.S.P. Woodhouse, *The Heavenly Muse*, ed. Hugh MacCallum, Toronto, University of Toronto Press, 1972, p. 200.

syntactic transformations of this paradise, as it were, are so little understood, or that puritan *sententia* sometimes appear to be devouring myth and narrative.[24] In the seventeenth century, however, doctrinal *sententia* never left biblical narrative very far behind. Scriptural narrative could be mentally appropriated by a single doctrine, but a doctrinal tenet could just as easily exfoliate into narrative. Michael demonstrates this convertibility of the word when, at the beginning of Book XI, he expands Adam's restatement of the *protevangelium* (11.154-155) into a narrative covering all history, a narrative that is folded up again, like an accordion, into the *protevangelium* as they enter the wilderness. Eve enunciates the essential doctrine—not in abstract formula, but in the poetic phrasing of Genesis 3:15:

> This further consolation yet secure
> I carry hence; though all by mee is lost,
> Such favor I unworthy am voutsaf't,
> By mee the Promis'd Seed shall all restore.
> (12.620-623)

Here, framed with personal pronouns, is the judicial sentence that had first devastated Adam and Eve hiding under the banyan tree and that in turn had gladdened them when they saw its promissory face. Now fully explicated, it is a mnemonic key to a rich "literary" lode deposited in their memory, which in turn will serve as the hermeneutic key to future experience. Henceforth all true experience, as Luther explained, will be experience with the word.[25]

Milton's most astonishing coup occurs in the last one hundred

[24] U. Milo Kaufmann, *"The Pilgrim's Progress" and Traditions in Puritan Meditation*, New Haven, Yale University Press, 1966, p. 107.

[25] For the paradox that what one believes becomes an object of experience, but that one gains experience by what one believes, see *LW* 24.10-11 and *LW* 25.370: "For we understand things metaphysically, that is, according to the way we understand them, namely as things that are apparent and not hidden, although He has hidden His power under nothing but weakness, His wisdom under foolishness, His goodness under severity, His righteousness under sins and His mercy under wrath. Hence they do not understand the power of God when they see infirmity, etc."

lines of the poem, when the primal Promise on the lips of Eve overcomes, in a purely literary way, "Satan's perverted world." When the couple depart, the narrator declares,

the World was all before them.

The word "World," surprisingly, does not seem synonymous with "woes," as it has every right to be after Michael's recital of history. Instead, we read the line as if it were "The *future* was all before them." It is not that our awareness of woeful contingency has been annulled, but that it is now dominated by the primal Promise. Milton's narrative performs one last time the "overturning" that he claims as the perennial promise of history. Adam had wondered where, if exiled, he could see God's "blessed count'nance." Now he knows that he can always see God's face "mirrored" in promissory words—concealed under exile thus is the Kingdom of God (*LW* 25.382).

▦ 7 ▦

The Secret Agent

thoughts of things divine, are intermix'd
With scruples and do set the word itself
Against the word.
                                  (*Richard II* 5.5.12-14)

In the final books of *Paradise Lost*, Adam and Eve are armed
for the wilderness, but *Paradise Regained* shows what the battle
of the wilderness is to be like and how it is won. If the Paradise
Within consists of a heartfelt knowledge of biblical theology,
then Milton's brief epic shows why this new paradise is safe
against the thief of Eden. *Paradise Regained* is a classic example
of the Reformation tendency to refer biblical imagery and points
of salvation history to verbal action. On many occasions, Luther
stressed the word over the work of Christ and typically claimed
that the Son of God is "sent by the Father to preach, not to
fight. For He has His strength in His mouth, not a sword in
His hand" (*LW* 12.46). Michael had told Adam that the Son
would fight a duel that had no "local wounds/Of head or heel"
(*PL* 12.387-388), and in *Paradise Regained* Milton presents this
duel and depicts the Son as a verbal *vindex veritas*.

Just as in *Paradise Lost*, "Scripture" initiates the action, and
the antagonists take up their positions for battle with reference
to God's spoken words—"This is my Son belov'd" (1.85). As

199

before, Satan responds with hostility and attempted subversion. This time Milton does not indicate Christ's extraordinary power by describing a fabulous war machine, but instead leaves it conspicuously invisible. Mainly it is the power, as Calvin put it, to detect when Scripture's "meaning is wickedly corrupted and mutilated by Satan."[1] Lewalski has shown how skillful Satan is at typological exegesis and how Christ is yet more skillful at detecting misapplied typology.[2] Satan's attack, however, is not confined to perverted typology, as we see in the last round of hostilities above the temple. He hurls at Christ a verse that Calvin saw as offering assurance "to all believers" ("He will give command/Concerning thee to his Angels");[3] Christ returns fire with one from Deuteronomy 5:16 that belongs under the rubric of the law ("Tempt not the Lord thy God"). Both combatants use Scripture throughout, but in the end Satan falls by it while Christ stands. The hero's ultimate weapon, then, is not Scripture itself, nor even the Gospel rather than the Law; his secret weapon is a hermeneutic mystery.

Satan's interpretive practices, on the other hand, could well be summed up by Milton's caveats in *Christian Doctrine*. He reads God's announcement of the Son with reference to human passions, for he sees it as revealing a heavenly nepotism:

> And what will he not do to advance his Son?
> His first-begot we know, and sore have felt.
>
> (1.88-89)

Nor does Satan submit his understanding to the word (*CD*, p. 136). Instead of resting with God's words in their "literary" sense, he presses beyond the given word for metaphysical distinctions, for the precise "degree" in which the hero is God's son; and he presses for information upon which the Scripture

---

[1] *Commentary on a Harmony of the Evangelists, Matthew, Mark, and Luke,* trans. William Pringle, Edinburgh, Calvin Translation Society, 1845, I, 219, cited hereafter as *Harmony of the Evangelists.*

[2] *Milton's Brief Epic,* Providence, Brown University Press, 1966, p. 181.

[3] PR 4.455-457; Psalm 91:11-12, *Harmony of the Evangelists,* I, 219.

is notably silent—the timetable for the inauguration of the Son's kingdom.

The hero, by contrast, accepts the pronouncement, "This is my Son belov'd" (1.85), as confirmation of his identity. The detailed accounting that the hero gives of his previous study is important because much of what he allegedly "learns" during the course of the epic is known to him from the outset. He muses thus on his mother's account of the curious events at his birth:

> This having heard, straight I again revolv'd
> The Law and Prophets, searching what was writ
> Concerning the Messiah, to our Scribes
> Known partly, and soon *found of whom they spake*
> *I am*; this chiefly, that my way must lie
> Through many a hard assay even to the death,
> Ere I the promis'd Kingdom can attain,
> Or work Redemption for mankind, whose sins'
> Full weight must be transferr'd upon my head.
>
> (1.259-267, *author's italics*)

Having discovered his identity (1.259-267) from Scripture, the hero readily takes the voice issuing from the clouds and the "strong motion" leading him into the wilderness as a divine signal (1.290, 286-289). Some details about his calling are yet obscure to him because he does not know "How best" to begin the mighty work and "to what intent" he is being led into the wilderness (1.186, 291). As one might expect from Milton's penchant for complicated irony, the second puzzle is the answer to the first, for this "leading" of the Spirit is both the beginning of Christ's mighty work and its epitome. At first, however, the heroic battle of *Paradise Regained* appears to be a purely defensive one in which the Son fends off repeated attacks upon his verbally bestowed identity. Can he cling to it without knowing *precisely* what it will mean in the future?

The question is tautological because the gift of the Holy Spirit is also an important part of the hero's identity, having been conferred upon him at his baptism, together with the title "Son

201

belov'd." This gift of the Spirit is the one piece of information that Satan does not have about the hero (he has seen only a dove), but it is the one that is crucial to solving the Messianic riddle. Milton not only accepts the prevailing exegetical tradition that Christ received the donation of the Spirit at his baptism (CD, p. 551), but presents a hero whose identity is that of the unique bearer and sender of the Holy Spirit. From the outset, Milton emphasizes the role of the Spirit: there are three accounts of the Dove's descent (1.30, 83, 282), an invocation to the "Spirit who led'st this glorious Eremite/Into the Desert" (1.8-9), and at least eight references to the "leading" of the Spirit in the first hundred lines of the poem. By the time that Christ makes his first reply to Satan, it comes almost as an open admission of where his secret strength lies:

> Who brought me hither
> Will bring me hence, no other Guide I seek.
> (1.335-336)

Yet another indication, early in the poem, that Christ's secret weapon is the Holy Spirit comes when the hero penetrates the disguise of the shepherd "in rural weeds." Satan has only to speak once for Christ to observe, "I discern thee other than thou seem'st/. . . I know who thou art" (1.348, 356). The Holy Spirit was understood to provide a faculty for testing all spirits,[4] and it is no wonder that the Son never credits any of Satan's perversions of Scripture: he has ready access to what Bunyan called the Interpreter. Thus, *Paradise Regained* is an epic *a clef*, for the gift of the Spirit not only explains the hero's hermeneutic shrewdness, but also the curious emptiness of his character, the curious negative action that is so spectacularly unspectacular, and, finally, Milton's overarching didactic intent.

[4] LW 16.130; LW 26.331; Calvin, *Commentaries on the Catholic Epistles*, trans. John Owen, Edinburgh, Calvin Translation Society, 1885, pp. 230-231, and CD, p. 588.

––––––––––––––– II –––––––––––––––

The law of the kingdom [is] the gift of the
spirit.

(*CD*, p. 436)

If *Paradise Regained* presents Christ as the unique bearer of
the Spirit, it seems curious that the brief epic is Milton's least
numinous poem, and curious also that he gives the Spirit cur-
sory treatment in his doctrinal tract. It is tempting therefore
to conclude that Milton displays the growing rationalism of the
seventeenth century simply because his conception of the Holy
Spirit is far from that of Christopher Feake[5] and the mechanic
preachers of the 1640s. Milton, however, does not follow the
Cambridge Platonists in their quietist equation of the Holy
Spirit with reason. His conception is much closer to that of
Calvin, who was less concerned with affect than with the sheer
fact of, and the precise content of, belief. To be sure, a rationalist
bent was implicit in the Reformer's thought. Faith, as Luther
remarked on many occasions, has to do with what can be taught[6]
and so necessarily involves the mind and the understanding.
Milton's conception of the Holy Spirit is rationalist in this sense:
the Spirit's main work was to preside over the right grasp of
doctrine and Scripture—and over its specific application to life.
In the latter area lay the incalculable or superrational compo-
nent. Calvin and Milton put relatively little stress upon the
Spirit's promptings to specific action, but impulse to action was
to take on ever-increasing importance among the sectaries, until
the Quakers, for example, valued the Spirit's promptings be-
yond and apart from Scripture. Though little prompted to bi-
zarre actions, the Cambridge Platonists also tended to leave the

[5] See B. S. Capp, *The Fifth Monarchy Men*, London, Faber and Faber, 1972,
pp. 73, 101.

[6] See, for example, *LW* 9.184 and *LW* 16.30: "Christians cannot read the
same teaching enough." Cf. *CD*, p. 287.

203

Bible behind in favor of the Spirit, which they identified with reason and their own meditative cogitation.[7]

Milton, unlike both the Quakers and the Cambridge Platonists, saw the Spirit's work mainly as that of "literary" (biblical) enlightenment. Despite his divergence elsewhere, he remains firmly within the Calvinist tradition on this point. He may have wished to deny that the Spirit is a separate "person," but his apparent dismissal of the Spirit in doctrinal formula is belied by the extraordinary number of verses that he amasses mentioning the Spirit. The juxtapositions indicate that Milton takes "the communication of the Spirit" and Christ's "dwelling within" as equivalents.[8] The Greek verbs for "to proceed" and "to go forth," Milton notes, do not properly distinguish between the Son and the Spirit (CD, p. 298). There had been, even from the time of the Ante-Nicene Fathers, a tendency to conflate the Son with the Spirit, some scholars even suggesting that the proper term for the early doctrine of God should be "Binitarian," not trinitarian.[9] Milton had been reading the early Fathers

[7] See Ernst Cassirer, The Platonic Renaissance in England, trans. James P. Pettegrove, London, Nelson, 1953, pp. 31-45, and Hugh Barbour, The Quakers in Puritan England, New Haven, Yale University Press, 1964, p. 245.

[8] The following passage, for example, shows the kind of equivalence that Milton is making between Christ and the Spirit: "The COMMUNION which arises from this union consists of a participation, through the spirit, in all Christ's gifts and merits. John vi.56: He who eats my flesh and drinks my blood, lives in me, and I in him; Rom. viii.9: if any man has not the spirit of Christ, he is not his, and viii.32: how shall he not give us all things, also, with him?; I Cor. i.9: God is faithful, through whom you are called into the communion of his Son Jesus Christ our Lord; Eph. iii.17: that Christ may dwell in your hearts through faith; Rev. iii.20: if any man hears my voice, and opens the door, I will come in to him and will dine with him and he with me; II Cor. xiii.13: communication of the spirit (CD, p. 499).

[9] K. E. Kirk, "The Evolution of the Doctrine of the Trinity," in Essays on the Trinity and the Incarnation, ed. A.E.J. Rawlinson, London, Longmans, Green, 1933, p. 207. For a detailed discussion of the way in which doublets like "God and Christ," "God and the Spirit," and "Christ and the Spirit" predominated over trinitarian formula in the New Testament, see Harry Austryn Wolfson, The Philosophy of the Church Fathers, Cambridge, Harvard University Press, 1956, I, 155-176. Milton also notices a lack of scriptural evidence for the Trinity; cf. CD, pp. 283, 281, and 420.

during his Horton days and no doubt found confirmation there for the "Spirit-Christology" that he first encountered in the Calvinist piety of his childhood. In this tradition, the word becomes the sacramental medium when *and only when* the Holy Spirit moves the mind to understand and embrace the scriptural word, so that it is not surprising to find Milton most often mentioning the Spirit on hermeneutic matters. Every believer, he insists, is entitled to interpret Scripture for himself because "he has the spirit, who guides truth," because "he has the mind of Christ" (*CD*, p. 583). In *Paradise Regained*, Milton attempts to show how the Holy Spirit operates: "No one teaches us more plainly what the nature, source, and functions of this Holy Spirit are than the Son of God himself" (*CD*, p. 286).

The hero's first soliloquy seems designed to show the difference before and after receiving the gift of the Spirit. As Calvin explained, it was not that Jesus was without the Holy Spirit at first, but that "as man, when he commenced a warfare of so arduous a description, he needed to be armed with a remarkable power of the Spirit."[10] All his life, Milton's hero recalls, he had been "Serious to learn and know, and thence to do/What might be public good" (1.203-204):

> yet this not all
> To which my Spirit aspir'd; victorious deeds
> Flam'd in my heart, heroic acts; one while
> To rescue *Israel* from the *Roman* yoke,
> Then to subdue and quell o'er all the earth
> Brute violence and proud Tyrannic pow'r,
> Till truth were freed . . . .
>
> (1.214-220)

At Jordan, the hero lays aside these admirable plans of his own in favor of those motioned by God's Spirit. He has walked forth into the wilderness, "the Spirit leading" (1.189)—away from the world of men he knows he is to redeem. The hero lays aside not only his good plans, but even his very last desire, his desire

---

[10] *Harmony of the Evangelists*, I, 203.

to understand the divine plan—and he has done so quietly, easily, and completely. To be in the Spirit, Milton remarks in his doctrinal tract, "is also called self-denial" (CD, p. 478). Hence arises the curious emptiness of the hero's character, literarily considered, for there is an almost chilling lack of appetite, an absence of the basic claims of the self that we expect in ordinary human beings. Satan, by contrast, is full of himself.

The hero's language consistently reflects this self-emptying because, as Stanley Fish has shown, Milton's hero eschews self-assertion and refuses to claim any efficacy of his own apart from God.[11] He is a model of reticence, not to say divine cunning, being almost as silent as the speechless babe in the Nativity Ode. Indeed, one important class of temptations is that in which Satan urges Christ to speak as if he were God the Father. The very moment after the tempter has been "undisguised," he asks permission to return the next day—an innocent enough question, it would seem. To give a yes-or-no answer at this point, however, would be to rule upon the parietal privileges of an acknowledged devil. It would be to pronounce as the Almighty. But Christ sidesteps the devil's categories by referring the matter to higher authority:

> I bid not or forbid; do as thou find'st
> Permission from above; thou canst not more.
>
> (1.495-496)

The sense of power behind Christ's speeches comes partly from his refusal to assert his own authority because in rhetoric a becoming hesitancy on the part of the speaker to advance claims for himself carries great force to convince. The hero's reluctance to parade his own authority suggests enormous reserves of power, but more than a principle of rhetoric is at stake because this reluctance is bound up with his identity. *Christian Doctrine* firmly notes that in the New Testament, Christ never speaks

---

[11] "Inaction and Silence: The Reader in *Paradise Regained*," in *Calm of Mind: Tercentenary Essays on "Paradise Regained" and "Samson Agonistes" in Honor of John S. Diekhoff*, ed. Joseph Anthony Wittreich, Jr., Cleveland, Press of Case Western Reserve University, 1971, p. 36.

anything of himself or on his own account (*CD*, pp. 259-260, 265-266, 294), and Milton follows this principle in constructing the dialogue. This pattern of speech is one that the hero happens to share with the Holy Spirit, who, Milton likewise points out, never speaks anything of himself or on his own account (*CD*, pp. 276-277, 288, 292-294).

The hero's dazzling strategies for evasion, especially the "what if" construction and the semidetached aphorism, all require the reader to make large and uncertain leaps of reference. The hero's language has what one might call "oracular reach," in that it *may* include, but not necessarily so, reference to specific future events.[12] A good example of its clairvoyant resonance occurs when Satan presses the hero to seize the throne of David at once. Christ brushes him off with:

> *What if* he hath decreed that I shall first
> Be tried in humble state, and things adverse,
> By tribulations, injuries, insults,
> Contempts, and scorns, and snares, and violence,
> Suffering, abstaining, quietly expecting
> Without distrust or doubt, *that he may know*
> What I can suffer, how obey? *who best*
> *Can suffer, best can do*; best reign, who first
> Well hath obey'd; just trial e'er I merit

[12] Prevailing critical opinion finds a developing awareness in the hero. Woodhouse, in *The Heavenly Muse: A Preface to Milton*, ed. Hugh MacCallum, Toronto, University of Toronto Press, 1972, p. 328, holds that "from the experience in the wilderness [the hero] is gaining a progressively deeper insight into his own nature as well as into God's purpose"; Arnold Stein, in *Heroic Knowledge*, 1957, reprint Hamden, Conn., Archon, 1965, sees the action as "a positive process of self-definition" (p. 131). The self-knowledge is arrived at "by uniting intuitive knowledge with proved intellectual and moral discipline" (Stein, p. 17); Lewalski in *Milton's Brief Epic*, p. 162, argues: "Yet it is in Christ's consciousness, not Satan's, that real development and change take place: the challenges of the temptations provide the occasion for Christ's progress through somewhat uneven stages to a full comprehension and definition of himself and the various aspects of his role . . . ." However, Jasper Burton Weber, in *Wedges and Wings*, Carbondale, Southern Illinois University Press, 1975, contends that Milton's hero "changes only in fortune" (p. 91).

My exaltation . . . .

(3.188-197, author's italics)

Is this merely clever fencing to avoid a yes-or-no answer? Or does this passage show that under the pressure of Satan's demands Christ is learning the purpose of the wilderness venture, which was still a puzzle to him in Book II, line 245?

If only the hero had said "that he may *show* . . ." instead of *know* (3.193), one could claim that the Son has come to share the mind of the Father. God had announced that the purpose of the wilderness episode was revelation: that all "may discern/. . . [the] consummate virtue" of the Son (1.164-166). The hero's remarks, on the contrary, seem to assume a human, somewhat skeptical father who must be convinced ("that he may *know* . . ."). However provocative mention of "scorns" and "violence" and "suffering" may be to someone who knows the events of the Gospels, the passage offers no certain indication that the hero intends anything beyond the ordinary wisdom that a soldier needs to prove himself in the ranks before being promoted. Even the apparent hints of the Crucifixion cannot be said to represent a growing prescience, as they are more general than Christ's earlier musing that his "way must lie through many a hard assay even to death" (see above, p. 201). Christ's speech remains stubbornly, oracularly general. We can never say until some literary doomsday precisely what the content of his consciousness is here or elsewhere after Book II, line 245.

The generality both conceals and reveals—conceals the content of his consciousness, but reveals the power of the Spirit to foil the devil's shrewdest probing. The studied generalities force the reader to make an interpretive choice. One must decide whether the hero's speech shows a canny but very human reliance upon common sense, displays a growing clairvoyance, or simply reveals his obedience by refusing to reveal himself. Of the spheres of possible reference here—the military or political life, the unfolding of a consciousness, the temptation itself, the Crucifixion, the doctrine of faith—some are more probable than others. The first may be ruled out altogether, except as a metaphor. The second is highly problematic. But the temptation, the Crucifixion, and the doctrine of faith are concurrent possibilities. The controlling referent, however, most likely is the doctrine of faith, which happens to be the broadest one. At the end of Book II, the midpoint in the poem, Christ emphatically widens the scope of reference:

> to give a Kingdom hath been thought
> Greater and nobler done, and *to lay down*
> *Far more magnanimous than to assume.*
> (2.481-483, *author's italics*)

"Laying down" embraces both the cross and the hero's claims for himself. Man's sin, thought Calvin, is covered by Christ's obedience, an obedience stretching unbroken from the wilderness to the cross.[13] This continuity is mirrored in the general language that the hero uses to ward off Satan's queries. In speech, he enacts an immediate giving up of (claims for) the self and so prefigures future surrender of life.

This self-denying pattern suggests the solution to the great interpretive crisis of the poem. The hero's last and climactic utterance is "Tempt not the Lord thy God." Lewalski admits that the referent for "Lord" is ambiguous, but constructs a persuasive case that the hero intends himself, "that he is now given to understand . . . the full meaning of his divine sonship."[14] Ambiguity notwithstanding, there is evidence that Milton himself took "Lord" as referring to God the Father only. In *Christian Doctrine*, Milton claims that the Son's speech in the Bible displays a subservience toward the Father, and sometimes Milton has to go to great lengths to preserve the consistency of the Son's speech. For example, he argues that in the Gospels "God" and "Lord" are never applied to Christ in a

[13] Christ has abolished sin for us "by the whole course of his obedience." It is "his death and resurrection, wherein the whole of perfect salvation consists. Yet the remainder of the obedience that he manifested in his life is not excluded. Paul embraces it all from beginning to end . . . . And truly, even in death itself his willing obedience is the important thing" (*Inst.* 2.16.5).

[14] *Milton's Brief Epic*, p. 316.

context that includes the Father as well (*CD*, p. 233). When on one occasion Thomas inadvertently cries, "Jesus, my Lord and my God" (John 20:28), Milton painstakingly argues that this is not a salutation, but an "abrupt exclamation" of surprise that should be read "as if he had said, 'Lord! What do I see?' " (*CD*, pp. 239-240).

From his doctrinal tract, no less than from the hero's pattern of speech, it appears that Milton would have referred Christ's words upon the tower to the Father, so as to constitute the last and most impressive self-denial. Whether the reader sees the moment as one of self-denial or of self-affirmation, he makes a doctrinal choice. It is little wonder that critics have drawn such different conclusions about the extent of the hero's knowledge and the related question of his humanity and his divinity.[15] That Milton never resolves the ambiguity of these points may indicate that the poem, like Scripture, is designed to be read aright with the aid of the Interpreter Spirit. After all, the hero would dismiss as futile the man who reads "and to his reading brings not/A spirit and judgment equal or superior" (4.323-324). Milton's doctrinal tract supplies the main lines of what he would have considered a Spirit-guided interpretation. In it he urges us to put away metaphysical analysis and to consider Christ as he is presented in Scripture (*CD*, pp. 275, 421-422), that is, as someone who is known by his dialogue. The important question, then, concerns not his consciousness, but his verbal action. When the hero comes under verbal attack by Satan, we see not so much how Christ understands himself, but how he understands God's word.

[15] Elizabeth Pope believes that Christ knows all along about the nature of his mission and is merely baiting Satan (*Paradise Regained: The Tradition and the Poem*, Baltimore, Johns Hopkins University Press, 1947, p. 38), but Woodhouse, Stein, and Lewalski find the hero growing into a full understanding of his nature and destiny (see note, above). Don Cameron Allen, however, finds a continual fluctuation in the hero's knowledge (*The Harmonious Vision*, Baltimore, Johns Hopkins University Press, p. 118).

——————— III ———————

In great zeal and fervor of the Spirit he speaks
sheer thunderbolts.

(*LW* 27.9)

While the hero of *Paradise Regained* is utterly passive about
himself, he is assertive, even aggressive, about Holy Writ. He
lashes out boldly at Satan whenever he uses Scripture to cam-
ouflage his wicked intentions or to paint the Father as a cosmic
blackguard. Satan, of course, is attempting something much
more subtle and much more demonic than simply pressing the
hero to give away secret information. The encounter in the
wilderness should not be seen as the polite scoring of points in
debate because the psychic pressure of Satan's arguments is
truly demonic. In human terms alone, Satan's object is a chilling
one—to destroy someone's identity, to destroy his psychic in-
tegrity, to shake his grasp upon reality, to make him believe
that white is black (or that God is evil). The object here, as in
the case of brain-washing, is to create a defector.

Satan's main tactic is to try to induce guilt. At the very first
meeting, he suggests that Christ has either a guilty identity or
a mistaken identity; either he is not the Son of God after all,
or his Father is a murderer, having led his son into the valley
of death from which no one returns (1.321-325). Suggesting
guilt by association is only one of many ploys. He tries to make
the hero's own responses seem guilty. Should he refuse the
command to make instant bread from stones, he will have the
blood of the famine-starved people of the desert on his head
(1.342-345). Should he refuse the lavish banquet carried by
waitresses whom Satan describes as "All these . . . Spirits of
Air, and Woods, and Springs,/Thy gentle Ministers, who come
to pay/Thee homage" (2.374-376), Christ will violate *noblesse
oblige*. The issue varies from the guilt of broken decorum to
the guilt of being utterly useless:

211

> What dost thou in this World? The Wilderness
> For thee is fittest place.
>
> (4.372-373)

The most insidious of all Satan's tactics is his attempt to make Christ guilty with respect to the very person of the tempter. Satan poses as Pitiable Human Frailty, the outcast who pleads for one last drop of compassion,[16] for the minimal acceptance of a passing notice. "Disdain not such access to me" (1.492), he whines. Or Satan becomes embarrassingly confessional in a shrewd attempt to make his very weakness a claim upon the charity of his would-be victim (3.209-214). The virtuosity of Satan's performance in this epic is that he plays the underdog so persuasively while still Prince of the Air, to whom the idolatrous nations of the earth have been given up. Satan's virtuosity is as much temperamental as forensic, and his performance is dazzling for the quick way in which he shifts his emotional ground. He is now wistful and ingratiating, now fierce and vengeful, now merely miffed at bad manners, now threatening like Jupiter. He presents the infinite variety of the indomitable and weasel-like ego, ranging from the merest whimper of injured merit—"but I see/What I can do or offer is suspect" (2.398-399)—to the most outrageous imperial command: "fall down,/And worship me as thy superior Lord" (4.166-167). Throughout, Satan bombards Christ with his emotions, discharging the full arsenal of his subjectivity at him, until Satan seems almost to be a principle of subjectivity. And so he is, the Protean self in all his emotional guises—shame, self-pity, hatred, arrogance—always claiming something emotionally of the other. He is the principle of the Self who always deserves something, if only a response.

In the face of such an emotional barrage, Milton's hero is not so much "cold" as tough-minded. The gift of the Spirit means the power to relinquish claims for the self, but it does not mean self-castigation. Milton follows Luther in noting that one of the

---

[16] See Arnold Stein's eloquent analysis of Satan's various appeals to charity in *Heroic Knowledge*, p. 91.

prime works of the Spirit and faith is a good conscience.[17] The Spirit's power is the power to resist debilitating guilt, to prevail against all the devil's attempts "to scruple" the conscience. The marvel is that the hero can remain unmoved and untouched by Satan's repeated psychic assaults. Mere human beings, as Conrad's Lord Jim discovered, find it almost impossible *not* to identify with the guilty when they ask for compassion. Mere human beings even find it difficult to reject the imputation of a clearly specious guilt. Milton must have known this, for though he vigorously denied the printed allegations that his blindness was God's punishment, he went on to write passionate soliloquies for Samson in which he bemoans his blindness as a badge of guilt.

The hero of *Paradise Regained* never flinches, because he has access to a secret weapon against any attempt at coercive persuasion—the Holy Spirit. Milton has chosen not to probe the hero's secret inwardness, as did the puritan journals that recorded so many "heartburnings"; his concern is different from devotional poets like George Herbert and Henry Vaughan, who celebrate the Spirit's work as a heightened affect, the former in metaphors of musical consort and the latter in metaphors of sexual intimacy—"A quickness, which my God hath kist" and "the secret favors of the Dove."[18] All Milton gives us to know about the hero's feelings is that they are not confirmed by the wilderness around him. "What from within I feel myself, and hear," says the hero, "Ill sort[s] with my present state compar'd" (1.198, 200). As elsewhere in his poetry, Milton focuses upon the Spirit's work in the "objective" arena of words, and it is here that Christ joins battle with Satan, his reticence then disappearing.

Christ's tone becomes sharply combative when correcting Sa-

---

[17] *LW* 9.184; *LW* 16.310: John Calvin, *Commentaries on the Epistles of Paul the Apostle to the Philippians, Colossians, and Thessalonians*, trans. John Pringle, Edinburgh, Calvin Translation Society, 1851, p. 161. Note Milton's equation of faith and good conscience in *CD*, p. 129.

[18] "Quickness," l.20, and "To the Holy Bible," l.29, in *The Works of Henry Vaughan*, ed. L. C. Martin, Oxford, Clarendon, 1957, pp. 538, 541.

tan's poisonous versions of Scripture. A classic example occurs after Satan tries to act as if he were playing Kent's part in *King Lear*—a servant still faithful in undeserved banishment. Satan claims to have undertaken God's dirty work, though in exile:

> I came among the Sons of God when he
> Gave up into my hands *Uzzean Job*
> To prove him, and illustrate his high worth.
> (1.368-370)

Likewise, he claims that he "undertook" the "office" of drawing King Ahab into fraud (1.374). He is, for all his banishment, still man's friend:

> Men generally think me much a foe
> To all mankind: . . .
> . . . .
> [but I] lend them oft my aid,
> Oft my advice by presages and signs,
> And answers, oracles, portents and dreams,
> Whereby they may direct their future life.
> (1.387-388, 393-396)

Satan attacks again and again with ever-new and astonishingly delicate perversions of Scripture. He is a devil of many semantic tricks, the *Tausendkünstler* of Luther's commentary on Galatians.[19] He concludes this bravura performance with a stunning point. Still playing the role of Kent, he complains:

> This wounds me most (what can it less?) that Man,
> Man fall'n, shall be restor'd, I never more.
> (1.404-405)

This statement is true (at least in Milton's literary universe). Satan *is* eaten up with envy on man's account, and he will *not* be restored. By contextual manipulation, however, he manages to insinuate a terrible indictment of God into a statement that is unexceptionable in itself. After his list of "errands" done for

[19] *LW* 26.196n.

God and "divinations" made for man, Satan hopes to make the Almighty appear unjust.

In response, the hero fires forth, "Deservedly thou griev'st, compos'd of lies" (1.407). Then he proceeds to a point-by-point correction of Satan's account: the devil himself had *chosen* to be the liar in the hundred mouths of Ahab's prophets (1.427-428); and in the case of Job, God had ordered him about like a thrall. The hero asks sternly,

> Wilt thou impute to obedience what thy fear
> Extorts . . . ?
> . . . .
>   That hath been thy craft,
> By mixing somewhat true to vent more lies.
> (1.422-423, 432-433)

This is an astonishing performance, from any point of view. Christ reveals himself to be "King of Scripture."[20] Such an unerring grasp of biblical doctrine, thought Protestant divines from Luther onward, comes only from the tutelage of the Spirit, whose "wisdom hidden in a mystery" ensured purity of teaching.[21] This ability "to judge about false doctrines, about the wiles of the devil," said Luther, was given to man in his inward parts; it was a "Golden Art."[22] Interpreting Scripture, Calvin explained further, was like a fire or touchstone trying gold. It was no mechanical process and could "only be done by those who understand the art."[23] The didactic intent of the epic is to demonstrate this Golden Art of discerning doctrine in Scripture and to show that the Spirit's help is invariably forthcoming whenever doctrine comes under attack. The iron confidence with which the hero rises to correct Satan is altogether different from

[20] *LW* 16.295. Luther held that when an insoluble question arose about a passage or when the devil or "stubborn hypocrites" put forth an irrefutably evil interpretation, one should ignore the passage. Scripture was but the "servant." Christ was "Lord of Scripture" and governed its meaning.

[21] *LW* 16.118, 120.

[22] *LW* 16.119; *TT*, p. 125.

[23] *Commentaries on the Catholic Epistles*, pp. 230-231.

the doubt and bewilderment he shows when alone (cf. 1.456 and 2.245). Don Cameron Allen related these fluctuations of tone to Satan's question about the nature of the hero, concluding that Christ seemed to be crossing and recrossing the boundary between the human and the divine.[24] His analysis, however, leaves us with Satan's big question unanswered. Barbara Lewalski has paid closer attention to Christ's tonal fluctuations. She argues that the hero withstands each major temptation and thereby immediately earns an illumination regarding his role as prophet, priest, or king.[25] The difficulty is that the tradition in which Milton was reared scarcely would have entertained the notion of "earned" illuminations. The Spirit was "free" and not tied to moral reciprocity of any kind;[26] his gifts were given according to need, not merit. Far from being rewards for staunchness, illuminations *constituted* staunchness, the Sword of the Spirit being the chief weapon against Satan. The discontinuities of the hero's tone—ranging from plaintive bewilderment to icy reticence to flaming denunciation—simply reflect the discontinuities of the Holy Spirit, whose "operations" were always mysteriously apposite.

Paradise Regained, then, is to be understood as a duel between Spirit and flesh, according to Reformation categories, not neo-Platonic ones. Satan offers all the means by which the self— that is, human identity—is usually established and maintained: creature comforts, wealth, acclaim, political power, political altruism, and learned knowledge. But Satan does not merely traffic in things material. For the Reformers, the flesh had nothing strictly to do with the body. It was only the popular consciousness that made a total identification between "the flesh" and

[24] *The Harmonious Vision*, p. 118.

[25] Of Christ's announcement that the oracles have ceased, Lewalski says, "I suggest that by withstanding this first temptation directed at his prophetic office he has *merited* from God a special revelation regarding this office and that the lines just quoted [1.454-464] show him receiving it. Christ cannot call at will upon divine illumination but it is granted after he has withstood, in all human vulnerability, the test posed" (*Milton's Brief Epic*, pp. 213-214, *author's italics*).

[26] *LW* 9.184. See *CD*, p. 293.

216

the body or sexuality; "the flesh" was the principle of the self that set itself up in opposition to God. The tempter in *Paradise Regained* appeals to the flesh in this sense. Leaving aside the question of beautiful women, Satan prefers invisible temptations that aim more compellingly at the ego, that is, at the "flesh" of the Reformation. In the last temptation before the tower, Satan offers all the wisdom of the ancients, first for fame (4.221), then for education to kingship (4.281-282), and finally for self-sovereignty:

> These rules [of the ancients] will render thee
> a King complete
> Within thyself.
>
> (4.283-284)

This offer is the quintessence of the flesh: self-mastery. It is true that the hero, from one point of view, does appear to be a man of iron self-control, and Satan seems very close to the messianic secret when he offers self-mastery by the tools of learning. Yet he could not be further from hitting its true nature. Christ's kingdom is characterized not by self-mastery, but by self-abnegation or self-emptying—and hence by the government of the Holy Spirit. The inner kingdom, then, is not the fetid tower of the Stoic retired into himself, but, in Milton's tradition, an inner room with windows thrown open, as it were, to "objective truth"—to "Light from above, from the fountain of light" (4.289).

There is one further aspect of the Holy Spirit's work to be considered, the one that shapes the dramatic structure of the poem. It is what one might call "a waiting." Particularly prominent in Quaker experience, a "waiting" concerned delay in some doctrinally sanctioned task, such as preaching or testifying, until a motion to do so was given by God.[27] All through Milton's career runs the temptation to peremptory accomplishment. At twenty-three he was not mature enough for his age, and at thirty-three he is impatient because the Reformation had

---

[27] See Hugh Barbour, *The Quakers in Puritan England*, p. 113.

not yet been reformed in England. There are occasions, however, when Milton's rhetorical appeal is to the fullness of time. On the eve of the Restoration, for example, he announces a consummation of "waiting" when he writes his pamphlet against a paid clergy. "Whereof," he explains, "I promised then to speak further, when I should finde God disposing me, and opportunity inviting. Opportunity I finde now inviting; and apprehend therein the concurrence of God disposing" (*CE* 7.47).

The climax of *Paradise Regained* turns upon this notion of "waiting" at a point when lexical interpretation per se is not at issue. The word itself becomes the vehicle of temptation. From the start, the hero has known that he is to be King of David's throne. To proceed to action, however prophetically sanctioned, at the behest of Satan would be to lose the battle after all. With desperate cunning, Satan urges the surety of the prophecy: "But to a Kingdom thou art born, ordain'd/To sit upon thy Father *David's* Throne" (3.152-153). Satan then purports to throw up his hands and abandon all argument based on selfish appetite, like appeals to glory, and, as if aping Christ's stance, rests with the word itself:

> So shalt thou best fullfil, best verify
> The Prophets old, who sung thy endless reign.
> (3.177-178)

"Reign then," he concludes.

This is the most dangerous temptation thus far, and it demonstrates why the Reformers insisted that Scripture was not understood and interpreted aright in the abstract. In the application of Scripture, there was always a unique component, and the best lexical interpretation could become gross disobedience if one acted hastily upon it. Christ, however, chooses to wait and will not obey the word without the Holy Spirit: "so when [my reign shall] begin/The Father in his purpose hath decreed" (3.185-186). With each temptation it becomes clearer that "holding to the word" involves more than lexical apprehension. Right application of the word to action, or inaction as is here the case, depended upon the secret and mysterious motions of the Holy Spirit. Milton may well appear a rationalist when compared to the Ranters, but he nonetheless always reserves a small area of mystery in which the Spirit's motions cannot be deduced from Scripture.

IV

The temple was a figure of Paradise; for if
nature had remained perfect, Paradise would
have been the temple of the entire world.

(LW 1.230)

On the pinnacle of the temple, the final temptation becomes
in itself a sign that confirms and explicates the hero's identity.
At the same time there is a corresponding revelation of Satan's
strength, because he now draws most heavily upon the powers
granted to him as an evil Spirit with some scope in the world.
Ironically, he uses his supernatural powers to put the hero into
a *physical* dilemma. Though Satan's tone ("To stand up-
right/Will ask thee skill" [4.551-552]) indicates that standing
on the pinnacle is a feat humanly impossible, the conditions of
Christ's physical footing do not touch the main issue, or Milton
would have clarified them. What is important is that the hero,
once he is placed atop the temple, is physically *within* Satan's
power when he commands, "Now show thy Progeny; if not to
stand,/Cast thyself down" (4.554-555). Christ no longer can
deny Satan's either/or categories by making a rhetorical side-
step. Standing and falling exhaust the alternatives of nature.
Human and corporeal, Christ must, according to the categories
of the natural world, either stand or fall. Yet anything he *does*
will be obeying Satan. Here Milton presents the ultimate terror,
not a physical one, but the terror of facing an infallible temp-
tation. The ultimate invitation to despair is to see an inescapable
trap in the conditions of life, to conclude that life in the world
necessarily defeats faith.

What the hero does, without showing the slightest flicker of
disquiet, much less terror at his impossible position, is to rely
upon his usual weapons—the word and the Spirit. He merely
says:

Also it is written,
Tempt not the Lord thy God; he said and stood.
(4.560-561)

This reply is the most spectacular of Christ's verbal self-denials, for the hero once again defers to higher authority. Yet his reply combines both humble passivity and a militant defense· of the word. Satan has offered the scriptural promise of ministering angels, not as a reward for faith, but as a lure toward presumption. When the hero repudiates this application of Scripture, the poisonous exegete falls away in amazement, leaving the temple, the mind, and the Paradise Within to the exalted Christ. "The true holy water with which to exorcise the Devil," Luther was wont to say, is God's word and Spirit. [28]

The episode demonstrates that the Spirit and the word triumph over the categories of common experience, over all the conditions of corporeal existence. A single speech motioned by the Spirit triumphs over all the realm of nature. This point seems to be confirmed by the epic simile immediately following, in which Milton compares the triumph of his epic hero to that of Hercules, who had strangled Anteus in the air (4.563-572)—a triumph, common enough in Renaissance allegory, for the victory of the spirit over the flesh. [29] The second simile, suggesting much the same point, sets the fall of Satan parallel to that of the Sphinx, who had devoured the Thebans when they could not solve his riddle. Oedipus had at last supplied the answer "man," at which the Sphinx, defeated, cast himself headlong down the Ismenian steep (4.572-580). In a similar way, Satan is cast down from the temple in defeat when Christ answers the tempter's question aright. But wherein exactly does the correctness of the Son's answer lie? What answer does he in fact give Satan?

---

[28] Cited by Roland H. Bainton, *Here I Stand*, New York, Abingdon-Cokesbury, 1950, p. 337. Luther claims throughout his work that the Devil is "overcom with God's Word and *Spirit*" (*TT*, p. 379).

[29] Carey and Fowler, p. 1164n.

221

The question that Satan poses as he brings Christ to the tower
has three variants following hard upon each other:

> In what degree or meaning [art thou] call'd
> The Son of God, which bears no single sense?
> (4.516-517)

Milton apparently does not intend the same answer that Oedipus
gave the Sphinx. His hero has just denied that the wisdom and
literature of the ancients hold any useful answers to life: "what
can they teach, and not mislead" (4.309)? Since Christ does not
answer the question, Satan refines it:

> I beforehand seek
> To understand my Adversary, who
> And what he is; *his wisdom, power, intent* . . . .
> (4.526-528, *author's italics*)

Again, Christ stands silent; but for the reader, the question as
formulated here is easy enough. The hero's wisdom is that of
the Holy Spirit; his power also comes from that source. And
as to his intent, we have seen that all Christ's noble purposes
have been given up to the intents and purposes of the Holy
Spirit. Because the hero is still silent, Satan poses his question
one last time, sharpening its metaphysical cast:

> *what more* [art thou] *than man,*
> Worth naming Son of God by voice from Heav'n . . . ?
> (4.538-539, *author's italics*)

What more than man? Christ never answers the question—and
thereby answers it. What more than man? The Holy Spirit who
never speaks anything of himself.

The tacit answer that Milton gives to Satan's question is a
brilliantly tactful one because it sidesteps the categories of "God"
and "man" and all metaphysical analysis based upon "hypos-
tasis," an approach that Milton denigrated (and according to
Lewalski, also misunderstood).[30] If Milton could not quite bring

---

[30] Milton notes that there is "not a single word in the Bible about the mystery

himself to see Christ in an orthodox way as coessential with the Father, he does see the Son as possessing the Spirit in no "measurable degree" (CD, p. 265). Not even an orthodox Calvinist could object. Milton goes on to add, however, on the authority of I John 2:20, that "the faithful also are said to know all things" by the Spirit—a position that nevertheless owes much to Calvin's christology.

Milton may eschew the Crucifixion as a poetic subject because Royalist apologetics link the martyrdom of Charles I with the passion and death of Christ,[31] but if so, political considerations were underscored by Calvinist habits of thought. Like Calvin, Milton seems to assume that it is Christ's total obedience— through life and death—which covers man's sin. This assumption allows the poet Milton to present the temptation as a synecdoche of the mediator's sacrifice and to focus less upon the hero's unique action than upon the dangers and weapons shared with all believers. To show Christ in the wilderness, rather than on the cross, is consonant with the tradition that puts much more emphasis upon overcoming sin than overcoming death. According to Calvin, Christ was tempted "as the public representative of all believers." The Son chose "to sustain assaults in common with us, that we might be furnished with *the same armour*, and might entertain no doubt as to achieving the victory." Hence we are to understand that our temptations are not "accidental," but that "the Spirit of God presides over our contests as an exercise of our faith."[32] This tradition takes a pneumatological view of the Son, presenting him as the prime bearer and sender of the Spirit, an identity suggested by the hero's prophecy about Pentecost:

---

of the Trinity" (CD, p. 420), and in regard to the earthly Christ one should "pay attention only to [clear] texts" and be "willing to be satisfied with the simple truth, ignoring the glosses of metaphysicians" (p. 421); Lewalski, *Milton's Brief Epic*, pp. 138-139.

[31] Florence Sandler, "Icon and Iconoclast," *Achievements of the Left Hand: Essays on the Prose of John Milton*, eds. Michael Lieb and John T. Shawcross, Amherst, University of Massachusetts Press, 1974, p. 183.

[32] *Harmony of the Evangelists*, I, 210, 214 (*author's italics*), 210.

God hath now sent his *living Oracle*
Into the World to teach his final will,
And sends his Spirit of Truth henceforth to dwell
In pious Hearts, an *inward Oracle*
To all truth requisite for men to know.
                              (1.460-464, *author's italics*)

Christ in this tradition, moreover, is more Promise than example, for "set forth in Him [are all] the virtue and power of the Holy Ghost" and "all the treasures of wisdom" that accrue to the believer.[33] The Son displays more clearly in life than in death what Milton terms "the gift of God, peculiar to the gospel" (*CD*, p. 524). It is this promise that Milton, aware of his "power beside the office of the pulpit," is proclaiming in *Paradise Regained*. He attempts no metaphysical definition of the incarnate Christ nor even provides any clear line of demarcation between the Messiah and the ordinary Christian. What is important is to demonstrate the gift that they share—"For as many as are led by the Spirit of God, they are the sons of God" (Romans 8:14).

[33] According to Calvin's doctrine, *insitio in Christum*, one would view Christ, the literary character of the Gospels, with proprietary eyes: "When we become possessed of this knowledge that the Son of God is joined to us, we should cast our eyes upon that which is so highly set forth in Him . . ." (*The Mystery of Godliness and Other Selected Sermons*, p. 22).

⬛ 8 ⬛
Peculiar Grace

I

Some I have chosen of peculiar grace
Elect above the rest . . .
(PL 3.183-184)

Samson, David, and many other celebrated men
who were full of the Holy Spirit fell into huge
sins. Job and Jeremiah curse the day of their
birth: Elijah and Jonah are tired of life and
pray for death. Such errors and sins of the
saints are set forth in order that those who
are troubled and desperate may find comfort.
. . . No man has ever fallen so grievously that
he could not have stood up again.
(LW 26.109)

In *Samson Agonistes*, Milton most artfully exploits the pos-
sibilities of the Protestant hermeneutic so that the line of dra-
matic action is bold and simple, yet has a pervasive oracular
character. More than any other work by Milton, this drama is
amenable to alternate routes of interpretation, both at moments
of allusive density and at times when the dramatic action is
considered as a whole. The drama may appear to be a retreat

from Christian affirmation toward a more profound and dread accounting of life's darkness, it may appear as a typological affirmation of the ultimate victory of Christ, or it may be taken as the legend of a Hebrew hero who is an honorary puritan saint. In Milton's treatment, however, the latter line of interpretation dominates and subsumes the first two interpretive routes.

At the end of his career, Milton is still unseating pagan oracles just as he was when he wrote the Nativity Ode. In casting the story of Samson in the form of "Greek tragedy," he manages to make the genre itself "speak" doctrine. The use of Sophoclean form establishes, tacitly and immediately, the power and supremacy of Jehovah's oracle. Milton thereby avoids the poetic liabilities of God's generalized speech in *Paradise Lost*, as well as the theological dangers of attempting to contain the Almighty within the shape of any literary "character." When Samson's promise is given at a flaming altar (23-29), Milton at once suggests something about the mysterious way in which God's promise presides over the hero's life, suggests that its transcendent power can neither be evaded by human ingenuity nor understood by human reason. The Judeo-Christian oracle, unlike the remote word of Zeus, is personally demanding. It is not enough to refrain from trying to circumvent it; God requires both specific deeds and inner motions. It called Samson to faith, discipline, and action, and finally wins out in both the arena of history and in the consciousness of the hero.

Milton examines closely the way in which God's oracle presides over the conscious experience of his hero. In the Old Testament story of Samson, Milton found a hero, like Adam, whose identity and consciousness had been molded early by God's word; Milton found a story in which God's promise is very specific regarding the hero's life; and Milton found a hero of martial accomplishment (131-132) who at first is completely faithful to the task demanded by the oracle. Though it is tempting to see Samson's sin as that of mistaking a sensual impulse for a divine one,[1] God's word is the measure of human sin in this drama just as it is in Milton's other major poems. Milton is explicit that Eve, whatever her spousal demerits, is "sinless" until she breaks God's one prohibition. Conversely, fidelity to God's pronouncement from the clouds in *Paradise Regained* is accompanied by a supernatural feat of endurance. In *Samson Agonistes*, Milton adjusts the scriptural account so that the hero's sin will be defined as an offense against God's word and so that his ultimate triumph (like that of old Oedipus at Colonus) will be defined by his embrace of the oracle. In the biblical account God does not require Samson to keep his Nazarite vow a secret, but Milton invents, or assumes one, so that the hero's violation of a divine injunction will constitute his great lapse.

Just as in *Paradise Lost*, divine and creaturely words compete for the mind of a saint. Samson confesses that he has been "vanquisht with a peal of words" (235), because Dalila's "Tongue batteries," like those of the Wife of Bath, had come "at times when men seek most repose and rest" (406). Both Manoa (428-429) and Samson see the offense clearly as one of breaking a divine injunction to silence:

> [I] have profan'd
> The mystery of God giv'n me under pledge
> Of vow, and have betray'd it to a woman,
> A *Canaanite*, my faithless enemy.
> (377-380)

Samson's fall remains something of a mystery even to himself because he clearly understood the issues involved and never intended to betray God (392-399), yet succumbed to provocation anyway. Violating God's injunction nevertheless estranges Samson from every tenet of his oracle. How can a blind man

[1] See, for example, Irene Samuel, "*Samson Agonistes* as Tragedy," *Calm of Mind: Tercentenary Essays on 'Paradise Regained' and 'Samson Agonistes' in Honor of John S. Diekhoff*, ed. Joseph Anthony Wittreich, Jr., Cleveland, Press of Case Western Reserve University, 1971, p. 250.

in prison become God's deliverer of Israel? It is precisely Samson's despair over the "impossible" promise that makes him an honorary puritan saint, for Samson's dilemma intertwines the great existential questions of Protestant piety: the persistence of sin and infidelity despite the most earnest of commitments and the "contradiction" that God's promise poses to ordinary human experience. Milton uses the story of Samson, just as Luther used the story of Abraham and the sacrifice of Isaac, to pose the problem of faith in "literary" terms: how can the "contradictory" oracle come true (*LW* 4.95)? Luther imagines Abraham on the way to Mount Moriah explaining the problem thus—"Isaac will be the seed and father of kings and of peoples; Isaac will die and will not be the father of peoples. Those contradictory statements cannot be reconciled by any human reason or philosophy. But the Word reconciles these two" (*LW* 4.113). At the beginning of *Samson Agonistes*, the oracle appears just as unfathomable as God's command to Abraham, but the story of Samson puts the contradiction of God's word even more sharply because the "impossible" word is not countermanded by a second one, as when Abraham is told to substitute the ram in the thicket for Isaac on the altar. Samson's oracle ultimately calls for an interpretive *metanoia*, or turnabout, of the sort that Luther's Abraham provisionally ponders: "he who is dead lives, and he who lives dies . . . . We are reckoned as dead because of sin, and though we have died, we are reckoned as living" (*LW* 4.113).

The Chorus, who serves a number of standard dramatic functions, like furnishing exposition and intensifying community reaction to events, has the important theological function of providing a negative definition of God's word. The Chorus wavers like Shakespeare's vulgar or like leaves on the surface of a stream. Immersed in the flotsam and jetsam of history, the Chorus provides the perfect foil for the immutability, transcendence, and inscrutable clarity of Jehovah's word. Most of all, their reasonable judgments and their grasp of experience by prudent aphorisms make an important contrast to the way in which Samson relates all experience to God's promise. The Chorus admirably demonstrates the triviality of human reason in the face of ultimate issues and marks the distance between a reasonable grasp of experience and the paradoxical depths that Samson discovers in God's Providence.

For the first time, Milton succeeds in showing by literary means that God's word is a source of poetic energy and power. Nothing could be clearer than God's promise that Samson will deliver his nation, but nothing could be more mysterious than the overt and covert means by which it is fulfilled. Nor could anything be more equivocal than the personal gain and loss involved in its working out. Oedipus was promised by his oracle that he would become King of Thebes, and this good fortune came true in tandem with the commission of violence and out-rage. The accomplishment of Samson's oracle similarly will have an unforeseen component of terror, pain, and loss. Milton com-bines the oracular ironies of *Oedipus Rex* with those of *Oedipus at Colonus*, because Samson's martial triumphs issue in a great loss that will yield yet another great loss and triumph. In *Areo-pagitica*, Milton saw life confidently as a contest in which virtue grows and flourishes upon trial by what is contrary, but here he sees life less as a series of ethical trials than as enduring the contradictions—or paradoxes—at the heart of his biblical faith. From an early confidence in the powers of human reason and choice, Milton moves in his last work toward a recognition of human failure in which the mystery of the human will is as dark as the mystery of Providence[2]—and hence arrives at a profound submission to the power of God's oracle.

[2] For a different view, see Mary Ann Radzinowicz, who finds Milton moving away from a "passive" acceptance of God's word toward "the assertion of reason" and an emphasis upon "the superiority of rationality" (*Toward 'Samson Agonistes': The Growth of Milton's Mind*, Princeton, Princeton University Press, 1978, p. 354). For a critical review of the arguments that Gilbert, Parker, and Shawcross give for an early dating of *Samson Agonistes*, see pp. 387-407. Radzinowicz adduces autobiographical and historical references for a Restoration date (pp. 403-407) that seem to me to comprise the more probable case. If so, there emerges a progression in Milton's canon from an analytic to a synthetic treatment of the character of the divine and the demonic, as I discuss below.

II

Purgatory is other people.
(Anonymous)

Decoction of the adder's tongue is sovereign
for the bite of the adder.
(Seventeenth-century Herbal)

At the beginning of the drama, Samson's fall has left him scornful of the oracle and estranged from his God, whom he sees as a liar, or worse. Samson's picture of the Almighty fluctuates and shifts, demonstrating the principle *fides facet personam*, for his view of the Almighty mirrors the state of his own soul, not the God who watches over Israel without slumber or sleep. Considered as dramatic action, *Samson Agonistes* is a Protestant *Purgatorio* during which all the hero's sin is purged— all the negative views of God, all the negative attitudes and psychic dodges that stand between him and a full embrace of his oracle. Samson's sin is purged, not by moral effort and penitential tasks, but by experience in this life mysteriously arranged by God. Milton is interested in Samson's story primarily as *theologia pectoris*, as the drama of a fallen saint, whose most straitened circumstances and blackest moods are ordered by God's Providence so that they work his recovery. Both the hero's despair and the providential workings to which he is quite blind are rendered intelligible by the Protestant hermeneutic as "Christian" experience. (Only at the conclusion will Milton overtly invoke typology, or conceptual analogy of Samson's life with the central event of the New Dispensation).

From the very first, Milton reminds us that he is presenting an "opened" version of Old Testament history when he weaves a vocabulary of Pauline doctrine into the fabric of dialogue and incident. For example, the concern of Manoa and Dalila over the question of ransom and intercession (604, 920) reminds us of the metaphysical mechanics by which Samson is presumed to gain eternal life. When Samson bemoans his blindness and complains that he is exempt from God's prime decree (85), the reader remembers that in Milton's accounting, God's prime decree concerns the Son rather than physical sunlight ("This day I have begot whom I declare . . ." [PL 5.603]). Similarly, at the close of the drama, when the maidens are summoned to wash the hero's body (1725-1728), we are reminded that Samson's sin is understood to have been washed away by "the blood of the Lamb slain from the foundation of the world" (cf. CE 15.403-405). The doctrinal vocabulary never yields a consistent allegory, but it does provide the latent instruments for analyzing Samson's experience in Christian terms. This Old Testament saint's legend offers a pastoral simplification, as it were, because it focuses upon the central issue of Christian experience—belief in God's promises—without overt consideration of catechetical matters or discussion of the metaphysical mechanics by which the Crucifixion rendered faith salvific in any age. The constant pressure of doctrinal allusion in *Samson Agonistes* emphasizes the metonymic connection (via the doctrine *insitio in Christum*) between the hero's faith and the Christ of the Incarnation.

Samson's first speech, for example, contains a doctrinal allusion that is particularly important for understanding the drama. In a way that recalls the opening of Dante's *Purgatorio*,[3] Samson comments upon "The breath of Heav'n fresh-blowing, pure and sweet,/With day-spring born" (10-11). This remark, taken together with his instruction to the boy—"A little onward lend thy guiding hand" (1)—intimates that "Heav'n's breath," or the Holy Spirit, is to guide the blind hero through the encounters that follow, though perforce nothing explicit can be said of the Spirit's hidden work. Both Luther and Calvin were convinced that the Holy Spirit moved in the lives of the patriarchs, and Milton may have chosen the story of Samson because it lent itself well to the theme of "divine impulsion." The account

---

[3] In Canto I, l.20, of the *Purgatorio*, Dante rejoices over having emerged from the "dead air" (*de l'aura [aria] morta*, l.17) into the freshening dawn that was "making the whole East smile" (*faceva tutto rider l'oriente*).

in the Book of Judges introduces each of Samson's feats with some variant of the formula "And the Spirit of the Lord came upon Samson . . ." (Judges 13:25; 14:6, 19; 15:14, 19). In any case, the climax of each of Milton's major works turns upon a well-known "operation" of the Spirit. In *Paradise Lost*, Adam's redemption coincides with the "opening" of his oracular sentence (10.1028-1095); in *Paradise Regained*, the hero's victory coincides with a "waiting" for a motion to act on his scriptural authority to reign (3.396-397); and in *Samson Agonistes*, the climax coincides with God's "leading" the hero to perform a specific and unexpected action of deliverance (1382-1389).

At the beginning, however, Samson is in no condition to respond consciously to any "leading" of the Spirit. Hence the Spirit's immediate therapeutic work is a homeopathic cure[4] administered by Samson's visitors, though disguised under the "realism" of their ego-concerns—family pride, female power,

---

[4] James Holly Hanford first applied Milton's prefatory remarks on purgation to the action of the drama, pointing out that it contained an Aristotelian diagnosis of Samson's tragic plight as a lingering disease that must find purgation "in deeds" ("*Samson Agonistes* and Milton in Old Age," *Studies in Shakespeare, Milton, and Donne, by Members of the English Department of the University of Michigan*, 1925, reprinted in *Twentieth Century Interpretations of Samson Agonistes*, ed. Galbraith M. Crump, Englewood Cliffs, N.J., Prentice-Hall, 1968, pp. 30-31. Arthur Barker sees the temptations, like that of Manoa's offer of ransom, to be parodic versions of his own earlier acts, with the central theme being dispensation from the law ("Structural and Doctrinal Pattern in Milton's Later Poems: *Samson Agonistes*," *Essays in English Literature from the Renaissance to the Victorian Age presented to A.S.P. Woodhouse*, 1964, reprinted in *Twentieth Century Interpretations*, p. 81). Arnold Stein mentions in passing that the homeopathic principle is at work but focuses upon Samson's temptations to espouse an inferior morality (*Heroic Knowledge*, Minneapolis, University of Minnesota Press, 1957, pp. 137-213; especially 210). Martin E. Mueller centers his discussion upon the purgation of Samson's death, citing T. S. Eliot's "Little Gidding" as a gloss for Milton's Phoenix image: "The only hope, or else despair/Lies in the choice of pyre or pyre—/To be redeemed from fire by fire" ("*Pathos* and *Katharsis* in *Samson Agonistes*," *ELH*, 31, 1964, 167). Raymond B. Waddington ("Melancholy Against Melancholy: *Samson Agonistes* as Renaissance Tragedy," *Calm of Mind*, pp. 259-287), works out the details of Barker's view and adds an analysis of Samson's despair according to the Renaissance theory of melancholy.

officious curiosity. In doctrinal terms, the drama traces the up-
ward, though somewhat jagged, course of Christian sanctifica-
tion,[5] as "like purges like." The homeopathic process, however,
is but one figure in the carpet, and until recently critical atten-
tion has focused upon the threat and temptation that each visitor
represents. Now, however, so many likenesses have been noted
between Samson and his visitors that it is hard to find any moral
difference between them. That Samson and his enemies are so
much alike in conventional moral terms[6] makes it clear that it
is only their relation to God's word that differentiates them.
After all, it is a given of the legend that God has called Israel
to be a peculiar people and Samson to be his Nazarite and chosen
champion. The hero is right or wrong, innocent or guilty, ac-
cording to the way in which he responds to God's Promise.
Though Samson's homeopathic cure raises strong passions that
are quelled or converted,[7] the curative process is verbally me-
diated and works precisely and inexorably along the sinews of
the dialogue.

We shall chart its course in some detail, not merely to show
how Dr. Johnson missed the chain of causation that gives the
drama its structure, but to show how God works "through the
creatures" verbally. *Samson Agonistes* is a logomachy between

[5] See John M. Steadman's view that "Samson is actually conforming to the
law of the Spirit" in " 'Faithful Champion': The Theological Basis of Milton's
Hero of Faith," *Anglia*, 77 (1959), reprinted in *Milton: Modern Essays in
Criticism*, ed. Arthur E. Barker, New York, Oxford University Press, 1965, p.
471.

[6] Irene Samuel, for example, in "*Samson Agonistes* as Tragedy," *Calm of
Mind*, severely criticizes Samson's moral discernment: "We have to observe
that the most profoundly evil of the Philistine Lords did not kill their murderous
enemy when they could have" (p. 252).

[7] See Sherman Hawkins, "Samson's Catharsis," *Milton Studies*, 2 (1970),
211-230. He also finds homeopathy to be the key structural principle (p. 223),
but focuses upon the visitors as tempters, each of whom rouses in Samson a
tragic passion—Manoa seeks to comfort his son, Dalila hopes to evoke Samson's
pity, and Harapha tries to excite Samson's fear. Hawkins emphasizes a con-
version, not a purgation, of the passions: "Self-pitying remorse becomes a true
repentance, wrath turns to righteous indignation, contentious pride to zeal for
Israel's God" (p. 224).

God's promise and human ones, during which the hero's rehabilitation is concealed under the uneven shape of personal crises concerning parental overprotection, marital failure, and the collapse of a career. The promises that the visitors offer him in his troubles—political intercession and ransom, paternal coddling, or connubial indulgence—are ones that do not touch Samson's real need, which goes to the core of his identity. If Samson were to accept any of these promises of help, it would constitute a final renunciation of God's oracle in favor of someone else's design for his life. Thus, his rejection of the human promises is important because he thereby avoids the final pitfall, and at least keeps the residual faith that makes his consciousness so painful.

All the while, a relentless homeopathic cure is at work, for Samson's affirmations come when, and only when, the speeches of his visitors echo his despairing thoughts. To show the relentless way in which Samson's cure proceeds apace whenever homeopathic theory obtains, we shall have to ignore for a moment a great deal of what the visitors say. None of them is merely a mirror of Samson. Though Milton's play was never intended for the stage and is a forerunner of symbolic dramas like *Manfred* and *Prometheus Unbound*, its personae remain "historical" characters with a distinct life of their own. The care that Milton takes to establish their individuality is important to a major theme: the working out of grace within the particulars of personal and national history. Milton demonstrates the simplicity of divine intention working contrary to and yet through complex human intention. In *Paradise Lost*, Sin and Death believe they are drawn over the causeway from chaos by mystic affinity with Satan, though we see Providence drawing them to help effect an Eden happier far. Similarly, we see Dalila come to Samson from dubious motives—it matters little whether they be anxious guilt, lust for female power, or outright malice—and help return the hero to his destined role. Unlike Adam in *Paradise Lost*, Books XI and XII, the reader of Milton's Greek tragedy must "observe God's providence" on his own without the prompting of an angelic interpreter.

Before we chart Samson's cure, a word must be said about his disease—a desperate guilt that has shattered his identity. In a moment of stress, one lapse has turned the champion into a traitor. Samson has acquired a negative identity, that is, one consisting of images diametrically opposed to what his rearing has taught him to be and one that he never can become with his whole heart.[8] Samson cannot deny the fact of betrayal, for he lives with the consequences—darkness and chains—but he resists his guilty identity nonetheless. Repeatedly, he thrusts the blame elsewhere, questioning God's providence both in regard to history and in regard to himself. He complains of nothing less than a divine betrayal:

> Why was my breeding order'd and prescrib'd
> As of a person separate to God,
> Design'd for great exploits; if I must die
> Betray'd, Captiv'd, and both my Eyes put out,
> Made of my Enemies the scorn and gaze;
> To grind in Brazen Fetters under task
> With this Heav'n-gifted strength? O glorious strength
> Put to the labor of a Beast, debas't
> Lower than bondslave! Promise was that I
> Should *Israel* from *Philistian* yoke deliver . . . .
>   (30-39)

Samson's image of God is shattered together with his cherished image of himself, but he cannot wholeheartedly entertain doubts about God, for something of the champion still remains to plague him. The hero's identity, like Adam's, is bound up with "Divine Prediction" (44) and his consciousness rests upon the memory of receiving a "command from Heav'n/To free my Country" (1212-1213). The assumptions of faith therefore remain to define his despair and intensify his pain. In this tradition, despair is always related to faith because it provides the reasonable framework that faith must defy.

---

[8] See Erik H. Erikson, *Young Man Luther: A Study in Psychoanalysis and History*, New York, Norton, 1962, p. 102.

Samson's torn identity manifests itself as a contest of voices echoing the cosmic adversaries of Milton's earlier poems. Samson's first voice is reminiscent of the stern God in *Paradise Lost*, Book III: "That plea therefore/With God or Man will gain thee no remission" (834-835). The other voice fluctuates between the injured merit of Satan in *Paradise Lost*, Book I ("Promise was . . ." he says over and over) and the extreme self-denigration of the Tempter in *Paradise Regained* ("the vilest here excel me . . . " [74]). With the first voice, Samson rages against himself with ever fresh accusation; with the second voice, he thrusts the blame away. But guilt hounds him, regardless of whether he thinks at the moment like a champion or a failure. Before Samson can function again, he must both accept *and* reject his negative identity. Presumably the contest of his interior voices would have gone on endlessly if there were no visitors to interrupt.

The cure begins with the arrival of the Chorus. None of the platitudes that they offer as "Balm to fester'd wounds" has any salutary effect. Their advice—"Deject not then so overmuch thyself" (213)—only exacerbates Samson's despair, setting him off on a tirade of bitter self-condemnation. When, however, the weak-minded Chorus forgets its nostrums and joins for a moment the current of Samson's thinking, they unwittingly administer the first drop of physic. When they recall an entire catalog of God-appointed leaders whose efforts, like Samson's, were foiled by tribal politics, he perceives that the Chorus has joined him in taxing divine disposal and counters with his first, qualified affirmation: "Of such examples add mee to the roll,/Mee easily indeed mine may neglect,/But God's propos'd deliverance not so" (290-292).

Manoa provides even stronger physic, for his outpouring of despair over the family disgrace more nearly matches Samson's in its intensity. Like his son, he makes a perfunctory avowal of human guilt, which subtly gives way to blaming God. Recalling his son's past exploits, Manoa cries:

O ever failing trust
In mortal strength! and oh, what not in man
Deceivable and vain! Nay, what thing good
Pray'd for, but often proves our woe, our bane?

(348-351)

Here "Deceivable and vain" seems to encompass both Samson
as Dalila's dupe and Manoa as God's dupe. Manoa not only
restates Samson's paradox of the accursed blessing in general
terms, but goes far beyond him in imputing sheer malignity to
the heavens. Whereas the son had merely accused God of or-
dering events to no purpose, the father cries out against God
as a cosmic sadist:

Why are his gifts desirable; to tempt
Our earnest Prayers, then, giv'n with solemn hand
As Graces, draw a Scorpion's tail behind?

(358-360)

The quarrel with God that Samson had framed as a question,
Manoa states boldly as a moral judgment: God "should not so
o'erwhelm" his chosen champion (370).

It is precisely when confronted with his own outrage against
God, made explicit on the lips of his father, that Samson first
firmly exculpates the Almighty:

Appoint not heavenly disposition, Father,
Nothing of all these evils hath befall'n me
But justly; I myself have brought them on,
Sole Author I, sole cause. . . .

(373-376)

Manoa also presents Samson with his own doubts concerning
God's governance of history, as they are amplified in the mouths
of the populace, both Philistine and Hebrew. Despair of God's
national providence had been implicit in Samson's earlier la-
ment. Now Samson meets his doubts writ large in the com-
munity—the Almighty "Disglorified, blasphem'd, and had in

237

scorn" (442). Only when Manoa shows Samson his doubt raised to the level of public consensus is he roused to give a ringing affirmation of God's power over history:

> [God], be sure,
> Will not connive, or linger, thus provok'd,
> But will arise and his great name assert:
> *Dagon* must stoop . . . .
>
> (465-468)

These ringing tones are far different from the uncertain way in which he earlier had defended national providence with a qualifying "haply," and indeed strike Manoa as "a Prophecy."

From this time forth, Samson never blames God nor doubts his power, but his cure is far from complete. His trust in Providence is historical rather than personal, and his guilt has been enlarged to include betrayal of all the "feeble hearts, propense enough . . ./To waver" in the wake of his apostasy (455-456). Hitherto, Samson's guilt has been primarily that of having betrayed himself; now he begins to feel deep guilt with respect to his people. But such staggeringly inclusive guilt he will not take on himself. He is still torn between blaming himself and excusing himself. Doggedly, he determines to remain in prison in order to expiate his guilt, but resorts nevertheless to a much more subtle strategy for evading it. He begins to particularize the' extent of his provocation in an attempt to show how the "importunity" he met provides an extenuation (393-410). Samson's self-exculpation and self-condemnation appear more deadly now. Compared to his first manly rage against God, this querulous recital of provocations smacks of the infantile, being very like the child crying that the table should not have been allowed to hit him. Samson's despair is likewise more devastating. It is terrible enough to give God a guilty face, but even more terrible to give God a closed, averted face—to have a "sense of Heav'n's desertion" (632). Of course, God's supposed wrath and his supposed rejection of the champion say nothing about God.

Just when prognostication for Samson's cure seems darkest, Dalila arrives with potent medicine. In her appeal, excuse comes

prologue to offers of renewed domesticity, and it is her excuse
that proves therapeutic. Like Samson, she purports to accept
full blame for betraying a trust. She asserts that she "merited,
without excuse," the severest condemnation (734) and protests
that she has no wish "To lessen or extenuate [her] offense"
(767), but very much like Samson she begins to expatiate upon
her great provocation. Her recital of the "aggravations" (769),
the "importuning" (797), and the "assaults" (845) of the Phil-
istine elders echoes Samson's rhetoric of the "importunity"
(397), the interminable "feminine assaults" and "Tongue bat-
teries" (404, 403) that he had met from Dalila. Indeed, she
seizes upon weakness in the face of extreme provocation as a
point of common identity:

> Let weakness then with weakness come to parle
> So near related, or the same of kind,
> Thine forgive mine; *that men may censure thine*
> *The gentler*, if severely thou exact not
> More strength from me, than in thyself was found.
> (785-789, *author's italics*)

She is really asking for excuse, not forgiveness. The antifeminist
chorus is right in one sense: insofar as Dalila represents the
effeminacy of wallowing in excuse, she is the primal enemy of
man in need of regeneration. But providential homeopathy here
leads Samson to reject in cruel and irrevocable terms his own
plea of extenuation:

> Such pardon therefore as I give my folly,
> Take to thy wicked deed . . . .
> . . . .
> All wickedness is weakness: that plea therefore
> With God or Man will gain thee no remission.
> (825-826, 834-835)

Once Samson has denounced weakness as a spurious plea, he
never utters another word of excuse. In acknowledging kinship
with Dalila the betrayer, but in denying identity with Dalila
the self-excuser, he has made significant progress toward whole-

ness. Indeed, by the time she finally gets round to the matter of Samson's welfare, her providential work has been done. Her proffers of "domestic ease" and her proposal to intercede with the elders have no further effect upon Samson's spiritual recovery. The hero's final response to his wife indicates what yet has to be purged from his diseased soul. He sees her visit, not as part of a divine cure, but as further evidence of God's repudiation: "God sent her to debase me,/And aggravate my folly" (999-1000).

In view of the homeopathic principle at work, it is not surprising that Harapha, whose speeches reflect those of Samson to an extraordinary degree, works the most spectacular part of the cure. Much like Samson's opening soliloquy, Harapha's first speech reveals his pride of name and national identity:

> I am of *Gath*;
> Men call me *Harapha*, of stock renown'd
> As *Og* or *Anak* and the *Emims* old
> That *Kiriathaim* held: Thou knowst me now
> If thou at all art known.
>
> (1078-1082)

Like Samson, who felt "Design'd for great exploits" (32), Harapha laments that the possibilities for truly heroic action lie only in the past, though of course it is Fortune he blames for his missing the chance to fell Samson at the peak of his glory. The giant refuses a fight now upon the very ground that Samson despaired of being Israel's champion: blindness rules out a fight (1101-1103). As Harapha continues to resist the prisoner's challenge, it becomes clear that it is not fair play that deters him, but decorum. To Harapha, there can be no heroic contest involving a slave, and Samson is now declassé. As one doing the labor of a beast, he is "no worthy match/For valor to assail" (1164-1165). The giant's fastidiousness may be that of a *miles gloriosus*,[9] but it is a faithful mirror of Samson's own fastidi-

---

[9] See Daniel C. Boughner, "Milton's Harapha and Renaissance Comedy," *ELH*, 11 (1944), 298.

ousness. Earlier, Samson had given up all possibility of heroic action, bemoaning that he had lost caste, that he was

> Put to the labor of a Beast, debas't
> Lower than bondslave!
>
> (37-38)

and that he was

> Inferior to the vilest now become
> Of man or worm. . . .
>
> (73-74)

In this interview with the reluctant giant, the pride behind Samson's determined disengagement becomes clear. He would not consider fighting for the God of Israel unless he could dictate his own heroic terms. He would not fight unless he could be an aristocrat of the soul, a "petty god." When he became a sinner with a blot upon his escutcheon, he despaired of contest, thereby becoming a *miles gloriosus* of the soul.

Providentially, the very attitudes and arguments that the hero had used to avoid engagement bring about his engagement. Samson had disparaged his qualifications as hero, complaining that God had tied his strength to his hair in order to point out its worthlessness (58-59). Now when Harapha disparages this strength as worthless magic (1132f.), Samson rises to reject the charge and asserts the reliability of his strength and its real source: "My trust is in the living God" (1140). To underscore his claims, Samson forthwith proposes a duel to show the supremacy of God over Dagon; and so, almost before he knows it, Samson has become God's champion again.

Harapha's next demurrer echoes Samson at the nadir of his despair:

> Presume not on thy God, whate'er he be,
> Thee he regards not, owns not, hath cut off
> Quite from his people, and delivered up
> Into thy Enemies' hand . . . .
>
> (1156-1159)

It is precisely when Samson's "sense of Heav'n's desertion" comes to him as a bald taunt from the enemy that Samson rejects his negative identity as a God-forsaken man and at last makes an emphatic, unequivocal declaration of faith:

> yet [I] despair not of his final pardon
> Whose ear is ever open; and his eye
> Gracious to re-admit the suppliant;
> In confidence whereof I once again
> Defy thee to the trial of mortal fight,
> By combat to decide whose god is God,
> Thine or whom I with *Israel's* Sons adore.
>
> (1171-1177)

The homeopathic cure is nearly complete: blaming God has been used against blaming God, self-excuse against self-excuse, reluctance to be committed against reluctance to be committed—pride against pride.

─────────── III ───────────

Healthy heroes [*Wundermänner*] are rare, and
God provides them at a dear price.

(*LW* 13.164)

Faith . . . attributes the supreme glory of ve-
racity . . . to God. John 3:33.

(*CD*, p. 473)

This man with the dangerous fists has come a long way from
his first appearance "lying at random." It would be a mistake,
however, to pronounce Samson completely restored here. Only
moments after joining himself to God's cause, he is wishing for
death:

> But come what will, my deadliest foe will prove
> My speediest friend, by death to rid me hence.
> (1262-1263)

The hero seems to be relapsing into despair. Samson's improve-
ment thus far appears to be a tenuous and unstable one, or what
Milton called "natural renovation," when the mind and will are
"partially renewed [and] for a time, at least, undergo alteration
for the better" (*CE* 15.354-355). Samson's faith at this point
owes more to events than to his own intention. His responses—
especially those to Dalila and Harapha—are emotionally charged
and quite unconsidered. His challenge to the giant seems to be
a reaction triggered automatically by the stress of the moment,
and Samson becomes God's champion literally before he knows
it. Once we see the homeopathic principle at work, all Samson's
early responses seem determined, because he invariably casts
aside his negative attitudes when he meets them on the lips of
others.

In sharp contrast to these early changes, Samson's last glo-
rious act stems from a conscious decision and demonstrates

243

"supernatural renovation," which, Milton explains, "create[s] afresh, as it were, the inward man, and infuse[s] from above new and supernatural faculties into the minds of the renovated" (CE 15.366-367). Samson's initial refusal to attend the feast of Dagon indicates that he sees the issue as one of obedience to God. The subsequent reversal of a carefully made decision suggests that the hero's responses are anything but automatic. With the access of the "rousing motions," Samson appears to have gained a new inner freedom, for he disregards both the prudent counsel of his people and Hebrew law. He now seems to be freed from the pressure of environment—free to respond to some "infusion" from above. Milton's *Purgatorio*, like Dante's, moves toward a freeing of the hero's will as its climactic event. As Vergil explains to Dante, once the will is free and upright, it is wrong not to follow its pleasure.[10] Hence comes the joy, the relish—the pleasure—with which the old fighter resists all kinds of advice and leaves the stage affirming, "This day will be remarkable in my life/By some great act . . ." (1388-1389).

A hiatus occurs in the drama when Samson receives the "rousing motions." Hitherto, his recovery has come in response to his natural setting. When he begins to respond to something beyond the natural setting, we begin to feel the inadequacy of Milton's chosen form and see him adjust it accordingly. Given his *dramatis personae*, he can show a free response to God only as a puzzling, isolated one that disrupts the established pattern of dramatic interaction. How exactly he makes the decision remains a mystery, and the content of the "rousing motions" can only be inferred, but this fact is itself important. The man who once "gave up his fort of silence" to a woman has learned not to betray the intimate counsel of the Lord of Hosts. All we can say with confidence is that Samson's decision appears both as a choice and as a "given" enlightenment that does not follow from any circumstance or previous action. Once the natural stage has been opened up to allow direct response to the divine,

[10] *Libero, dritto e sano è tuo arbitrio, è fallo fora non fare a suo senno* (*Purgatorio* 27, 190-191).

the drama is resolved on a symbolic plane where historical, psychological, and theological categories fuse. The mysterious change that has come over Samson is illuminated by the symbol of his death. Historically, his death is a hero's work that saves Israel for one era and vindicates God's governance of history. Psychologically, Samson's death epitomizes the method of his cure. We have seen the painful and negative process by which Samson's despairing attitudes are purged as he responds to like attitudes, but the negative process is complete only when Samson responds to God. We may now complete the homeopathic formula with respect to supernatural renovation. The wish for death (despair) is finally purged by willing death at God's command—an heroic and fearful feat even at the level of the spirit.

Theologically, Samson's death clarifies his newly-found identity, which is neither that of sinner nor champion, but one that takes both into account. As a man of faith his identity is more than a composite of his former selves and is radically different in that it includes identity with Christ. This need not be, however, an exclusively typological identity.[11] Milton treats the image of the Phoenix (1689-1710) in such a way as to recall the first utterance of the oracle and to emphasize the relation of God's Spirit to his word. In his opening soliloquy, Samson had described how his birth was foretold

> Twice by an Angel, who at last in sight
> Of both my Parents all in flames ascended
> From off the Altar, where an Off'ring burn'd,
> As in a fiery column charioting
> His Godlike presence . . . .
> (24-28)

[11] For typological analyses, see T.S.K. Scott-Craig, "Concerning Milton's Samson," *Renaissance News*, 5 (1952), 45-53; F. Michael Krouse, *Milton's Samson and the Christian Tradition*, Princeton, Princeton University Press, 1949; William G. Madsen, *From Shadowy Types to Truth*, New Haven, Yale University Press, 1968, pp. 181-202; Barbara Lewalski, "*Samson Agonistes* and the 'Tragedy' of the Apocalypse," *PMLA*, 85 (1970), 1050-1062. Lewalski notes that generally "in Protestant formulations the Christic reference becomes much less prominent" in typology (p. 1055). Waddington in "Melancholy Against Melancholy," *Calm of Mind*, p. 281, stresses the alchemical and therapeutic

The motions of God's Spirit are described similarly at the moment when Samson receives his "intimate impulse" from on high about how to overcome his Philistine captors. The hero

> Despis'd and thought extinguish't quite,
> With inward eyes illuminated
> His fiery virtue rous'd
> From under ashes into sudden flame,
>
> . . . .
> Like that self-begott'n bird
> In the *Arabian* woods embost . . . .
> (1688-1691, 1699-1700)

Given the pneumatological understanding of the Son that Milton displays in *Paradise Regained*, it is not surprising that he should employ a traditional image for Christ, like the Phoenix, to Samson's "rousing motions." But even if the image is read more traditionally, the christological associations that arise may be read in a metonymic as well as a typological way. Given the pervasiveness of doctrinal allusion throughout the drama, Milton's application of the Phoenix image to the hero suggests that he is transplanted in Christ like a latter-day believer—and like Milton's Adam and Eve (*PL* 11.35). Only at the point of full faith is a conventional image for Christ affixed to the hero, so as to indicate that faith effects an identity with the Son (*insitio in Christum*) and to remind us that the drama has moved from the symbol of the common prison to the symbol of the Phoenix, as we see Samson *liberi a servitute peccati ad imaginemque divinam restituti . . .* (*CE* 15.370).

The Protestant hermeneutic, which allows for a figural pull toward the beginning of time as well as toward the end, creates a web of dramatic ironies much denser than that in Sophoclean drama. If Samson is an honorary puritan saint, the dramatic irony is no longer just a matter of our knowing what will happen

---

aspects of the Phoenix, while Carey and Fowler stress the association of immortality (p. 277n). For political uses of the Phoenix, see Christopher Hill, *Milton and the English Revolution*, New York, Viking, 1978, p. 445.

at Dagon's feast, though Milton deals shrewdly in such ironies, even arranging Samson's last speech so that exclusive alternatives come true.[12] The compounding of dramatic ironies is one of the striking qualities of *Samson Agonistes*, and the arrangement of ironies ultimately depends upon how the reader relates the Old Testament to the New. If allusions in the drama to "intercession" and "ransom" serve only to remind the reader of an impassable gulf between the two Dispensations, then Anthony Low is right in suggesting that the immediate "world of the play" is a tragic one set within the larger framework of a history that is comic. If Samson is only a "barbarian" who breaks God's law and meets "immediate adversity and early death" and who unwittingly serves as a type for the Savior,[13] then the chief irony of *Samson Agonistes* is one of tragic timing, like that which occurs in *King Lear* when Cordelia dies minutes before the order arrives countermanding her execution. Such a reading, however, is at odds with the prevailing Protestant hermeneutic. Luther and Calvin held that the patriarchs were illuminated by God's Spirit and saw through their dark oracles to the promise of immortality (*LW* 4.96), if not the day of the Redeemer himself (*Inst.* 2.10.13). Milton has not indicated here, as he did in the case of Adam, just what this Old Testament saint sees in the future or knows about his reward. Such visionary particulars do not belong to "the science of the saints," which is always blind: saints have "the sublime knowledge" that somehow "in the midst of death we are in life" (*LW* 4.120). The blinder Samson's faith happens to be, the more heroic it is, and the more sensationally comic its reward. If the hero's faith makes him a full beneficiary of God's Prime Decree regarding the lamb sacrificed from the beginning (cf. *CD*, p. 475), then the main dramatic irony lies between partial and full knowledge of the triumph.

What Manoa and the Chorus celebrate at the close of the

---

[12] Joseph H. Summers, "The Movements of the Drama," *The Lyric and Dramatic Milton*, New York, Columbia University Press, 1965, p. 158; Anthony Low, *The Blaze of Noon*, New York, Columbia University Press, 1974, p. 86.
[13] Low, *The Blaze of Noon*, pp. 51, 60, 134.

drama may be a tribal victory with "Enemies/Fully reveng'd" (1711-1720) and honor brought to the "Father's house" (1717)—but they do celebrate. The puritan reader would easily discount the emphasis upon revenge and mass slaughter as belonging to the ethics of a bygone age and focus instead upon the unchanging spiritual issue: faith in God's words. Samson's important action is not that he killed so many Philistines, but that he reaffirmed God's promise in the face of an "unsearchable dispose." Even Manoa, with his tribal consciousness, celebrates Samson's faith as the preeminent fact of his life, that he died "With God not parted from him, as was fear'd,/But favoring and assisting to the end" (1719-1720).

Samson's nationalistic victory over the Philistines is tiny compared to that which he will have in heaven and the long run of history. The emphasis upon "fame" suggests that, like the fame of Lycidas, it will win him attendance at the marriage supper of the Lamb. But most important of all to the puritan, who wants to be useful within history, Samson will have a long, rich literary immortality, his "copious Legend" becoming part of the word of God to the Christian era as a prefiguration of the Messiah and the Apocalypse. His highest fame, from a puritan perspective, will be not the proleptic schema he unwittingly bears, but the way in which his Legend reveals the rich and paradoxical texture of "true experience" with God's Promise. Indeed, Samson's "literary" immortality as a puritan saint overcomes the dramatic irony most immediate to the story: that the hero's coup of liberation is undone and the Israelites soon taken captive again. However ephemeral Samson's political achievement, the *story* of his faith perseveres, useful over the ages. The more intricately and "realistically" copious it is, the more useful. Milton's *Purgatorio*, like Dante's, assumes an ongoing connection between Christians living and dead, though not the mystical one celebrated in the *Commedia* between the Saint in heaven, the sinner on earth, and the Soul in Purgatory. In Milton's tradition, there is an exclusively "literary" invocation of saints. Samson and Abraham and David (and even

Milton's beloved Waldensians) were understood to have no di-
rect power to affect a man's metaphysical destiny. Their legends,
however, testified to the power of God's word and Spirit and
thus, like sermons and the New Testament itself, could become
vehicles of grace—at the pleasure of God's redeeming Spirit.

IV

Milton, that glory of our English nation!
(Henry Stubbe, *Clamor, Rixa* . . . , 1657)

John Milton is their goose-quill champion, who
. . . had a rams head and is only good at tongue
batteries.
(Anonymous pamphlet, 1660)

I have [written], with a view not only to the
deliverance of the commonwealth, but likewise
of the Church.
(*CE* 8.67)

In *Samson Agonistes*, Milton integrates his own voice more completely into the matter of the fable than in any of his previous works. In *Paradise Lost*, the bard is a choric observer, except when he joins the angel choir round the throne of God. In *Paradise Regained*, the poet's serious childhood is visible in the Son's first soliloquy about his early aspirations to quell violence and falsehood. But in *Samson Agonistes*, the poet's biography is woven into the texture of Samson's experience throughout, and even elaborates upon the epithets with which the popular press, including his own pamphlets, characterized him. Who has not, like Hanford, found in the poem some remarkable correspondence to a detail in the poet's biography and thought he found Milton momentarily baring his soul? With regard to the Chorus' description of man's fate (687-709), Hanford remarks:

> The personal note here is too distinct to be mistaken.
> "Unjust tribunals under change of times," "their carcasses
> to dogs and fowls a prey" are certainly echoes of the Res-

toration, with its brutal trials of men like Henry Vane, and
the indignities to which the bodies of Cromwell and Ireton
were subjected. The parallel and no less wretched fate of
poverty and disease is Milton's own. He goes so far as
almost to specify the rheumatic ills from which we know
him to have suffered—"painful diseases and deformed"—
with the bitter reflection that these afflictions, justly the
fruit of dissipation, may come to those who, like himself,
have lived in temperance.[14]

It is virtually impossible to read *Samson Agonistes* without
adducing something of the poet's biography, and in consequence
any reading will compose Milton's life into a fable that is com-
pelling in its own right. Milton seems to have designed *Samson
Agonistes* as an oracle, for the contemporary allusions are all
terribly dark and terribly obvious. It is impossible to establish
whether Milton intended the hero to represent the leadership
of the elect minority, the army, the Parliament,[15] the poet him-
self, England—or all of the above. If Milton's contemporary
allusions cannot be identified with precision, it seems beyond
dispute that *Samson Agonistes* bespeaks his judgment upon a
Philistine Restoration and his firm persuasion that England is
still God's favored people, who, like ancient Israel, will undergo
recurring reformations after periods of servitude (cf. YP 1.602).
In a similar way, the drama conceals and reveals Milton's in-
timate experience. In the episode with Dalila, one cannot con-
clude with any degree of probability whether Milton is deploring
his early league with the Presbyterians, undoing his reconcili-
ation with Mary Powell, or drawing more generally upon his
experience of marriage as a dungeon (cf. YP 2.258). As with
the doctrinal allusions, the biographical ones come as persistent
but momentary glances, which resist arrangement into a co-

[14] *"Samson Agonistes* and Milton in Old Age," *Twentieth Century Inter-
pretations*, p. 29.

[15] See Mary Ann Radzinowicz, *"Samson Agonistes* and Milton the Politician
in Defeat," *PQ*, 44 (1965), 467; Christopher Hill, *Milton and the English
Revolution*, p. 430; YP 2.585.

herent allegory. Just as persistently, however, they challenge the reader to arrange them into a saint's legend, with or without complete historial evidence.

Frank Kermode speculates that Milton had to sign an oath of allegiance to the hated new monarchy in order to survive and that abjuration must account for the gigantic load of guilt that Milton's last hero displays.[16] On the other hand, Milton's treatment of Samson's suicide may be an apologia for the literary "suicide" of bringing on his own blindness. Against the advice of his physicians, Milton had continued to write as an apologist for the Cromwellian regime, claiming that he wrote the *First Defense* at the prompting "of some diviner monitor within" (*sed divinioris cujusdam intus monitoris viderer mihi audire* [CE 8.69]). If so, Radzinowicz is probably right in suggesting that since Milton aspired to reach "something of prophetic strain" in old age, *Samson Agonistes* itself—written when he was totally blind—is the heroic coup that fulfills his destiny.[17] Hints within the drama tend to confirm such a reading because Milton is virtually alone in calling the site of the Dagonalia a "Theater" (1605), though in the Bible it is simply a "house" and in other accounts, a "temple."[18] Samson hesitates to join all the theater crowd—"Dancers, Antics, Mummers, Mimics" (1325)—but finally goes to the theater to be among them but not of them, and yet to triumph in their midst. He stands like Milton in the preface to *Samson Agonistes*, who insists that his drama was never intended for the stage, as if he wished to dissociate himself from the profane levity of the Restoration theater, yet who appears confident that his work will triumph in its literary achievement and ideology. Opposition between the sobriety of

[16] Kermode, however, considers the punishment that Milton's God metes out for purely "ceremonial submission" to Charles II so extreme that it could only come from a "god of madness" like the one described in the famous Freudian case of Schreber ("Milton in Old Age," *The Southern Review*, 11, 1975, 529).

[17] Radzinowicz, "*Samson Agonistes* and Milton the Politician in Defeat," p. 463.

[18] A. W. Verity, *Milton's Samson Agonistes*, Cambridge, Cambridge University Press, 1949, p. xxviii.

the Nazarite hero and the drunken Philistine lords seems to carry the same polarity that it does in *Comus*.

Samson Agonistes is a consummate example of Reformation biblical exegesis because to an extraordinary degree Milton has followed Luther's injunction to amplify the biblical story and fill in the "lattices" of the narrative with his own experience. In any number of ways, a reader can fashion a myth, or saint's legend, from the life of Milton as glimpsed through the experience of his Samson, but it will inevitably be one of spectacular failure and faith. However opaque in detail, the drama is profoundly revealing in those larger outlines upon which most readers can agree. The most striking fact of the drama is the hero's monumental sense of failure and guilt, the purging of which comprises the central action—and the important self-revelation of the author. There is no question of Milton's thinking himself to be a reincarnation or fulfillment of the Old Testament warrior. Rather, the fusion of the poet's biography and his fable suggests the public confession and the ultimate devotional act of a poet.

If exegetical identification with biblical personae is a matter of spiritual exercise and personal testimony and if Milton's identification with the antagonists of his works may be taken for granted, then one can deduce a further point from his poetic testimony considered as a whole. In *Paradise Lost*, Satan and Christ remain a cosmos apart for most of the epic, and Abdiel stands in for the Son during a debate with Satan about the Primal Word. In *Paradise Regained*, Christ and Satan draw closer, meeting on the same ground for a verbal duel over God's proclamation at Jordan. In *Samson Agonistes*, however, the demonic and the divine no longer are presented as separate characters. The word of God appears chiefly in the tortured memory of the hero who discounts it; yet the divine promise battles and overcomes despair within a single human consciousness. The course of Milton's canon is itself confessional because it increasingly acknowledges the extent to which the evil voice is enmeshed with the self.

253

Samson Agonistes reveals the dread but glorious consequence of purging such a mixed self. During the drama, the voice of the Old Man is systematically mortified as "sanctification" proceeds steadily, a process never complete in this life. Not until moments before the hero's departure for the Philistine theater is the Satanic voice of rage and despair stilled—completely stilled for the first time in Milton's poetry—as the sanctification and death of the hero coincide. Milton seems to be composing himself for death. His affirmation that Samson's end is victorious and that even his failure performs an on-going literary service comprises a final statement of faith for the poet—a faith that appears heroic in exact proportion to the felt pain and private loss that the affirmation countermands.

Index

Abel, 170, 176
Abraham, 69, 73, 106n, 137, 138, 145, 170
Achilles, 84, 86, 196
active life, 9, 10
Actus Purus, 4. *See also* God
adding to the word, 18, 154
Aeneas, 62-79, 86, 172-74, 196
Aeneid, 18, 59-79, 88n, 172-73, 196
Agamemnon, 75
Agathon, 34n
Ahab, 214
Ajax, 84
Alcibiades, 34n
Aldridge, William, 34n
allegory, 5, 9, 13, 34n, 73, 95-96, 221
Allen, Don Cameron, 31n, 73n, 210n, 216
Althaus, Paul, 106n
Ames, William, 12, 19
Anabaptists, 141
Analogy of Being, 74, 148, 175
analogy of Evangelick doctrine, 4. *See also* analogy of the word
analogy of faith, 4, 14, 74
analogy of the word, 4, 6, 13, 74
Anglican liturgy, 33
antifeminism, 156
Antony and Cleopatra, 109
Apollo, 67
Apollodorus, 52
apostolic address, 106-107, 144
Aquinas, Thomas, St., 5-6, 42, 97, 118, 148n
Aratus, 72, 77

Ariosto, 18
Arthos, John, 51n, 52n
Ascham, Roger, 40n
Athanasias, 18
Athena, 76, 95
Athenaeus, 34n
Atkins, Samuel D., 72n
Atreus, House of, 75
Auden, W. H., 18
Auerbach, Erich, 68
Aurifaber, Johann, 96n

Bacchus, 35n
Bainton, Roland H., 221n
Baldwin, T. W., 40n
Barbour, Hugh, 170n, 204n, 217n
Barker, Arthur, 232n
Beatrice, 74, 175
Bell, Captain Henry, 96
Benoit de Sainte-Maure, 65
Berry, Boyd, 103n, 127n
Bible, 8, 101. *See also* Scripture.
  Acts, 72, 77; Colossians, 125, 130; I Corinthians, 35n; Daniel, 82n; Deuteronomy, 120, 154n, 200; Exodus, 121; Galatians, 109; Genesis, 13, 137-39, 144, 146, 154n, 167n, 170; Hebrews, 16, 91n, 121, 179; Hosea, 8; Isaiah, 9, 101; Jeremiah, 120; John, 136n, 168n, 210, 243; Leviticus, 121; Luke, 29, 35n, 49, 88n, 136n, 171n; Matthew, 5, 122; Numbers, 5; I Peter, 10; Psalms, 8, 88n, 90-92, 94, 102, 116, 121, 128, 138, 140, 200n; Revelation, 154n; Ro-

255

Index

Index

Holy Spirit, passim; activating biblical commands, 218; above the church, 13n; and Adam's redemption, 171; authentication for Scripture, 6; and communion, 123; as Daemon, 32; and deference to higher authority, 209-10; demonstrated by the Son, 223, 224; as exorcist, 221; and freedom, 216; as gift of the Gospel, 224; and good conscience, 213; as Interpreter, 202, 210; as inward consolation, 189; as the law of God's Kingdom, 203; as Messianic secret, 201-202; and narrative gaps, 190; and the Old Testament, 111, 170; and the patriarchs, 231, 247; as pugnacious, 109; as Remembrancer, 170; as rhetorician, 7, 15; and the Son's speech, 206-207; and self-denial, 206; and silence, 222; and syntax, 21; uniting heaven and earth, 110; unpredictable, 17, 170; as wisdom, 222; as a weapon, 216, 220; and tropes, 123, 127
homeopathic medicine, 233 and passim
Homer, 64n, 65, 72, 75, 78, 172
Hooker, Richard, 97
Hunter, William B., Jr., 33n, 132n
hypallage, 5. See also tropes
hyperbole, 95. See also tropes

icon, 22
Iliad, 64, 65, 75, 79, 86
illumination, 161-63, 182
imagination, 66
Incarnation, 102, 139, 175, 187
innovation, 179
insitio in Christum, 39, 224, 231, 246
irony, 5

James I, 55
Jayne, Sears, 51n
Joachim of Westphal, 121
Job, 215
John the Baptist, 137
Johnson, Samuel, 123n, 233
Jonson, Ben, 33n
Joseph of Exeter, 65
Joshua, 186
Juno, 66
Jupiter, 67, 70, 72, 76

Kaufmann, U. Milo, 105n, 170n, 197n
Keats, John, 151
Kelley, Maurice, 34n, 72n
Kermode, Frank, 252
Kerrigan, William, 32n, 124n, 126, 127n, 179n
Kierkegaard, Soren, 195
King Lear, 17, 83, 193, 214, 247
Kingdom of God, 8 and passim
Kirk, K. E., 204n
Krouse, F. Michael, 245n

Lady Sin, 96. See also Devil's whore
Landino, 73
Lewalski, Barbara Kiefer, 5, 13n, 135, 136n, 142n, 143n, 177n, 185n, 200, 207n, 209n, 210n, 216, 222, 223n 245n
libertines, 55
"literary" theology, 142. See also biblical theology
logomachy, 160, 233
Logos, 3, 105, 140
Lord Jim, 61, 213
Lord of Misrule, 55
Lot, 11
Lot's wife, 143
Low, Anthony, 247
Ludus Coventriae, 90
Luther, Martin, The Bondage of the Will (1526), 7, 109, 114n, 128,

259

Index

Index

Whitaker, William, 11, 13n, 20n
Williams, Arnold, 168n
Williamson, George, 182n
Wittgenstein, Ludwig, 112, 180, 191
Wolfson, Harry Austryn, 204n
Wollebius, 19
Woodhouse, A.S.P., 33, 42, 44, 196, 207, 210, 232
works of the Law, 13-14, 45

Wright, B. A., 51n
Wyclif, John, 192n

Young, Arthur M., 65n
Young, Thomas, 17, 67
Yu, Anthony C., 152n, 163n, 164n

Zacharias, 88n
Zeus, 75

Library of Congress Cataloging in Publication Data

Christopher, Georgia B., 1932-
    Milton and the science of the saints.

    Includes index.
        1.   Milton, John, 1608-1674—Religion and ethics.
2.   Reformation in literature.   3.   Theology, Puritan, in
literature.   4.   Calvinism in literature.   I.   Title.
PR3592.R4C56   1982   821'.4   81-47911
ISBN 0-691-06508-X   AACR2

*Georgia B. Christopher is Associate Professor of English and Director
of Graduate Studies at Emory University.*